LANGUAGE IN SOCIETY 18
Language, Society and the Elderly

Language in Society

GENERAL EDITOR
Peter Trudgill, Professor in the
Department of Language and
Linguistics, University of Essex

ADVISORY EDITORS
Ralph Fasold, Professor of Linguistics, Georgetown University

William Labov, Professor of Linguistics, University of Pennsylvania

Language, Society and the Elderly

Discourse, Identity and Ageing

*Nikolas Coupland, Justine Coupland
and Howard Giles*

BLACKWELL
Oxford UK & Cambridge USA

First published 1991

Basil Blackwell Ltd
108 Cowley Road, Oxford, OX4 1JF, UK

Basil Blackwell, Inc.
3 Cambridge Center
Cambridge, Massachusetts 02142, USA

British Library Cataloguing in Publication Data

A CIP catalogue record for this book is available
from the British Library.

Library of Congress Cataloging in Publication Data
Coupland, Nikolas, 1950–
Language, society, and the elderly: discourse, identity, and
ageing / Nikolas Coupland, Justine Coupland, and Howard Giles.
p.   cm. – (Language and society; 18)
Includes bibliographical references and index.
ISBN 0–631–18004–4 – ISBN 0–631–18279–9 (pbk.)
1. Sociolinguistics.   2. Aged – Language.   3. Intergenerational relations.
4. Aging.   I. Coupland, Justine.   II. Giles, Howard.   III. Title.
IV. Series: Language and society (Oxford, England); 18.
PB40.C64   1991
306.4′4–dc20   91–10514
                                                    CIP

Typeset in 11 on 12.5pt Ehrhardt
by Hope Services (Abingdon) Ltd.
Printed in Great Britain by T. J. Press Ltd, Padstow, Cornwall

Contents

For Ray, June, Bill, Muriel and Alex

Editor's Preface

The pioneering research on which this book is based represents an intersection of insights, knowledge and methodology from two important areas of work in the field of language in society: the social psychology of language; and discourse analysis. As the title suggests, however, *Language, Society and the Elderly: Discourse, Identity and Ageing* is primarily concerned with reporting on and drawing conclusions from the discourse analytical aspects of the research. The book is also concerned that the wider implications of work on the language used by and to the elderly should be acknowledged and acted on by those who are involved in social work and other forms of interaction with older people. Of major interest to decision makers, linguists and social psychologists – as well as to the rest of us who are or hope to be elderly – is the finding that conversation both between and within generations contains discourse strategies which reflect and reinforce beliefs and stereotypes concerning different age-groups and the ageing process. The authors' hope is that sociolinguistic work of this type may help to counteract the marginalization to which the elderly are subject in many western communities. If, as seems likely, this volume succeeds in opening up this area to public discussion, it will surely signal the beginnings of a research programme in what should prove to be one of the most socially important new areas of sociolinguistic research for some time.

Peter Trudgill

Preface

The status of the elderly as a social group is an ambiguous one. Ironically, one factor that pulls together what is in reality an enormously diverse and rapidly changing population is that older people, corporately, are severely under-represented in the sociolinguistic and communication literatures. In an academic climate where gerontological issues are at last coming to receive the attention they deserve, what then might sociolinguistics offer to gerontology, and how might studies of later life enrich sociolinguistics?

The principal existing tradition of linguistic research on ageing, which we review in the book's first chapter, attempts to identify distinctive characteristics of age-related speech and language competence in later life. This approach explores decremental effects, though with inconsistent findings. Such studies have operated with varying definitions of the category term 'elderly', but also, we would argue, with a limited agenda for ageing research itself. Language-based research, and particularly *socio*linguistics, should address itself to more fundamental issues than whether or not older people's use of (intrinsically rather insignificant) features of the language code are measurably different from, or supposedly inferior to, their use by younger people. Social ageing is too intriguing a process, and too loaded with implications for social policy, for this to be the limit of investigative aims.

In the body of the book we explore the emerging finding that talk between the generations may have characteristic configurations, that cross- and within-generation talk can be modelled in terms of recurring discourse strategies that intersect in important ways with beliefs and ideologies of ageing. Talk can usefully be considered a forum for enacting and modifying generational attitudes, goals and aspirations, where social evaluations and attributions are made that are significant components of age-groups' identities. So the agenda we propose is an ambitious one: for sociolinguistics to access ageing as a rhetorical as much as a biological formation. We assume that if there is a social consensus in defining 'the elderly', it will be one constituted interactionally, and therefore amenable to be studied.

As with other, better-established areas of sociolinguistic study, there is also a political dimension, which we openly acknowledge. Our most general aim for the book is to make some headway in understanding how a culture, in part through patterns of social interaction, comes to marginalize its older members and to define them as a minority group (though certainly not in the numerical sense). Conversation is the medium through which all the 'isms' and most social group-level tensions and problems are endorsed or challenged, aggravated or relaxed. Patterns of intergenerational talk – for example, in the management of self-disclosure – for us constitute a part of this cyclical movement. They seem to offer a factual kernel to sustain stereotypic myths of elderly egocentricity and conversational grouchiness. But they also offer a dimension of interaction through which some doubtless well-intentioned younger interlocutors can draw out age-stereotyped behaviours from the old.

Following this general line of argument, we suggest that sociolinguistics has a critical role to play in the analysis of societal agesim. Although the mainly qualitative, text-based analyses we present are exploratory, and although they inevitably relate to a limited range of data contexts, we show how they do cross-reference to many different applied concerns – for example, in training initiatives for people working with and caring for the elderly, and in the day-to-day routines of providing care for old people in residential and community settings. It will become clear that there is still very much to be achieved through empirical research and interpretation, but we hope this book will at least provide a stimulus for systematic consideration of older people in future sociolinguistic studies.

Acknowledgements

The research on which this volume is based has been suppported by an award from the Economic and Social Research Council (ESRC, UK), reference number G0022220022 to Howard Giles and Nikolas Coupland ('Communication and the Elderly: an Interdisciplinary Approach', 1985–9).

The book represents the discourse analytic component of this research. As such, it integrates (in revised forms) several existing papers and chapters. Overviews of the more socio-psychological and experimental phases of the research are available in Giles and Coupland (1991a, 1991b), and Williams and Giles (in press). Specific sources for the present volume are: for chapter 1: N. Coupland and Coupland (1990); for chapter 2: N. Coupland, Coupland, Giles and Henwood (1988); for chapter 3: J. Coupland, Coupland, Giles and Henwood (in press); for chapter 4: J. Coupland, Coupland, Giles and Wiemann (1988); for chapter 5: N. Coupland, Coupland, Giles, Henwood and Wiemann (1988); for chapter 6: N. Coupland and Coupland (1989) and N. Coupland, Coupland and Giles (1989); for chapter 7: N. Coupland, Henwood, Coupland and Giles (1990) and N. Coupland, Coupland, Giles and Henwood (1991); and for chapter 8: K. Atkinson and Coupland (1988); N. Coupland, Grainger and Coupland (1988) and Grainger, Atkinson and Coupland (1990).

As the citations above indicate, we owe very substantial debts to colleagues who have been involved in all phases of the research reported here. Particularly to Karen Henwood, who participated fully in the design and implementation of all the programme's empirical studies and in the authoring of research reports on which several of the chapters here are based. Karen Grainger and Karen Atkinson conducted studies in parallel to those we report below, and participated in many key phases of the programme research, data transcription and analysis; aspects of their independent doctoral research are summarized in chapter 8. John Wiemann provided much needed guidance in the planning stages of the programme and has made crucial contributions to those aspects of our work relating to health communication and self-disclosure. Penny Rowlands and Bob Dumbleton have also offered us sustained help and criticism.

Many of the studies we report in the book were made possible through the ready cooperation and advice of the directors of the two day centres with which we were involved between 1985 and 1989. Confidentiality needs do not allow us to mention them by name, but we are very grateful indeed for the help of these individuals. Most importantly of all, we thank all the volunteers who gave their time, interest and much of themselves in participating in these studies. We learned more from time informally spent with them – at home, at the day centres and at the university – than we are able to capture by way of 'findings' from research studies.

The manuscript was prepared while two of us (NC and JC) held visiting appointments at the Department of Communication at the University of California, Santa Barbara. We are most grateful to faculty and staff of UCSB for providing all necessary resources, and particularly to graduate students at UCSB (session 1989/90) for the opportunity to discuss and refine many of the data analyses summarized here. Barbara Horn gave most valuable advice at the copy-editing phase. Not least, Jon Nussbaum has helped us forge connections between our own work and literatures in social gerontology, and has on many occasions offered us insight from his own research on ageing.

We extend our thanks to all these friends and colleagues.

NC, JC and HG
December 1990

1

Language and Later Life:
Incipient Literatures

The language sciences have generally been slow to contribute to our understanding of social ageing. There is a dawning recognition (which has come later to the UK than to the USA) that academic research, like the broader community, must revise its assumptions and upgrade its knowledge about a rapidly ageing population. It is common to come across statistical predictions of profound demographic changes in Western societies producing an enduringly large 'elderly' segment of the population living longer into a healthier old age. Gravell (1988), for instance, notes that 11.3 per cent of people in the UK in 1980 were over 65, while it is predicted that this figure will rise to 18.3 per cent by 2030 (for an overview of trends, see Tinker, 1984). From a specifically generational perspective, these trends are establishing vividly new patterns of within-family relationships. Hagestad (1985), for example, reminds us that until very recently it was only a lucky few young adults who had living grandparents. Now we assume multigenerational ties are normal, and count on them to be durable (p. 34). Patterns of family composition are changing so rapidly that, Hagestad argues, the grandparenting role no longer has any clear normative expectations attached to it (p. 36). In many senses, then, we are, societally, in the process of rediscovering and even reconstituting cross-generational relations, and even ageing itself.

But demography alone does not explain the absence of a sustained literature upon which this book and the developing field of 'gerontological sociolinguistics' might have drawn. After all, if we are only now rediscovering the elderly, it is because we have studiously overlooked them in the past, for what McCready (1985) calls 'murky and ineffable reasons' (p. 49). Our academic neglect of older people has perhaps mirrored society's own reticence to engage with older people and ageing concerns. For whatever cause, the elderly do not as yet feature at all consistently as a visible social group within the paradigms of sociolinguistics, the social psychology of language, conversation and discourse analysis – indeed, within the language and communication sciences as a whole. When language research has considered age and human development, this has almost uniquely been taken to mean *child* language development.

Still, several important overviews of 'communication and ageing' have appeared. It is, in fact, the (predominantly North American) tradition of communication research – for example, the work of the Speech Communication Association's Commission on Communication and Aging – that has been most conscientious in thematizing life-span concerns and ageing itself as appropriate and necessary issues for linguistic research. But in many cases it has been the clinical psychological and psycholinguistic traditions that have dominated in published overviews – for example, Bayles and Kaszniak, 1987; Maxim and Thompson, 1990; Obler and Albert, 1980; Wilder and Weinstein, 1984. For more interdisciplinary perspectives, see also N. Coupland, Coupland and Giles, in press; Giles and Ryan, 1986; Nussbaum, Thompson and Robinson, 1989; Oyer and Oyer, 1976; and Shadden, 1988. Despite these efforts, the research we shall survey in this chapter, as a backdrop to the volume's own contribution, is incipient and partial in several respects. At the same time, it should be seen as raising issues that no other sociolinguistic domain can afford to ignore. Inevitably, the life-span perspective (explicitly argued for by Nussbaum, 1989) will both inform and challenge established findings in the study of virtually any context of language use. Generalizations made in other research areas are, no doubt, skewed by under-representing elderly populations' behaviours, beliefs, orientations and assessments.

In this chapter's introductory review we shall mainly be concerned to identify general orientations to language and later life that have emerged or are emerging. In doing this we hope to contribute to a debate about the appropriate priorities for gerontological linguistic and communication research, and to introduce and defend the essentially qualitative, interactionally grounded methods exemplified in later chapters. Although we shall see that there is a valuable fund of existing empirical work to draw upon, there is a need to reconsider theoretical and ideological foundations before significant, concerted progress can be made. In particular, we shall review existing work in relation to two key concepts: *diachrony*, the perspective on change over time, and *decrement*, progressive decline in health or competence. These concepts are bound to be relevant to sociolinguistic studies of ageing, but they can be invoked in crucially different ways.

A whole tradition of existing work, the deficit paradigm, is in danger of adopting a stereotypically based set of assumptions about how diachrony and decrement 'naturally' relate to ageing as a process. The deficit perspective itself determines what we should know and research about elderly populations; it predisposes us to investigate how older people's linguistic competence may be lacking in certain regards, and how their involvement in conversational interaction may be problematical. The second and converse orientation, which we discuss under the heading 'The anti-ageism paradigm', articulates a more liberal ideology, and resists assumptions about 'natural' decline with years. It treats these assumptions as pernicious and ill-founded.

We review empirical studies in these two traditions after a more detailed discussion of how diachrony and decrement surface as themes in research on language and ageing.

Invoking Diachrony and Decrement

The study of linguistic and communicative impairment is in some ways an obvious component of gerontological linguistics. Specific pathologies and syndromes of impairment, such as Alzheimer's (Emery and Emery, 1983) and Parkinson's disease, Huntington's chorea, and related aphasias (cf. Cummings, Benson, Hill and Read, 1985), are probabilistically associated with late life (Beasley and Davis, 1981). But, from another perspective, it is at least as important to establish the normal elderly as a population open to language and communication research, and to resist the assumption that the normal linguistic condition of late ageing is predictably and progressively decremental; it clearly is not. Boone, Bayles and Koopmann (1982) are adamant that 'the typical person over age 65 communicates very well. Age per se is not a deterrent to "good communication"' (p. 313). It is, of course, true that studies of impairment are necessary, both in their own right and to establish the boundaries of some specific dimensions of normal language and communication in ageing. But there is also an obligation upon *socially* based research to redress the balance and move away from the cognitive and psycholinguistic concerns that have come to dominate the literatures. It is ultimately inadequate to characterize the linguistic and communicative dimensions of normal social ageing as the avoidance of decremental pathologies.

Concern with change over time also appears to surface 'naturally' in gerontological contexts, if only because older people's most obvious defining characteristic is the fact that they occupy a certain band of the life span. But, again, this perspective can be unnecessarily limiting. It is just as feasible to approach the elderly as a relatively stable social group as to assume that ageing is inherently a decremental process. The issue is not merely terminological. Important implications follow from old age being researched in relation to earlier and later time periods, not least that such treatments impose an essentially *transitional* character upon the condition of old age.

Even where the focus of interest is apparently a more static phenomenon – a social group, 'the elderly' – some diachronic focus can be implicit. Research questions are often generated relating to the group's language or communication behaviour, but framed by past or projectable changes in those behaviours. And since change, for the old, is represented in stereotyped formulations as ineluctable progress towards incapacity and, eventually, death, the keyword is not generally development but in fact, again, *decrement*.

Therefore, our own starting point is that the diachronic perspective and the associated expectation of decremental change are built in to the mythology of ageing and in the ideologies and common practices of linguistic research into normal ageing. If we leave them unchallenged, these assumptions systematically misrepresent the conditions and experiences of later life. Linguists, sociologists and psychologists are in danger of asking excessively narrow questions about elderly language and communication: questions about declining competence. On the other hand, there is also a naivety in the converse position, which explicitly or implicitly denies the importance of diachrony and decrement as elements of our experiences of ageing. Later chapters will show how the social identities of many elderly people are bound up with *precisely these* parameters, influencing their conversational goals and styles, and those of younger people they interact with. So, perhaps ironically, diachrony and decrement come to be crucial factors in the interpretation of elderly talk; but as themes in its constitution, and not as premisses for its interpretation.

Approaches to the Elderly as a Social Group

We have suggested that it can be damaging to approach the elderly exclusively as a social group in transition. There is certainly a need to give attention to older people as an independent social collectivity, for reasons parallel to those that have led to the existence of, for example, a feminist sociolinguistics, a discourse and racism paradigm, or a (child) developmental linguistics. We can point to unique issues of social practice and policy affecting the elderly as a group: the characteristic communication networks of some elderly groups (for example, in retirement, Mutran and Reitzes, 1981); their particular needs from the health and caring services (Montgomery and Borgatta, 1987); persistent (predominantly negative) social attitudes to old people, and associated stereotypes (Braithwaite, 1986; Crockett, Press and Osterkamp, 1979) and social inequalities (Ward, 1984). All of these factors act together to generate recurring patterns of elderly and intergenerational language use, which research has only recently begun to explore.

Where we find stable group characteristics or processes, objective or subjective, we can draw on at least three distinct interpretations of intergroup variation. First, we might suggest that the very condition of being elderly is enough to explain behavioural configurations: that is, an appeal to *inherent causes*. From this perspective it might seem natural to look to cognitive factors at the root of, for example, 'deficiencies' that are taken to reflect elderliness itself.

Second, it is possible to make derivative inferences, assuming that the roots of elderly speech or language characteristics lie in the absence of change, or in limited change from time past: appeal to *historical causes*. A clear instance of this line of interpretation is Labov's 'apparent time' methodology for the study of dialect change. Labov (1972), for example, has used elderly informants to identify changes in the pronunciation of postvocalic /r/ in New York City coinciding with the Second World War. In this methodology old speakers are not under investigation in their own right, but are taken as exemplars (within recognized limits) of 'the way it was' dialectally. The technique is highly informative in its own terms, though it risks marginalizing specifically gerontological issues in language.

A study by Clyne (1977) raises the possibility of a third set of interpretive possibilities. The pattern of L1 regression (reverting to first-language use in a second-language community setting) that Clyne finds among elderly German-English and Dutch-English bilinguals may, he suggests, be best interpreted as the consequence of one or more factors in the elderly's current social circumstances: that is, an appeal to *environmental causes*. Elderly people, as in the case of Clyne's data, may revert to their first languages because they participate in less extensive or less diffentiated sociolinguistic networks of the sort that would require multiple language use or code-switching. (Clyne, in fact, considers several different explanations for L1 regression.) Kutner (1962) has likewise distinguished social/ socio-psychological from physiological/cognitive dimensions of intrinsic elderly characteristics.

Socially and socio-psychologically based interpretations of elderly language use are remarkably rare. Yet, the *contexts* of communication across age-groups can be demonstrably distinct, even to the extent that we can reasonably regard the generations as culturally distinct groups (cf. Giles and Coupland, 1991a). Bengston and Kuypers (1971) argue that the 'drama of generations' is sustained by unique drives and anxieties, particular 'generational stakes' that each group holds in relation to other groups.

A recent investigation of different generation groups' beliefs about talk itself as an activity suggests that these cultural differences may show up quantitatively in elicitation tests. For example, in interviews, some groups of older people (British, in their 60s) were found to construe talk in more positive terms than younger groups (Giles, Coupland and Wiemann, in press). The younger (student) groups in the study appeared to have negative stereotypical conceptions of the elderly's own beliefs about talk. They thought elderly people valued small-talk greatly, with a strong tinge of perceived egocentricism. The older groups believed that young people were more sceptical about the value of small talk than older people in general. These subtle differences in belief structure, which need to be refined and clarified in new studies, may well lie at the root of the sorts of cross generation differences in styles and contents of talk that we are only now starting to become aware of.

A social group perspective on the elderly does not in any way stop us recognizing *diversity*, and often extreme diversity, within populations we decide to call 'elderly'. Age in years, chronological age, of course offers us scope for differentiating elderly populations, given that 'elderliness' by some token can comprise at least three decades of life for many people. It is conventional to distinguish at least two numeric elderly age-groups, the 'young-old' and the 'old-old' (distinguished by an age boundary in the mid-70s). Socio-economic class, sex, generational position (grandmothers versus great-grandmothers, etc.) and many other cross-cutting dimensions could, within their own limitations, provide further independent variables, few of which have been successfully controlled in contrastive studies. But age in years itself, or, for that matter a classification based on cohort membership (groupings by birth dates), may be a poor predictor of generation placement. Hagestad (1985) illustrates this by saying that 'an 18-year-old can have maternal and paternal grandfathers who are not only strikingly different in age and vigor, but who also represent sharp contrasts in life experiences' (p. 32).

Another perspective on diversity is the ecological one developed by Bengston, Kasschau and Ragan (1977) in considering the impact of life events, triumphs, disasters and changes upon behaviours through the life span. Ethnicity and intercultural variation are further crucial areas (cf. Markides and Mindel, 1987; Palmore, 1975) where we have very little language variation data as yet.

But an important observation for the approach we shall adopt in this volume is that objective criteria for differentiating elderly populations may often take secondary place to subjective processes in their explanatory value. Smith (1985) has noted that individual men and women must not be assumed to be perfect exemplars of their gender groups. In the same way it is likely that purely objective dimensions of ageing will have low predictive value in accounting for patterns of language use and communicative behaviour in general. There is little agreement about the earliest age in years at which it is reasonable or necessary to consider individuals to be 'elderly', except when our social institutions impose arbitrary boundaries, such as statutory retirement ages or the age-bands used by life-insurance companies. In fact, important departure-points for our own studies are that age category labels are: (a) socially constructed by particular communities, for particular purposes; and (b) subjectively interpreted by individuals (cf. Cole and Gadow, 1986). Therefore, a person's 'psychological age' (Montpare and Lachman, 1989) may be a better candidate for interpreting behavioural differences. Similarly, A. M. Rubin and Rubin's (1982, 1986) measure of 'contextual age', an aggregated index of life-circumstantial and subjective factors, has proved to be a useful predictor of patterns of television viewing.

Some research has focused explicitly on typologies of elderly personality prototypes, as in the work of Brewer, Dull and Lui (1981). Neugarten, Crotty and Tobin (1964) empirically derived a typology of grandparenting styles, which they labelled 'formal', 'fun-seeking', 'distant figure', 'surrogate parent' and 'reservoir of family wisdom'. Although these typologies still adopt a more deterministic view of middle age and elderly identity profiles than seems appropriate for interactional research, they are a valuable reminder of how inadequate, and often ageist, simple group designations of 'the elderly' can be.

There are many challenges here for future language and communication research to explore these dimensions of potential variability among middle-aged and older people. Indeed, we want to argue that analyses of interaction have a key role to play in the social scientific study of ageing generally. A discourse analysis perspective recognizes the constitutive potential of talk as a vehicle for *formulating* life positions, and responses to them by old and young alike, interactively and relationally. This is the case we argue at the end of this chapter and then illustrate in the analyses of intergenerational talk presented in later chapters. Before that, we review the linguistic perspectives that have come to dominate ageing research.

The Deficit Paradigm

In the existing literature, language and communication in normal ageing are most often characterized through an appraisal of residual competence, with research focusing on precisely those dimensions of language use that are known potentially to show, or are suspected of showing, decrement. As a result, language use in normal ageing tends to be represented by providing evidence of an adult group's non-impaired competence in some respect, or sometimes their achieving a higher score on some index than an impaired group achieves. Sometimes, the 'normal elderly' themselves will be shown to have declined on some psycholinguistic measure in relation to a younger group. Very many facets of speech production, linguistic knowledge and processing have been investigated from these perspectives over more than three decades, producing complex and sometimes inconsistent results. We refer below to only a sub-set of representative studies.

One band of research has characterized the acoustic and articulatory characteristics of the ageing voice. Studies have shown that elderly voices are regularly discriminable from younger voices. Ptacek and Sander (1966), for instance, showed that people over 65 and under 35 could be identified even on the basis of single prolonged vowels. Ramig (1983) found that physiological ageing is associated with increased vowel spectral noise, stemming from degenerative changes in the larynx. In Liss, Weismer and Rosenbek's (1990) study, 87- to 93-year-old male voices sometimes showed notable similarities to the voices of Parkinson's disease patients. Clearly, then, voice quality, just like pitch perturbation and pitch itself (see below) has the potential to act as a social marker of elderly speech (Helfrich, 1979, gives a useful general review).

On the issue of receptive processing and recall of language, Obler, Nicholas, Albert and Woodward (1985) report a linear decline by age (across decades from 30s to 70s) in scores on a sentence-comprehension and -completion task. In Feier and Gerstman's (1980) study declining scores were again found among people in their 60s and 70s (and not in younger groups) on a task requiring comprehension and production of complex sentences. Goodglass and Kaplan (1972) found an age effect on levels of comprehension of written sentences and paragraphs, but none on an auditory comprehension sub-test.

In an influential series of studies of discourse comprehension and recall, Ulatowska and colleagues (1985, 1986) found significant differences between young-old (64–76) and old-old (77+) subjects on test items requiring inferencing from the original text. S. K. Gordon and Clark (1974) similarly found lower levels of information recall among older subjects. More recent studies have continued to report older people's inferior levels of understanding (for example, of information about medical prescriptions (Morrell, Park and Poon, 1990)) and recall relative to young adults. But some have pointed to how effects are mediated by the particular types of language texts involved. Tun (1990) shows that age-related differences in recall are partially reduced when the task involves remembering *narrative* texts. Petros, Norgaard, Olson and Tabor (1989) report similar findings.

In terms of sentence production, Obler (1980) found older speakers (50–80) used more elaborate and indefinite terms than younger speakers. Gold, Andres, Arbuckle and Schwartzman (1988) identified so-called 'off-target verbosity' among elderly speakers, when speech 'quickly becomes a prolonged series of loosely associated recollections increasingly remote from, relatively unconstrained by, and irrelevant to the present external contextual stimuli' (p. 27). The authors found no direct association between such talk and age itself, but suggest that it 'becomes manifest in older people who are extroverted, socially active, not concerned with others' impressions of them, undergoing more stress and experiencing declining performance in nonverbal cognitive functioning' (p. 32). While Gold et al. are not able to commit themselves to a single interpretation of their findings, they consider cognitive impairment once again as a candidate explanation for behavioural characteristics of elderly talk.

From a series of formal tests of sentence comprehension and manipulation (including many varying in syntactic complexity), Emery (1986) reports no significant age differences, at either phonological or lexical levels, except in speed of response. But in morphological respects and on every measure of syntactic function she finds repeated, significantly lower levels of performance among the normal elderly (aged 75–93) than among the pre-middle-aged (30–42). Kynette and Kemper (1986) likewise report that subjects in their 70s and 80s produced more syntactic errors and used less complex syntactic structures (which impose lower memory demands) in interview responses than people in their 50s and 60s. Kemper (1986) also reports that elderly adults (70–89) were less able to imitate complex syntactic constructions than young adults (30–49).

Nebes and Andrews-Kulis (1976), on the other hand, report no decremental age effects in subjects' construction of grammatical strings. Cooper (1990) finds no relationships between age (across people aged 20–78) and several measures of speech production, elaboration, complexity dysfluency, conciseness or information imparted. Adams, Labouvie-Vief, Hobart and Dorosz (1990) report that older people (mean age 66 years) used a 'more integrative and interpretive' style (p. 17) than young adults (mean age 19 years) in written tests of narrative recall.

Bayles and Kaszniak's (1987) balanced conclusion, after a thorough review of a good deal of the available experimental psycholinguistic research on ageing, is that 'The study of possible age effects on the ability to communicate is extremely demanding because effects, when present, are generally subtle, and most tasks are influenced by the subject's intelligence, education, life history, motivation, sensory integrity, mental status, and vigor. Few researchers have been able to control all of these variables in a convincing way' (p. 152). The authors single out comprehension and inferring as the areas of most clearly documented differential performance between young and old: 'Age effects are most obvious when information to be comprehended is new, complex, and implied and the time allowed for processing is short' (p. 153). but they suggest that, in terms of linguistic production, evidence is more difficult to interpret, again suggestive of some decline with age, though not necessarily through deterioration of the lexicon. Contra the findings of Emery (above), Bayles and Kaszniak conclude that 'An individual's knowledge of grammar is well preserved across the life span' (p. 153).

Generally, the deficit paradigm of later life research interprets the notion of 'normality' in confusing ways. In most studies the 'normal' elderly (labelled this way according to criteria of general health, and particularly absence of specific sensory problems) are shown to be performing 'abnormally' in some linguistic/communicative respect, if the norm is defined by young adult performance. So, Emery (1986) concludes from her study that 'diminished linguistic processing appears to be a concomitant of normal aging' (p. 60). In ways that are reminiscent of early and problematical studies in the area of language and social class, ageing research produces results that are very difficult to interpret in any socially sensitive frame. There is generally no consideration of attitudinal or motivational factors that might mediate different levels of performance (why do older people respond more slowly in some experimental conditions?); or of contextual factors (in what range of test circumstances do older people use less complex syntax, understand or remember less?); or of real-life implications (do measured differences have any socially contrastive or 'emic' significance (cf. Robinson, 1972) to everyday people in everyday settings outside of the test situation?); or of semiotic impact (which elderly characteristics, in fact, connote 'elderliness', to whom, and with what evaluative weighting?).

As a rule, the rationale behind the studies we have examined so far is the assumption that there is a 'normal' continuum of decrement during ageing. Differences in linguistic performance can indeed be shown to exist, if selectively and variably, and we do not mean to suggest that the investigation of linguistic performance (or 'under-performance') during normal ageing is not interesting. Our point is that the very design of this sort of research presupposes that decrement is normal. Even if specific findings do not themselves offer evidence of decrement, the studies have oriented to decrement as the researchable question in linguistic gerontology. The research is framed within the scope of a decrement model, and therefore legitimizes it.

A more elaborate conceptualisation of decrement in later life is the *inverted-U* model, which implies that elderly linguistic and other behaviours are in some specific respects not only moving towards lower levels of competence but moving *back* to the levels and types of behaviour associated with the early years of life. The model feeds off the more general mythological association of the old with children in our society – old age as a 'second childhood'. Realizations of this myth include visual images of the old as physically smaller and stooping (for example, as portrayed on UK road signs near residential old people's homes), and the conventional grouping of elderly people with children – for example given reduced-cost bus and rail-fares and cheaper admission to cinemas, theatres, etc. Myths of the 'success' and 'naturalness' of interaction between elderly people and children are perhaps to be interpreted similarly.

In matters to do with language, explicit claims are sometimes made about regression in later life. Emery (1986) concludes that there is 'a direct relationship between language deficits and age, a direct relationship between language deficits and linguistic complexity, and what appears to be the concomitant inverse relationship between sequence in language deterioration and sequence in [child] language development, i.e. the more complex the linguistic form, the later the development of that form . . . the quicker the deterioration of that form' (p. 57). Even though this same claim has been discredited in aphasia research (Lesser, 1978) and in any case has no practical value for therapists, the elderly-as-child myth seems to recur in other dimensions of ageing research. Beyond syntactic complexity, several characteristics of elderly speech can, with some creativity, be taken to fit the inverted-U. Elderly males' higher vocal pitch and lower speech rate, as reported in some studies (for example Hollien and Shipp,

1972; Mysak, 1959), might be seen as regressive features and stereotypically associated with young children's speech. Egocentricity (one interpretation of Gold et al.'s (1988) verbosity data) is again stereotyped as both an elderly and child characteristic, and so on.

Societal Ageism

As researchers, we are not immune from societal stereotypes and myths (see Kite and Johnson's (1988) meta-analysis of stereotyping studies). Miller (1987) has expressed concern about 'the degree to which our society imputes social and moral meanings [e.g., of "rolelessness"] even to unconditionally legitimate behaviors in the aging role [for example retirement]' (p. 146). In the past, 'rolelessness' (Bengston, 1973; Rosnow, 1973) and 'disengagement' (Cumming and Henry, 1961) have been put forward as theories to explain social ageing, in a way that is very controversial today. Miller (1987), on the other hand, stresses how society itself problematizes the elderly: 'Medical and social control agents tend to construct an ageing role which emphasizes disengagement, pathology, and the development of secondary deviance . . . These processes tend to present the elderly as a deprived problem group based on the factor of age alone and to undercut the view of normal or healthy aging as part of the life-cycle' (p. 152). According to J. Levin and Levin (1980), an ageist ideological slant pervades gerontological research. They argue that the gerontology literature is 'shot through both with the assumption of decline with age and, perhaps partly as a result of this assumption, with the findings of physical, psychological and sociological deterioration in ageing individuals' (p. 2).

From this viewpoint, the deficit tradition in language research may therefore be just another branch of cultural prejudice against the elderly, with its selective designs and pervasive concern with linguistic decrement. The fact that only modest and qualified evidence of suppressed performance levels has been produced does not seem to have challenged the work's ideological assumptions. We have already referred to some instances where more positively construed elderly communicative characteristics have been evidenced; elderly subjects have sometimes been shown to 'outperform' young communicators.

Smith, Reinheimer and Gabbard-Alley (1981) found that elderly women (mean age 71) coped better with the demands of crowded and close communication environments than young women (mean age 20): 'Task performance among younger subjects deteriorated in close interaction conditions, whereas the performance of older subjects was improved by spacial intrusion. Further, older subjects exhibited positive communication behaviours [including friendliness and involvement] in response to close conversation' (p. 259).

Overall, it seems appropriate to remind ourselves of what Guggenbuhl-Craig (1980), in an intriguing analysis, has called 'the pitfalls of the health/wholeness archetype' (p. 21): the blinkered concern with perfect competence and with individuals' deviations from it to which Western society is prone. If we can remove these blinkers, we can begin to explore the diverse processes through which language and communication impinge upon the experience of old age and on society's orientation to the old.

The Anti-ageism Paradigm

In many approaches to sex/gender, social class and race across the social sciences we can identify a coherent perspective that assumes and tries to demonstrate that its research populations are disenfranchised and undervalued. In social gerontology there is no shortage of statements that elderly people are such a group. Tyler (1986), for example, argues that ageism is structurally integrated into contemporary British society. J. Levin and Levin (1980) review the diverse forms of societal ageism and its origins. As factors in the construction of an ageist climate they identify how social groups concerned with their own status and self-esteem show hostility to minorities they perceive as weak, powerless or inferior. Economic forces create further pressures in the form of competition between young and old over scarce resources and jobs. J. Levin and Levin also recognize a specific condition that they label 'gerontophobia', fear of one's own ageing, of the elderly and of association with death (p. 94; cf. also Bunzel, 1972). Butler (1969) similarly defines ageism as 'a deep-seated uneasiness on the part of the young and middle-aged – a personal revulsion to and distaste for growing older' (p. 243).

A critical manifestation of gerontophobia is to be found in the caring professions, where, according to Norman (1987), 'The poor image of old age inevitably rubs off on those who are working in this field. Work with old people is not a prestigious occupation and there is a vicious circle in that jobs with low prestige tend to attract unambitious or less-skilled workers' (p. 9). For J. Levin and Levin (1980), ageism shows up as a propensity to 'blame the [elderly] victim', to blame 'biology or the ravages of time' for the states and conditions of old age, rather than focus on the social forces that make old age 'a difficult, even dreaded stage of life' (p. 35). Age-prejudicial forces have been documented in several other domains too: literature (Berman and Sobkowska-Ashcroft, 1986), humour (Palmore, 1971), magazine fiction (Martel, 1968), television drama and commercials (Kubey, 1980).

Research has set out to demonstrate the ways in which parts of the language system itself play a part in the reproduction of ageist attitudes. Covey (1988) traces the changing meanings of terms relating to old age. The etymology of the word 'old' itself, for example, associates it with the meaning 'to nourish', and it has for a long time carried connotations of experience, skill and wisdom (p. 293). More recently, it has been associated with meanings of endearment ('old friend', 'Old Bright'), but also conservatism ('old guard'); it has been used in references to the Devil ('Old Harry', 'Old Nick') and very often in derogatory terms ('old hag', 'old fogy', 'dirty old man'). Covey claims that 'contemporary older people do not like to use the word old in describing themselves or their membership groups' (p. 293), and concludes generally that terminology in this area reflects 'a decline in the status of the elderly and the increased focus on the debilitative effects of aging' (p. 297).

Nuessel (1984) similarly argues that there is a vast lexicon of ageist language in everyday usage, within which most terms are used to describe or refer to the elderly in a pejorative way, or at least carry negative overtones. Instances relating to females, often prefixed by 'old', (most from Nuessel) include: 'biddy', 'crone', 'bag', 'hag' and 'battleaxe'; referring to males: 'gaffer', 'duffer' and 'geezer'; 'old fool', 'old fart' and others are also in wide currency. Pejorative adjectives often used to describe elderly people include: 'cantankerous', 'crotchety', 'fussy', 'garrulous', 'grumpy', 'rambling'. 'Wrinklies' has recently been adopted fairly widely in the UK as a demeaning group noun. Studying group labels experimentally in the USA, Barbato and

Feezel (1987) asked people of different ages (17–44, 45–64, 65+) to evaluate the connotative meanings of ten words referring to an older person. Some terms (including 'mature American', 'senior citizen' and 'retired person') were positively rated on the scales 'active', 'strong', 'good', 'progressive' and ' happy'. On the other hand, 'aged', 'elderly' and nouns using 'old' were evaluated more negatively. An interesting finding was that there were few differences between the responses of the different age groups.

There is much scope for further research, both observation and controlled experimentation, into the connotative content of age-related vocabulary. It will be important to distinguish terms of reference (ingroup and outgroup) from terms of address (cf. Wood and Ryan, in press), and to establish where, when and by whom they are used. By these means we should be able to produce better-founded and more particular statements of the distribution of age-related terms and expressions in everyday usage, and of the evaluative effects they produce in particular listeners. Research also needs to consider carefully the *discursive* contexts in which these terms are used; for example, whether in serious, glib or humorous talk, whether in general reference or perhaps particularly when speakers account for their reactions to interaction with elderly people. Our interpretation of the significance of these usages, and the extent to which we do in fact need to view them as ageist, depends on this more sophisticated approach. Certainly, the hope that Oyer and Oyer expressed in 1976 of making vocabulary relating to the elderly 'more accurate and complete' and so of reducing or eliminating ageism from language seems premature.

Talk to the elderly has been the subject of some of the most sustained research to date, mostly driven by concern for what is thought to be the proper treatment of older people in conversation. Ashburn and Gordon (1981) compared specific formal and functional characteristics of care-givers' and volunteers' speech among them-selves and to elderly residents in a nursing home. They found that staff and volunteers used more questions and repetitions to elderly residents than among their peers, and that staff used more questions to non-alert than to alert residents. Rubin and Brown (1975) found that students used significantly shorter utterances, and hence arguably simpler syntax, to explain the rules of a game to older adults (who they assessed to have lower intellectual abilities) than to young adults.

Again there is a need for more contextual sensitivity in work of this sort, and quantitative contrastive designs will inevitably tend to obscure the conversational dynamics involved. Multilevel research has, however, begun to produce important findings. Greene, Adelman, Charon and Hoffman (1986) found no differences in the frequencies of questions, compliments or negative remarks made by physicians to older (over 65) and younger (under 45) patients in medical interviews. But they still concluded that it was more difficult for elderly patients than for young patients to 'get their agendas addressed'; also that 'physicians were less respectful, less patient, less engaged and less egalitarian with their old than with their young patients' (p. 121). Greene et al. take these differences of approach by physicians as evidence of ageist professional practices in medical encounters (see also Adelman, Greene and Charon in press).

The focus of Caporael and colleagues' research (Caporael, 1981; Caporael and Culbertson, 1986; Caporael, Lucaszewski and Culbertson, 1983; Culbertson and Caporael, 1983) has been the use of secondary baby-talk (BT) by care-givers to the institutionalized elderly. BT, defined as a specific set of prosodic configurations including high and variable pitch, was found in the 1981 study to be frequent in care-givers' talk to residents (up to 20 per cent), and to be indistinguishable when content-filtered from primary BT (that is, talk actually addressed to children). As Caporael's term 'BT' shows, the research parallels other sociolinguistic traditions investigating simplified addressee registers, not only baby-talk (or 'motherese', cf. Snow and Ferguson, 1977) but also 'foreigner talk' (Ferguson, 1981).

While overlaps in language and communication styles to these diverse groups are of course interesting, and while there might be implications in these similarities for a universal theory of linguistic complexity and simplification, each demographic context has its unique considerations of social motivation, evaluation and consequence (De Paulo and Coleman, 1986). For example, Brown (1977) considers a possible pedagogic intent behind using simplified registers to children; descriptively similar styles of language used to non-native speakers may conceivably be intended to suppress linguistic and cultural integration (Valdman, 1981); simplified talk to the visually handicapped may be demeaning because it overgeneralizes from a particular sensory handicap (N. Coupland, Giles and Benn, 1986). Therefore, an approach that glosses 'talk to the elderly' as one of a family of speech registers will inevitably obscure the social processes at work. In fact, Caporael and colleagues' important research (to which we return below) clearly demonstrates the value of integrating sociolinguistic and socio-psychological analyses in specific research contexts.

The quantitative social evaluation paradigm has also considered age-discriminatory responses to vocal styles. The stimuli are audio recordings of elderly and young-adult speakers, either genuine or (most often) imitated, with vocal characteristics that differ along specified dimensions – the so-called 'matched guise' technique. Stewart and Ryan (1982), for example, found that younger adults can be rated more positively than older adults in competence-stressing situations (cf. also K. H. Rubin and Brown, 1975). Research findings have not been entirely consistent. Crockett, Press and Osterkamp (1979) found relatively favourable reactions to older speakers, and attributed the finding to the effects of judges' negative stereotypical expectations of elderly speakers being disconfirmed. In Ryan and Johnston's (1987) study the variable 'effective' versus 'ineffective' message was the only factor significantly influencing competence ratings across younger and older speakers, with no main effects emerging for age itself.

Ryan and Cole (1990) asked two groups of elderly women to evaluate messages addressed to them in different speech styles. They found that the younger group, who lived in the community, were less tolerant of styles used in speech to them; the older, institutionalized group perceived and preferred speech that was slower, simpler and clearer. Ryan and Cole identify a predicament for those wishing to speak most 'effectively' to older people: that speech styles that convey support and nurturance are also liable to suggest an expectation of diminished competence.

Giles, Henwood, Coupland, Harriman and Coupland (submitted) again found that, in a matched-guise design, speech rate was a more potent variable than either accent (standard versus non-standard voice) or age (older versus younger speaking guise). But there was also some evidence that an elderly voice in conjunction with a non-standard accent and a low speaking rate conspired to produce very high ratings of perceived 'vulnerability'. In an open-ended phase of the investigation respondents were found to invoke stereotypes of age and class to rationalize the evaluative rankings they had made across all conditions of the study. For example, while the non-standard speaking guises called up images of a homely, provincial speaker, the elderly vocal guises were associated with incompetence, forgetfulness and disaffection.

Other studies have shown detrimental age stereotypes intervening not only in abstract judgements but also in behavioural choices. Carver and de la Garza (1984) found that, after a supposed road accident, the sorts of information asked for from younger and older drivers varied in stereotype-consistent ways. Drivers labelled 'elderly' tended to be asked to give information about their physical, mental, sight and hearing competence; 'young' drivers tended to be asked whether they had been speeding or had drunk alcohol. In an extension study Franklyn-Stokes, Harriman, Giles and Coupland (1988) found similar patterns of differential questioning, though distributed incrementally across ages 22, 54, 64, 74 and 84 years (these were the ages given for the supposed addressee). Health and physical condition featured increasingly often in subsequent questions as the age of the driver increased. To this extent, information seeking can be seen to be ageist across the adult life span.

Generally, then, research in what we have been considering the anti-ageism paradigm has pointed to very different sorts of association between language and prejudicial beliefs about elderly people. Identifying speakers as 'elderly 'often results in downgraded evaluations of their competence, and causes people to act in discriminatory ways towards them. Perhaps even the language system itself has reified society's ageist assumptions in its vocabulary. There is growing evidence that people modify their speech to at least some groups of older people, and some suggestion that these styles can be unwarranted and demeaning. In medical encounters patients of different ages are at times treated differently by doctors, and this could in turn have profound implications for the success of health care (Kreps, 1986). It is not surprising that one of the major growth areas in social gerontology is study of the role of social support in elderly health and well-being, and of how relationships may be able to act as buffers against stress (for example Krause, 1986; Rook and Pietromonaco, 1987; see Giles, Coupland and Wiemann, 1990 for an overview). Certainly there is an important place for sociolinguistic research in this enterprise.

Discourse and Ageing: An Integrative Perspective

The studies we report in later chapters, and gerontological socio-linguistics generally, can find a useful basis in the wide-ranging research we have reviewed in this chapter. On the other hand, many of these studies have worked in laboratory settings; inevitably, most of them have approached language and social ageing in a rather fragmented way. As we have already suggested, much of the existing work is reminiscent of early eras in other sociolinguistic areas, with contrastive, decontextualized and non-interactional designs predominating. There have been very few attempts to cross-refer between research tradi-tions, although studies of attitudes, stereotypes, speech character – istics, addressee styles, interaction and social support all have their place in an adequate sociolinguistic perspective on ageing.

Caporael and her colleagues have shown the value of more intergrated research in their case for understanding the complexity of issues involved in the use of secondary BT styles to institutionalized elderly people. They found that even in one physical setting, speakers' goals and listeners' attributions and evaluations were highly differentiated. The Caporael et al. study established that care-givers predicted that residents with low functional ability would *like* to be spoken to with BT, and felt that *non*-BT speech would be ineffective for interacting with them. Also, it emerged that BT was indeed judged by some institutionalized elderly people to be demeaning, but to be *nurturing* by others. Dependent elderly people were more likely to hear BT as nurturing, and BT was found to be associated with a high frequency of 'encouraging comments'. Other dimensions of 'elderspeak' also may be facilitative in some social situations. Cohen and Faulkner (1986), for example, reported that speech styles with exaggerated primary word-stress had positive effects on elderly people's comprehension and recall. Findings like these mean that we need to be cautious in the claims and judgements we make in particular settings. What may appear a case of ageist behaviour, where negative stereotypes of ageing are taken to dictate language and communication choices to the detriment of elderly recipients, may at times be better described as well-judged and accommodative adaptation.

These contextual considerations show that a variety of research methods is needed, and that our interpretations will often need to reflect how talk is embedded in multiple layers of textual as well as social and psychological *con*textual considerations. Since quantitative, contrastive, survey-type designs cannot hope to control such considerations as variables, it seems inevitable that sociolinguistics will increasingly use more qualitative discourse analytic methods. And it is the label 'discourse analysis' that best characterizes the research orientation we adopt in the following chapters, however diffusely the term has come to be used (cf. Potter and Wetherell, 1987). Mainly through close examination of particular sequences of talk involving specific elderly people, speaking either to age peers or younger individuals, we explore a range of questions to do with the management of elderly identity and intergenerational relations.

Unlike most of the approaches we have reviewed in this chapter, we try to adopt a thoroughly interactional perspective. If we are to move beyond quite gross attempts to specify what 'elderly language is like' or how 'the elderly are talked to', we have to reflect the local organization of talk and its textualization – what Maynard (1988) has called the 'interaction order' (p. 312). Appreciating the sequential organization of talk – which has always been the primary goal of conversation analysis – is the basic means of exploring the relational possibilities and constraints of individual conversations as they develop in real time. In fact, a recurring theme of this book is that older conversationalists frequently have their interactional roles, and key aspects of their life-span identities, constructed *for* them by younger people. At many points we are drawn to the conclusion that important subjective dimensions of ageing itself are accomplished interactionally.

At the same time, we assume that conversation sequencing *alone* is too narrow a source for interpretation, and that the broader social and cultural frameworks in which talk is conducted exert powerful, if often unseen, influences on what is said and what is inferred. In talk between the generations there is always the possibility of speakers aligning as age-group members, with their talk being interpreted through a screen of 'intergroup' evaluations and attributions, in Tajfel's (1978) terms. So, our interpretations often appeal to macro as well as micro dimensions of context, to the life experiences, assumptions, priorities and goals of the people whose talk is under analysis. We recognize that this procedure can sometimes be uncomfortably subjective, but we find support in the ethnographic background work on which our analyses are based: the group discussions and interviews that are occasionally referred to in the text, and our own long-term interactions with the elderly people who constitute our principal research populations.

A Preview

In the next chapter we specify the range of interactional considerations that a discourse analysis, as we conceive of it, must encompass. We draw on case-study data and previous research to identify general strategies of intergenerational talk, and trace their psychosocial origins and their consequences. Using the general concepts of speech accommodation theory (Giles, Coupland and Coupland, 1991), we identify overaccommodative and underaccommodative modes of talk, which lie at the root of many intergenerational conflicts and problems. We use these and related concepts in analysing more extensive interactional sequences in later chapters.

In chapter 3 we examine data from 40 videotaped first-acquaintance interactions between women aged 70–87 and women in their 30s. This is the initial database for several of the discourse processes explored in the volume. We focus on a range of discourse strategies that are involved in the management of *age identity* in different interpersonal contexts. These strategies make salient, and even define, the 'contextual' life positions of older speakers, and of younger speakers relative to them. *Variable* age identities, as regards their independence, mobility, life satisfaction, and so on, are in fact projected by *and for* elderly people in different contexts. We interpret the data as showing the active role that interaction can play in the social construction of ageing.

The focus of chapters 5 and 6 is more particular: the management of so-called 'painful self-disclosure' (PSD) in cross- and within-generation talk. PSD refers to the revealing of personal and often intimate information about ill health, bereavement, immobility, loneliness, and so on. Chapter 5 develops a taxonomy of the interactional alternatives available to disclosers and listeners to introduce, encode, respond to and close PSD sequences. This taxonomy is then used in chapter 6 to overview how PSD is in fact managed in the 40 interaction corpus as a whole. The patterns we find suggest a range of *positive* identity functions for older people's disclosive behaviour, though such intimacy in first-acquaintance settings also incurs social costs.

In chapter 6 we consider patterns of *age-telling*, trying to account for the high frequency of this further type of self-disclosure in elderly talk. We again focus on the local management of age-telling, and show how age in years is structurally integrated with appraisals of own and other's health. Age-telling is therefore a further resource for projecting and modifying age identity in talk.

In chapter 7 we use data from group discussions *about* intergenerational talk, gathering further insights from what older people say about their priorities and goals for talk and how younger people react to the talk of their elders. Discourse analyses of group discussions show something of the intergroup divide across which intergenerational talk can proceed, a filter of generation-specific beliefs and predispositions.

Lastly, what broader implications follow? The final chapter reviews recent data from three institutional settings, all involved with forms of care for the elderly. The way age- and health-identity are construed can impinge very directly on health itself, perhaps particularly in medical and caring contexts (Kaplan, Barell and Lusky, 1988). Talk in these settings deserves attention – not least from professionals and care givers themselves. We therefore consider aspects of the training that is provided for home helps and nurses who will care for the elderly, and how conversations in fact proceed in long-stay caring institutions. We evaluate the potential for sociolinguistic research to influence day-to-day practices in these contexts.

Sociolinguistic priorities

At this point in this chapter's general argument, then, there is an irony. We argued early on that theory-driven explorations of elderly language and communication are often unduly narrow in being limited to considerations of diachrony and decrement. Now, in the data-driven, discourse analytic investigations into elderly and inter-generational communication that this volume will present, diachrony and decrement clearly underpin some of the most distinctive observable characteristics of talk: the thematizing of own ill health and decrement and the telling of age.

There is no contradiction in this. The discourse analytic approach, perhaps above all, invites an analysis of how social actors make sense of their social circumstances, and not least of themselves, through interaction. It is for these reasons that discourse theorists have for some time resisted deterministic assumptions about the constitution of social categories and their 'effects' upon linguistic performance (cf. P. Berger and Luckmann, 1967; Potter, 1988; Shotter and Gergen, 1989). In gerontology, as West and Zimmerman (1985) have suggested for gender research (p. 119), a shift of attention from a demographic category treated as an isolated sociolinguistic variable to speech as a mode of action between humans of varying situational identities allows us to develop a much richer understanding of how discourse helps to construct the fabric of social life.

Perhaps, then, the greatest challenge for studies of language and later life is to explore how themes of ageing, ageism and anti-ageism arise in social discourse where the elderly are participating or in question. If we see 'elderliness' as a collective subjectivity as much as a physiological end-point, it is important to explore the social construction and reproduction of old age through talk. An interactional focus is essential if we assume, as independent research suggests, that elderly people are prone to assimilate society's devalued appraisals of their own elderly group, and so lower their self-esteem (Bengston, Reedy and Gordon, 1985).

There is evidence in the following chapters that, for at least some elderly people, locating oneself in relation to past experiences, to one's own state of health, to chronological age and to projectable future decrement and death is functional at a profound level. Discourse can enact a negotiative process centring on life position and life prospects, with immediate consequences for morale and psychological well-being. If in these ways language has the potential to influence our most fundamental experiences of ageing, for better or for worse, the language sciences' historical neglect of elderly people seems all the more regrettable. Sociolinguistics may in future prove to have a key independent contribution to make to applied gerontological concerns.

2

Discourse, Accommodation and Intergenerational Relations

Sociolinguistics has not generally adopted the interactional, relational and constitutive perspective that we argued in favour of at the end of chapter 1. Many analytic frameworks in sociolinguistics, such as the widely used correlational approach associated with Labov's work, are too static to allow us to be sensitive to the local interactional processes that we suggest help to define experiences of ageing. But any coherent analysis at least needs a principled set of concepts, a repertoire of interpretive possibilities to draw on. Because we have argued that discourse analysis needs to reflect social and social-psychological dimensions of context as well as the organization of talk itself, it will be helpful to have a model that recognizes how linguistic variables intersect with speakers' and listeners' attitudes, goals and strategies, and with the outcomes of interaction.

Communication accommodation theory (CAT; see N. Coupland and Giles, 1988; Giles and Coupland, 1991a; Giles, Coupland and Coupland, 1991) has been developed as an integrated interdisciplinary model of discourse and context, and offers us some useful initial concepts and hypotheses. In this chapter we briefly introduce the CAT model and use it to sketch out how talk can be involved in one generation group's alignment to another, and some of the likely sources of intergenerational conflict. We review some theoretical research that has already used the accommodation model to describe 'young-to-elderly' speech styles; we then elaborate on this approach using data from a case-study of intergenerational talk. One value of CAT is that it allows discourse studies to engage with recent theory in social psychology, in line with our attempts to provide a multidisciplinary analysis.

The Accommodation Model

The original aim of accommodation theory was to specify the strategies of *convergence* and *divergence* (Giles, 1973; 1984; Giles and Powesland, 1975). These terms refer to the ways in that speakers modify their language (and other behavioural differences) to reduce or increase differences between them. A third possibility was said to be linguistic *maintenance*. Each strategy was then associated with a range of particular socio-psychological contexts – for example integrative motives in the case of convergence, and generally dissociative motives with divergence and maintenance. So, speakers' orientations to their listeners can themselves be said to be convergent or divergent. Figure 2.1 shows how such orientations are likely to be influenced by speakers' experiences, needs, and other states, and by the contextual demands upon them. The model allows us to make some testable predictions about communication strategies and their outcomes. When a speaker has particular relational goals for an interaction (for example wanting to gain the other's approval, wanting talk to be effective and efficient or, conversely, wanting to establish self or self's social group as distinct from the interlocutor or her/his group), she or he will select from a range of sociolinguistic (and non-verbal) strategies *attending to or anticipating the recipient's own communication characteristics*.

The sociolinguistic heart of CAT is this focus on processes of *communicative attuning*, adaptive and strategic moves made by interactants to increase and decrease social and sociolinguistic distance. Because it specifies processes of perception and evaluation, the model is useful to explain various forms of intentional or unintentional *mis*matches of communication styles. It can help us to trace their origins, effects and implications at both individual and group levels (see Giles and Coupland 1991a for a discussion of interpersonal versus intergroup dimensions of social relations). Convergence and divergence have been studied at very many linguistic levels, including segmental phonology and other dialect features, speech rates, pause and utterance lengths, choice of language code. These symbolic *approximation* strategies have been shown to function productively over a very wide range of social settings in almost two decades of empirical research (for reviews, see

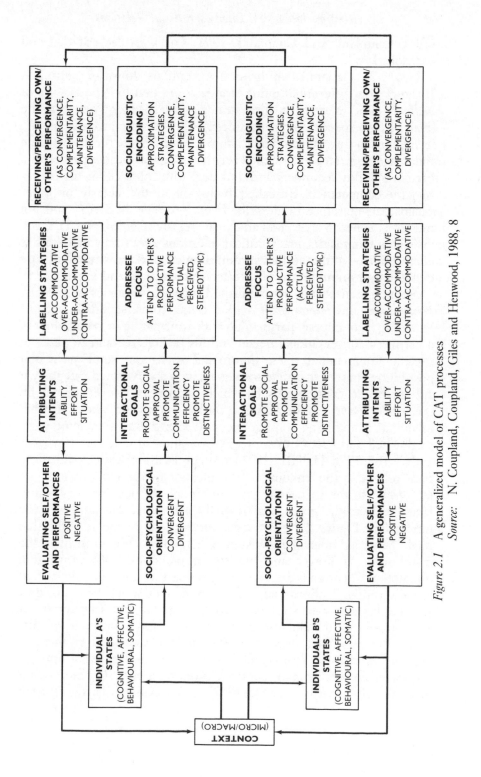

Figure 2.1 A generalized model of CAT processes
Source: N. Coupland, Coupland, Giles and Henwood, 1988, 8

Giles, Coupland and Coupland, 1991; Giles, Mulac, Bradac and Johnson, 1987).

Figure 2.2 elaborates on the strategic options shown in figure 2.1. It shows how different attuning strategies are tied to various sorts of *addressee focus*. In approximation strategies the speaker focuses on the hearer's own speech output, and designs his or her convergence, etc. in relation to this. Accommodation may alternatively (or at the same time) involve strategies designed relative to how a speaker perceives a partner's ability to understand and deal with interaction, his or her *receptive* competence. So-called baby-talk to the elderly or other groups can therefore be described very precisely by CAT, and not merely as a speech style or an addressee register (see chapter 1). CAT invites us to consider many critical questions about how baby-talk is contextualized – the attitudes, motivations, speaking situations, and cultures that promote it, *and* its effects, immediate and longer term.

Attuning can also be accomplished through strategies of *discourse management* and *interpersonal control*. Being conversationally accommodating is, of course, partly to do with anticipating or responding to a partner's conversational needs and his or her freedom to play out specific interactional roles. Figure 2.2 spells out some particular possibilities here. Discourse management is a very broad category. It subsumes the many means by which degrees of conversational fit, greater or lesser, can be achieved during interaction, and with what relational motives and consequences. We have drawn on some well-established approaches to contextual variation in language (Gregory and Carroll, 1978; Halliday, 1978) to suggest a three-way classification: *Field* relates to the building of the ideational/referential content of talk; *tenor*, to the management of interpersonal positions, roles and faces; *mode* to the procedural/textual dimensions that structure the interaction. Figure 2.2 gives some illustrations of the features that might be varied in each dimension. When talk is attuned through the distribution of power and control, a psychologically convergent orientation will often mean allowing your partner a reasonable level of role discretion. Authoritarian stances in interaction will be realized by severely limiting your speaking-partners' opportunities to initiate or develop topics, to follow their own agendas and fulfil their specific goals. For example, data from the institutional settings that we examine in chapter 7 indicates low attuning through what appears excessive constraint and control. Nurses appear to exert their institutional authority over elderly long-stay patients partly through

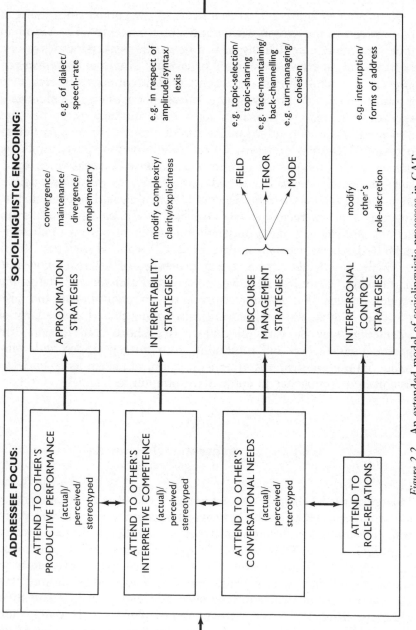

Figure 2.2 An extended model of sociolinguistic processes in CAT
Source: N. Coupland, Coupland, Giles and Henwood, 1988, 28

denying them certain conversational rights (Grainger, Atkinson and Coupland, 1990).

Returning to figure 2.1, we see some of the complexities that can be involved in interpreting accommodation strategies. For example, there are many potential disparities between speakers' and hearers' appraisals of their own and others' behaviour. The label *overaccommodative* is a useful one in intergenerational contexts. It refers to a miscommunicative process where at least one participant perceives a speaker (who may be herself or himself or another) to 'go beyond' a sociolinguistic style judged necessary for attuned talk on a particular occasion. Examples are speaking too loudly or too slowly, or being unnecessarily cautious and careful. *Underaccommodation* is when some style or quality of talk is underplayed (relative to needs or wishes). The model stresses *creative* aspects of listening and interpreting: it suggests that, as recipients, we are likely to make attributions for actions and evaluate them under the influence of our own culturally delimited experiences (cf. Bradac, 1982; Giles and Hewstone, 1982).

Finally, by feeding back these processes of interpretation into participants' cognitive, affective, behavioural and somatic states, the model implies that discourse processes in institutional, but also everyday, situations can be critically important. Experiences of interaction may be very relevant to our short- and longer-term personal satisfaction and fulfilment, even for our health and well-being. These are the sorts of consideration that seem to us to be an important rationale for an applied sociolinguistics.

CAT in Intergenerational Contexts

How might CAT help in characterizing some of the difficulties that are often reported as arising in cross-generation talk? A starting point is to be found in studies of social *stereotypes* of old age. In fact, a set of empirical studies (Thakerar, Giles and Cheshire, 1982) established the need for CAT to consider the role of stereotypical perceptions of speakers and their speech characteristics. The studies showed that stereotypes can mediate the language strategies we adopt and their effects on listeners (see also Street and Hopper, 1982; Hewstone and Giles, 1986). There is ample research evidence to prove that older speakers are often negatively stereotyped, perceived as relatively incompetent, slow, old-fashioned and inflexible (see, for example, Crockett, Press and Osterkamp, 1979; Stewart and Ryan, 1982). As we saw in chapter 1, there is also a tendency for people to confirm age-related stereotypes when another's elderliness is made explicit. This opens up the possibility that elderly people might regularly be addressed by speakers who are accommodating *not* to individuals' communicative characteristics *per se*, but rather to those they stereotype the elderly as possessing.

So, we might expect to find inappropriate and misconceived language styles being used to those elderly people – the vast majority – who are inaccurately included in the social stereotype (cf. Platt and Weber, 1984; and chapter 1). The predictable consequences might be irritation and dissatisfaction – ultimately for both parties involved – leading to the accentuation of perceived differences between the generations and perhaps to a mutual wish to avoid future contact (cf. Hewstone and Brown, 1986). Alongside these social consequences there are also predictable *individual* consequences. Where our relational experiences impinge on our age- and health-identities, a decline in life satisfaction and in psychological and even physical health can be anticipated (see the discussion below on linguistic self-stereotyping).

In CAT terms, then, we can derive the general hypothesis that younger speakers may regularly overaccommodate to the elderly, producing styles of talk targeted at the often inappropriate, stereotyped social persona of 'the elderly communicator'. In more familiar terms, older people are likely to suffer from being patronized, talked down to, or 'baby-talked' – evaluative dimensions of miscommunication that CAT can help to clarify, model and relate to specific sociolinguistic selections and their effects. For instance, Henwood and Giles (reported in Ryan, Giles, Bartolucci and Henwood, 1986) observed 33 elderly women (aged 65–94 years, living alone) in conversation with home helps (home-care assistants). What the elderly subjects considered baby-talk occurred quite frequently, and about 40 per cent of this (admittedly small) sample reported having been the recipients of demeaning talk. Similarly, Caporael and associates' research on talk to the institutionalized elderly (see chapter 1) fits the overaccommodation rubric particularly well.

The Ryan et al. Young-to-Elderly Strategies

Ryan et al. (1986) drew on observational research by Henwood and Giles and used CAT constructs to devise a typology of four young-to-elderly strategies (see table 2.1). The first of these they characterized as *overaccommodation due to physical or sensory handicaps*, which arises when speakers rightly or wrongly perceive their addressees to be specifically handicapped (for example, with hearing impairment) and adapt their speech beyond the optimal level. Even if the recipient does suffer some hearing loss, the younger person who overcompensates with much-increased loudness will be heard to be shouting. The perception of a specific handicap can trigger many different stylistic features, many of them associated with talk to children (Ferguson, 1977; Snow and Ferguson, 1977). They include lexical and syntactic simplification, decreased speech rate and the prosodic features (wide pitch range and rapid pitch variation) that Caporael and associates take as their primary definition of baby-talk.

The second strategy is labelled *dependency-related overaccommodation* and refers to overbearing, excessively directive and disciplinary talk to elderly people, as in the exclamation 'oh you naughty girl!' used by a carer to one elderly woman in the data who had made quite a minor mistake. Ryan et al. conjectured that this strategy is one way in that a younger person can control the relationship and (wilfully or not) induce an older person to become more dependent. The addressee may come to be classified as needy and so lose some of her rights to make autonomous decisions, unless these rights *are* vigorously protected and openly asserted. It is precisely these rights that *are* being asserted in the account below (extract 2.1, transcribed from Henwood and Giles' (1985) audio-recorded data)[1] that an older person (OP) gives to a researcher (K) of a problematic interaction she had with a relief home help; P is her regular carer. OP says that she was shouted at, told what to do in her own home, and generally, she felt, spoken to like a baby.

The third strategy identified, *age-related divergence*, draws on one of CAT's central predictions that speakers may seek to promote the distinctiveness of their own social group by differentiating aspects of their speech from the speech of their interlocutors. In talk between the generations young people who want to dissociate themselves

Table 2.1 Summary of the socio-psychological contexts and sociolinguistic instantiation of five processes of young-to-elderly miscommunication

Language strategies[a]	Sender					Receiver
	Social/socio-psychological trigger	Interactional goal(s)	Addressee focus	Sociolinguistic strategies activated	Judged strategies	Speaker performance labelled
Sensory over-accommodation	Assumption of physical/sensory handicap (e.g., hearing loss)	Promote communication efficiency	Other's interpretive competence	Interpretability (e.g., much increased amplitude)	Overcompensation	Overaccommodative
Dependency overaccommodation	Perception of social or institutional roles	Confirm or exert own control	Other's social role	Interpersonal control (regulative talk)	Authoritarianism	Underaccommodative or overaccommodative
Intergroup divergence	'Threatened identity (e.g., elder seen as superior)	Promote intergroup distinctiveness	Other's productive performance	Approximation (divergence)	Dissociation	Contra-accommodative
Intergroup over-accommodation	Perception of social stereotype (e.g., of 'aged communicator')	Promote social attractiveness, communication efficiency, nurturance	Other's conversational needs of interpretive competence	Discourse management; interpretability (e.g., simplification, etc.)	Depersonalization	Overaccommodative
Intergroup under-accommodation	Life circumstances	Presumably positive	Weak (egocentric focus)	Discourse management (lowly attuned)	–	Underaccommodative

[a] cf. Ryan et al. (1986)

Source: N. Coupland, Coupland, Giles and Henwood, 1988, p. 22ff.

EXTRACT 2.1

```
 1 OP: . . . and and and she told me off (.) she she said to me (.) go in
 2      she said (.) sit down (.) I don't want you to watch me washing (.)
 3      I said I'm not watching you washing (.) I'm only having a conversation
 4      like P_____ used to when she did the washing (.) and she said get in
 5      then she said I don't want you (.) ((watching)) me
 6 K:   so did she think you were angry at her and then she got angry?
                                        [    ]
 7 OP:                                  I I
 8 OP: yes she (.) she came in you see (.) to me (.) and she but she was angry
 9      at me first
10 K:   right
11 OP: she told me off first you see because I sat down (.) she didn't ((want))
12      she thought I suppose in her mind I don't know (.) that I was watching
13      to see if she was doing the washing properly ((it was)) far from my mind
14      (.) because I always was used to P_____ setting down ((into it)) I've
15      never complained to you have I P_____?(.) ever
                                         [
16 P:                                      not ((2 sylls.)) no
17 OP: and all I wanted was a kind of conversation as I sat down you see(.)
18      and yet she told me off(.) get in out of it she said get in she said(.)
19      I don't want you ((watching)) me(.) and of course that put my back up see
20      and I come in and I sat down and I thought to myself I'll never have you
21      again I'll rather sit on my knees and do the washing again and she come
22      in again she said shall I ring mister R_____? I said you can do what
23      you like (.) but I said tell him your attitude to me(.) whatever else
24      you do(.) tell him your attitude to me I don't want the likes of you
25      coming and doing washing for me and telling me off and treating me like
26      a baby I won't have it(.) I said I'm a sensible decent person(.) and
27      I'm not going to be told off because I happen to sit in my kitchen if I
28      want to (1.0) would you have it?
```

culturally, in terms of their value systems and lifestyles, from the old may achieve or mark this psychological divergence sociolinguistically. Though Henwood and Giles did not produce behavioural evidence of the strategy in action, there is a large literature over many years that demonstrates the social attitudes that underpin it (see, for example, Kogan, 1979; Lutsky, 1980; Tuckman and Lorge, 1954).

In a survey of our own (N. Coupland, Coupland, Giles and Henwood, 1988) we recorded age-stereotyped evaluations made by various groups of young people in the UK in group discussion sessions. A total of more than 100 young people of widely varying socio-economic and educational backgrounds, in three groupings (pre-employment trainees on the 1986 Youth Training Scheme, participants at a residential outdoor pursuits award course, and university undergraduates), expressed their views on the strengths and weaknesses of 'the young' and 'the old', and on the similarities and differences they perceived between the two categories. Vivid (though by no means homogeneous) stereotypical images of the elderly as an out-group emerged. The old were frequently seen as physically decrepit and inactive (including sexually), cognitively declining, and socially isolated. In speech, they were characterized as repetitious, grumpy, slow and dull, but knowledgeable and correct.

These group sessions were conducted as a pilot to more systematic, socio-psychological investigations of intra- and intergroup attitudes, beliefs and categorizations (studies reported in Giles, Coupland and Wiemann, 1990; Williams and Giles, in press). But they are interesting in themselves in showing very little overlap of perceived ingroup and outgroup attributes. When the elderly were assigned positive traits – namely experience, wisdom and gentleness – these were quite uniformly different from those assigned to the young: sense of humour, cheerfulness, strength and potency, good looks, concern for contemporary social issues such as world peace. Given this complementary distribution of in- and outgroup stereotypical traits (see Hummert, 1990), it would be surprising if some young speakers did not seek to reinforce and symbolize their distinctiveness, as they construe it, in social encounters with older people. They might achieve this through a dynamic communicative style (perhaps a faster speech rate), by expressing non-conservative ideologies and 'progressive' ideas and attitudes, through youth-cult slang and colloquialism, and so on.

Finally, Ryan et al. (1986) identified *intergroup overaccommodation* as the fourth, and, they argued, one of the most pervasive, young-to-elderly language strategies. Simply perceiving an addressee to belong to a social category – being elderly, independent of any particular handicap – is enough to invoke negative inferences for many younger people. This is the central case of failing to accommodate to elderly addressees *as individuals* through accommodating to perceived group norms. In fact, it is in these circumstances that we would expect to find an habitual and fixed mode of speech, an addressee register of 'elderspeak' (see Cohen and Faulkner, 1986, and chapter 1).

Presumably, this linguistic depersonalization would be especially characteristic of young people who had little knowledge of how the elderly community is structured (for example its demography and institutional support), particularly negative attitudes to ageing and older people, and little contact with them.[2]

There are many important hypotheses here for sociolinguistic studies to test empirically. Simplification and clarification, related but non-parallel processes (R. Brown, 1977; N. Coupland, 1983), are the predictable realizations of intergroup overaccommodation at many linguistic levels: phonological (for example, careful, little-assimilated articulation), syntactic (low complexity in terms of number of constituents and coding rules), lexical (familiar vocabulary), and discursive (a high level of explicitness and redundancy in encoding linguistic functions and in structuring interactions).

An illustrative fragment (extract 2.2) shows apparently overaccommodative speech by a 22-year-old female student clinician (C) to a 62-year-old functionally competent female patient (P) at an audio-taped university optometry clinic.

EXTRACT 2.2

```
 1  C: right (1.0) let's have a look and see what you can read (switches on)
 2      OK(.) if you just look there and er(.) don't read down the whole chart
                                    [    ]
 3  P:                             yeah
 4  C: but tell me one of the lowest ones yeah
           [
 5  P:             no I tell you one of the ((3 sylls.)) yeah(.) well I can
 6      see(.) something Z U Y
 7  C: mhm(.) that's right at the bottom is it?
           [
 8  P:             ((3 sylls.)) that's right at the bottom yeah
 9  C: mm
10  P: now then the one above that
                  [
11  C:            how about the l-line above?
12  P: yeah(.) now that's(.) R P B Z E P D N (( )) R O N
13  C: that's good(.) that's good(.) let's try this one
14  P: F U R E P H
15  C: mhm
16  P: can't see any more
17  C: you can't
```

18   P: no(.) no that's blurred that is but I can make it out(.) it's F U R(( ))
        [   ]   [ ]
19   C: right   OK

The patient is being put through a routine visual acuity test with which she is familiar. At line 6 the patient reads letters from the bottom line of the test chart, which the clinician follows with the seemingly highly redundant 'that's right at the bottom is it?'. That the letters Z, U and Y are right at the bottom of the chart is uncontroversial, evident to P and C alike; clearly to P who has just identified the letters. At line 11 C interrupts P's verbal lead-in to the identification of further letters with (the again apparently redundant) 'how about the l-line above?'. Again, P's fluent reading of the R, P, B, etc. sequence (line 12) is received with the overly commending 'that's good (.) that's good', with very high start-point to the falling intonation on each occurrence of 'good' conveying (?over)enthusiastic praise.

The concept of overaccommodation therefore appears to be useful for characterizing some aspects of miscommunication in young-old dyadic talk (cf. J. Coupland, Nussbaum and Coupland, 1991). It addresses a problem that is particularly prevalent for older people who may have relatively few social contacts and few alternative routes to self-esteem and satisfaction. But it is naive to see problematic intergenerational talk as a one-sided affair; Grimshaw (1980) appeals forcefully for a bilateral focus on miscommunication in general. In the case of overaccommodation, for example, *neither* participant can experience whatever satisfaction we assume to derive from 'balanced' accommodative interaction, certainly in the longer term. The notion of *relational competence* (as, for example, developed by Wiemann, Gravell and Wiemann, 1990) is an appropriate one, taking the view that whatever an interaction achieves is a matter of *joint* construction and negotiation. 'Competence' cannot therefore be simply interpreted in terms of the individual skills and sensitivities of the participants involved.

Following this line, we can supplement the Ryan et al. list of accommodation possibilities with aspects of the speech *of* older *to* younger people (see pp. 50–1). Certainly there are many circumstances where young adults report the elderly to be 'difficult' in conversation or 'not on their wavelength'. These sequences of miscommunication may well have their origins in the same socio-psychological factors that give rise to young overaccommodative speech. What we have been glossing as young-to-elderly talk is, of course, influenced by, and interconnected with, the strategies of elderly speakers themselves. And accommodation theory again allows us to specify some elderly strategies that may be enmeshed in what Ryan et al. have called the 'communicative predicament model' of intergenerational talk. In the following section we introduce potentially problematical aspects of elderly discourse through a contrastive study of two cross-generation interactions involving the same young adult. The two interactions contrast quite starkly in the extent and nature of 'discomfort' they cause to the younger speaker.

A Contrastive Case-study

It is important to repeat our observation from chapter 1 that there is, of course, *no* inevitability of intergenerational miscommunication, however we define this. In fact, the two conversations we shall examine provide striking evidence of both the problems and the possibilities of cross-generation conversation. The two instances involve one of us (JC) and, on separate occasions, two elderly females, each living alone. Many individual differences of personality and life history intervene in the following analysis. Still, we believe it illustrates how the life circumstances of different elderly people can systematically influence their own conversation styles and the options open to younger people conversing with them.

The methodology of participant observation of researchers' own interactions with family, friends or associates is, of course, a highly restricted one. We use it here merely to derive some conceptual categories for later use. The method does not allow any degree of generalization; nor do we have the basis to claim here that the interactional strategies we identify and interpret are unique to intergenerational contexts. In fact it would be surprising if similar 'problematical' patterns were not recognizable in, for example, the context of talking to the non-elderly infirm. (For an exploration of overlapping issues in interaction between the visually impaired and fully sighted people see N. Coupland, Giles and Benn, 1986). An obvious weakness is that the approach risks skewing 'natural' behaviours through the intrusion of research interests. Still, at the time when the relevant conversations were recorded, no explicit research questions had been formulated. Also, as a source of preliminary data and even in its own terms, participant observation has compensating strengths, allowing depths of insight and sensitivity that are not easily available to more traditional, objective sociolinguistic approaches. In any event, we are persuaded by Robinson's (1979) account of the 'layers of reality' surrounding 'the truth' (p. 217) in social scientific research. Similarly, Cicourel (1973) has recognized a process of 'indefinite triangulation' (p. 124) whereby apparently objective methods that seem to 'lock in' evidence and claim a level of adequacy can themselves be subjected to research inquiry. In this way, there are no ultimately authoritative or final accounts of communication data.

When the case-study data were gathered, the two elderly females – we refer to them fictitiously as Doris and Emily – lived in separate flats in the same house. Doris was 85 years old, a retired high-school teacher who had never married. Until ten years before, she had led an active life, attending coffee mornings, visiting friends to play bridge and so forth, but was then admitted to hospital for a serious abdominal operation. She emerged from this experience frail, partially sighted and quite immobile, and rarely left the house. Apart from the home-help who visited her once a week, she had only three regular visitors, two elderly female friends and a priest.

Emily, Doris's cousin, was 83 years old and had worked as a clerk in a garage until she married young. She had three children, six grandchildren and seven great-grandchildren. She was relatively healthy, though partially deaf, and very mobile; she often travelled long distances alone to visit friends and relatives and left the house every day to go shopping, visiting and so forth. In turn, she had many visitors, young and old, male and female.

Neither Doris nor Emily showed any significant cognitive or linguistic/communicative decrement, though Emily had an apparent tendency to be forgetful and her partial deafness sometimes obtruded. Despite this, it is the conversation with Doris that was regularly, and in the case we consider here, problematical for JC. Below, with data from the two complete audio-taped encounters, we isolate categories of conversational sequences in which JC finds the shared construction of meanings to be routine, easy and comfortable in the one case, but effortful, awkward and unsatisfying in the other. Both Doris and Emily were informed of the recording of the conversations after they had been made and gave full permission for their use in this context.

Phaticity and Topic Constraint

Phatic communion (Laver, 1974) is a convenient term to subsume the range of ritualistic devices conversationalists use in the establishment and maintenance of social encounters. Acquaintances commonly engage in predictable and semantically empty exchanges, for instance, introducing pseudo-topics that are highly conventional though, of course, still socially important. 'How are you?', 'how's things?', 'how've you been?' are thus usually taken as requiring some minimal, non-specific and therefore phatic response, though we might expect this response to have more substance among close friends and relatives (as in the case with our present data).

Consider JC's would-be phatic question of this sort in line 1 of extract 2.3, a question she asks knowing that Doris is rather frail, and Doris's response to it. The very asking of the question causes JC some discomfort in this context, though avoiding asking it might make the issue of Doris's age and health more rather than less salient at that point.

EXTRACT 2.3

```
 1 JC: how are you anyway?
 2  D: not too bad J_____
 3 JC: not too bad
 4  D: not too good either
 5 JC: you're not feeling very well?
 6  D: I don't know what it is(.) I suppose(.) I suppose it's old age
 7      I(.) it's such an effort to do anything
 8 JC: mm (3.0)
 9  D: still(.) (cheerfully) could be a lot worse
10 JC: mm(.) that's right(.) yes(.) you can get about a bit anyway
11  D: oh(.) I can(.) ooh yes I can(.) you see(.) E_____ does
12      the cleaning and that kind of thing(.) shopping ((3 sylls.))
                                                        [  ]
13 JC:                                                  mm
14  D: if I only can get my meals and that kind of thing well as long
           [  ]                                     [  ]
15 JC:      mm                                       mm
16  D: as I can do that
17 JC: mm(.) what's your appetite like nowadays?
18  D: well I *never* feel hungry(.) I never want to eat(.) I just eat
```

19   things at a mealtime(.) when I have to
20 JC: you've never been a *big* eater though(.) have you?
21 D: no(.) never
22 JC: no

At line 3 JC's follow-up move accepts Doris's response, but Doris reinitiates (line 4) with 'not too good either', going on to attribute this to 'old age'. From JC's viewpoint, these (nonformulaic) comments go well beyond phatic communion and appear to have reinterpreted 'how are you?' as a more specific request for an appraisal of physical and psychological well-being. We might say that the conversation is shifted in the direction of consultation.

In general, there are many conventional topic areas of this sort that JC perceives to be unavailable in, or at least inappropriate for, conversation with Doris. Many of the topics of phatic communion are based on responses to change, and it is *lack* of change above all that characterizes Doris's life circumstances. Her recent past and the future she can anticipate lack just those experiences that could otherwise make up conventional responses to 'what've you been up to?', 'what's been happening?', 'doing anything nice at the weekend?', 'going on holiday this year?', and so on. Doris would have great difficulty finding adequate responses to these apparently insignificant (though for her perhaps threatening) questions; accordingly, JC tries to protect her from the salience of lack of change. Matters relating to the future in general tend to be problematical, for example, discussion of medium and long-term plans and prospects. There is even the worry that talking about other people's (including JC's) plans for future activities may itself highlight Doris's contrasting circumstances, particularly because Doris herself very rarely asks JC questions about these things.

Another problem for JC here is that she recognizes that *protectionist* conversation strategies of this sort carry their own risks; she does not relish acting as the arbiter of an elderly person's communicative needs and potential. To adopt this protectionism on a large scale would, in fact, risk being overaccommodative, in the sense of this term we introduced in the previous section, unduly constraining and reinforcing stereotypes of elderliness.

In JC's parallel conversation with Emily, she feels free to indulge in phatic openings, and Emily responds by updating on past events and her plans for the future. She talks of family visits, two future births in the family and the gifts she has made (see extracts 2.4 and 2.5 as illustrative fragments). Her interest in the new births is bolstered by expecting to visit and be visited by family members. Doris on the other hand, though she is party to the same news, rarely raises these matters in conversation.

EXTRACT 2.4

```
1   E: um(.) what else(.) and er er I(.) I rang M_____last
2       night(.) I was in a panic
3  JC: why?
4   E: when I came home from(.) er from er(.) Gloucester(.) from
5       K_____'s birthday  I   took some snaps when I was there(.) and
                          [    ]
6  JC:                     mm
7   E: um(.) I couldn't find my *camera* and I *looked* and *looked*
                              [    ]
8  JC:                              ah
```

EXTRACT 2.5

```
1 EC: how um(.) when is H_____ expecting her ((baby))?
2  JC: oh it's not long *now*
3   E: my *god!*(.) I hope it's *not* she'll *burst*
                         [
4  JC:                        [laughs] it's er(.) her due date
5       is the eighth of August(.) so that's over a week(.) isn't it?
```

Lack of change seems to underlie a more general problem for JC with Doris's conversation. JC often perceives Doris's topic repertoire to be narrow and repetitive, talk that could be taken to confirm young people's stereotypical views about elderly conversation (see above) and that it is all too easy to ascribe vaguely to cognitive decrement. In extract 2.6 Doris has opened the topic of 'the price of things today' and she gives the example of biscuits, not for the first time in conversation with JC. JC is struck by the contrast between the mundane (as she finds it) content of this sequence and its assertive (she thinks *over*assertive) style.

EXTRACT 2.6

```
1   D: but in *all* ways prices are crazy(.) now(.) er for example
2       at breakfast(.) I never could eat breakfast(.) a couple of biscuits
```

3   are all I like for my breakfast
4 JC: mm
5 D: I like a plain biscuit I like an Osbourne biscouit(.) well Edna got
6   them for me(.) um(.) oh until about oh about two or three months ago
7   (.) she said to me well she said(.) I had a *real* shock today(.) she
8   said she'd always got the biscuits at such and such a place but she went
9   into an*other* supermarket that she doesn't often go into(.) and the *same*
10   packet of biscuits(.) Osbourne biscuits which she had been paying twenty-
11   five pence for(.) in this shop were fifteen (1.0) now(.) a *pac*ket of
12   biscuits(.) and *ten pence* variation on them
13 JC: gosh (.) that's a lot isn't it?
                 [
14 D: I think there should be some price control
15 JC: mm(.) mm(.) there isn't though(.) is there?

In the same conversation JC reacts similarly to an exhaustive, unsolicited account of Doris's daily routine and a familiar anecdote about a relative helping with some building repairs. It is entirely understandable that Doris should take whatever limited opportunities she has to be conversationally assertive and that, through a combination of limited topic repertoire, infrequent social contacts, and a largely non-changing milieu, she should misjudge the newsworthiness of issues to her interlocutors. JC does appreciate the social basis of this sort of miscommunication, and she is concerned and even guilty about her own periodically negative reactions to Doris's talk.

In the recorded conversation with Emily difficulties of this sort do not arise, though with her, JC feels she would have no compunction in interrupting a repeated anecdote and openly showing her negative response to it. The different addressees clearly need to be accommodated to very different extents, just as they, in turn, are differentially accommodative to JC.

Discourse Structuring and Topic Change

The two conversations differ in the mechanics of their discourse, so that the transcripts lend themselves to different extents to structurally based discourse analysis. For example, the conversation with Doris is relatively easy to analyse into moves, exchanges and transactions, following the model provided by Sinclair and Coulthard (1975). In

particular, the conversation is analysable as a series of typically two-
or three-part exchanges, mainly initiated by JC. There is relatively
little overlapping of turns except for very frequent follow-up and
back-channel responses from JC overlapping Doris's speech. Indeed,
it is the fact that JC 'leads' conversationally that produces the
relatively tightly structured discourse, just as Sinclair and Coulthard
argue that it is the teacher's powerful institutional role that primarily
accounts for the recurring patterns of classroom talk in their data. A
large majority of new topic units (what Sinclair and Coulthard call
transactions) are opened by JC here, consistent with the comments
we made earlier about Doris's restricted topic repertoire. Reviewing
the transcripts and tapes retrospectively revives JC's feeling that she is
generally responsible for 'managing' the discourse in that conversation.

This is again the background against which Doris's occasional
strongly assertive contributions need to be seen. On three of four
occasions when Doris does shift topic, JC perceives her contributions
to break the coherence of conversational development. For example,
during a series of exchanges about the merits and demerits of
television, Doris begins a protracted account of her daily routine
('because in the morning by the time (.) I get up and make my bed and
wash and dress and get my lunch (.) that's (.) that's the morning (.)
that takes (.) occupies the whole morning . . . '). It is not that this
opening is unconnected to the previous text, which has focused on the
time at which Doris switched on her television in the evenings, but
Doris does not make this account overtly coherent with the 'value of
television' theme, leaving JC to achieve what coherence she can.

The frequency of JC's follow-up moves in conversation with Doris
is also an indicator of her major conversational responsibilities here.
A large proportion of these moves are realized by acts where JC
confirms Doris's assessments and views and generally aligns herself
with Doris's opinions. In extract 2.3 for instance, we see acceptance
in the repetition of *not too bad* (line 3) and in the verbal and non-verbal
confirmation provided by 'mm', 'that's right, yes', 'no', and so on
(lines 10, 15, 21). Moves like these are not at all uncommon
interactionally, but JC feels more obliged to produce them with Doris
than with Emily, and she is strongly aware in talk with Doris of the
risk of sounding vacuous. JC follows an anecdote about a helpful
relative with 'that's worth (.) something isn't it really?', an empty
aphorism; at the end of extract 2.6, JC's 'there isn't though (.) is
there?' is said in the absence of a more pertinent available comment.

In instances like these, potential conversational lacunae appear where next utterances are problematical for JC (cf. Tannen and Saville-Troike (1985) on the conversational functions of silence), but they are not allowed to develop, because of an overriding need to maintain at least a superficial conversational flow. Again, in extract 2.3 Doris's self-disclosure recognizing that she is 'not too good' (line 4) demands some sort of follow-up, but preferably not the simple accepting move that would be realized by 'mm', 'yeah', or 'no'. It is not appropriate for JC to challenge the assessment fundamentally (Doris knows that JC knows of her frailty) or to convey even mild surprise ('really?'). (To this extent, response opportunities differ markedly from those available to non-familiar recipients, as in the self-disclosure data to be considered in chapters 4 and 5.) In the event, JC opts for the weak and potentially minimizing 'you're not feeling very well?' which might seem to reinterpret Doris's appraisal of an ongoing state as a temporary minor ailment. Doris's more global self-assessment over lines 6 and 7, where she invokes her elderliness (see chapters 3 and 6) – 'I suppose it's old age' – comes close to eliciting an actual silence. JC sees no alternative to a minimal 'mm', an impasse from which she is rescued by Doris's 'still (.) could be a lot worse' (line 9).

Paradoxically, actual silences in these positions are more frequent in JC's conversation with Emily, where JC does not feel the need to accommodate her interlocutor so comprehensively and so meticulously. With Emily, silence can play its more usual part as a rhetorical device, for example, indicating felt reservation, disagreement or disapproval. On one occasion Emily broaches the subject of a long-standing family disagreement and seems to seek support for her side of it. JC will not be drawn on this, which is implicit in her refusal to provide an immediate next utterance of any sort.

Ideological Matching

We noted earlier that CAT predicts convergence of many aspects of participants' communication in circumstances where speakers have integrative and supportive intentions. But we take it that a further characteristic of such interactions will be the recognized possibility of disagreement and *non*-matching of fundamental social beliefs, values and ideological standpoints.

In the example just quoted, JC found the communicative means to dissociate herself from Emily's perpetuation of a family feud. It is a general characteristic of JC's talk to Doris, and again problematical for JC, that she feels obliged to accommodate her values, opinions and ideological stances, on more or less trivial issues, to those of Doris. JC matches the biscuits anecdote in extract 2.6 with one about a relative who shops around for low-priced canned tuna ('she would know exactly which supermarket to go into to get a tin of tuna for fifteen pence less than in all the others . . . '). This complementary anecdote is not about JC, but it purports to espouse a similar valuing of thriftiness in the management of household affairs. When Doris gives her views on the low quality of most television output (in extract 2.7), JC agrees and even hears herself to be converging towards the style of Doris's criticisms.

EXTRACT 2.7

D: I(.) don't look at *any* programme that I can say *re*ally appeals to me(.) and
    you know those Crossroads and Emmerdale Farm and Coronation
    Street [soap operas](.) I think they're *bo*ring(.) and I *don't* like Westerns
    and I *don't* like science fiction(.) and quiz shows(.) those *si*lly quizzes(.)
    The Price is Right(.) (despairingly) oh

JC: really(.) if you think back to how funny Morecambe and Wise and
    people like that used to be(.) I mean(.) there's *no*body now to compare(.)
    and Paul Daniels(.) how on *earth* they manage to put him on on a
    Saturday evening(.) he *must* be very popular but for the *life* of me *I* can't
    understand why

JC edits her actual views of television to praise programmes that she assumes Doris will also express approval for (e.g. Princess Anne on the Terry Wogan show).

There is a hierarchy of ideological accommodation, which begins with avoiding articulating viewpoints that an interlocutor will predictably not share, through selective putting of one's own views and modifications of them, to outright falsification. JC's ideological adaptation to Doris is enough to produce a tension between integrity and accommodation; aspects of her talk to Doris do not allow her to 'be herself'.

Taken together, the communicative characteristics listed under the three broad and overlapping headings above lead to quite polarized perceptions of the two conversations. By comparison with the conversation with Emily, the one with Doris is in many respects an effortful and self-conscious event for JC. In CAT terms, JC sees herself as forced into a variety of overaccommodative strategies and finds her speaking partner underaccommodating to her own conversational needs. While every conversation presupposes various types of shared participation and involves some selectivity in the presentation of self, that sharing and the expression of personal integrity is far more apparent to JC with Emily. Beyond the immediate problem of sustaining talk with Doris, JC faces the problem that she tends to view her own discourse style as undesirably overaccommodating, and *still* inadequate. Even though she is prepared to modify her own perceived persona considerably in the interests of 'getting on', she is concerned about how Doris is, in fact, evaluating and attributing her accommodation.

Ultimately, discourse games like these are dangerous and the dissatisfactions of moving outside one's habitual styles and ideologies can lead to mutually dissatisfying interactions. This is either because JC's efforts may be recognized *as* efforts (Doris may then perceive her to overaccommodate), or simply because JC will have low expectations of future contact. The conversations we have considered certainly suggest that life circumstances can constrain topic repertoires and indirectly dictate aspects of the mechanics of interpersonal discourse in problematical ways for interactants. Also, a younger speaker who is sensitive to an elderly partner's life position may feel it necessary not to distance herself too far in terms of expressed beliefs and values, and therefore enter the maze of over- and underaccommodation possibilities.

A Typology of Elderly-to-Young Language Strategies

'Miscommunication' is not in itself a well-defined concept (cf. N. Coupland, Giles and Wiemann, 1991); how widespread the above instances and categories of interactional 'problems' are in inter-generational encounters remains to be established. An intercultural focus will be particularly important, because we are well aware that other communities are likely to foster quite different relationships, and so accommodation patterns between their generation-groups.

Even within our own cultural context it is quite possible that many features of Doris's discourse (and JC's moves relative to them) could be found in young-peer interactions, particularly when there is an imbalance across interlocutors' life events and experiences of change.

On the other hand, the general analysis that elderly people's talk can be construed as underaccommodative by many younger recipients surfaces at several points in the more substantial data analyses that follow in later chapters. But we shall show that other contextual factors are important also, not least that there is a range of more *positive* goals that underaccommodative talk can fulfil for elderly people in different circumstances. Therefore, to complete this largely theoretical discussion, we now consider four further candidate elderly-to-young language strategies, beyond and refining the *intergroup underaccommodation* pattern we have just considered (see table 2.2). Each derives from contemporary theoretical work in social psychology. Like the earlier set, the strategies are not to be seen as mutually exclusive, but as elements of a highly complex accommodative repertoire for (even one instance of) intergenerational talk. We shall return to them in later chapters in interpreting patterns of elderly self-disclosure.

Self-protective Underaccommodation

Many dimensions of JC's identity, beyond her status as a young adult, could have been at least as salient and perhaps threatening to Doris, such as JC's being married, employed, mobile, active, etc. These factors could have disposed Doris to avoid verbally invoking interpersonal evaluations likely to be uncomfortable. For instance, when she thematized television watching she kept conversation within a domain that was at least as salient to an elderly female living alone (see A. M. Rubin, 1986) as to a younger, married woman. The topic was to this extent 'safe' in that it did not raise issues of social comparison that might have disadvantaged her. Doris may have judged the risk of appearing conversationally insular and/or egocentric as a small price to pay for maintaining some measure of conversational control and keeping her identity intact. We should consider the possibility that strategic considerations may prevent Doris, too, from 'being herself'.

Age Self-handicapping

This is a propitiatory, face-saving strategy widely acknowledged in the social psychology of self-presentation (cf. Arkin and Baumgardner, 1985; see also Hewitt and Stokes (1975) on the use of disclaimers). We self-handicap when we excuse ourselves from performing adequately at future tasks and events by foregrounding illness, mishap or other forms of claimed disadvantage. In discourse self-handicapping is a strategy to lower anticipated evaluations of a speaker's performance, which will either mitigate criticism (for poor performance) or promote praise (for non–anticipated good performance). When an elderly speaker says such things as 'I can't do that anymore', 'these old bones . . . ', and 'I just can't remember as well as . . . ', she may be trying to elicit patience or sympathy and to propose inevitable biological attributions for her own circumstances and diminished competences. As well as excusing speakers from current loads and responsibilities, such strategies (as we show in later chapters) are also *rhetorically* productive, serving to elicit *denials* or *modifications* of self-appraised incompetences, and perhaps, therefore, to bolster an older person's projected identity. There is also the potential for self-handicapping to be consciously manipulative as a form of 'emotional blackmail' – a tactic for gaining compliance or services. These tactics, too, are understandable when used by people who, from one perspective, can legitimately marshall whatever limited resources for influence they have available to them. These, at least, are processes by which some elderly people might themselves legitimize the tactic.

Self-stereotyping

Turner (1982, 1986) introduces self-stereotyping as a particular process of depersonalization. He argues that when we construe a situation as an intergroup one, we not only homogenize the attitudes, cognitions and acts of out group members, through stereotyping (for example, 'they all sound and speak the same'), but we also attenuate presumed differences between ourselves and members of our own group (cf. Doise, 1978). In other words, we take on the characteristics of what we believe to be, or stereotype as, prototypical ingroup members.

Table 2.2 Summary of the socio-psychological contexts and sociolinguistic instantiation of five processes of elderly-to-young miscommunication

Language strategies[a]	Sender				Receiver	
	Social/socio-psychological trigger	Interactional goal(s)	Addressee focus	Sociolinguistic strategies activated	Judged strategies	Speaker performance labelled
Intergroup under-accommodation	Life circumstances (probably little intergenerational contact)	Presumably positive	Weak (egocentric focus)	Discourse management (lowly attuned)	Passivity or overassertion, high self-disclosure, egocentricity	Underaccommodative
Self-protecting	Threatened identity (e.g., actual or anticipated negative interindividual comparisons)	Exert control guardedly positive or defensive	Other's productive performance	Interpersonal control (indirect); discourse management (field: topic deflection)	As above	Underaccommodative

Self-handicapping	Threatened identity (e.g., anticipating poor performance)	Promote positive face	Other's attributions and subsequent productive performance	Discourse management (field: accounts or excuses; tenor: negative face)	Apologizing/over-compensating	?Overaccommodative
Self-stereotyping	Perception of social stereotyping (e.g., of 'aged communicator')	Presumably positive	Weak (group-centred focus)	Discourse management (lowly attuned)	Stereotypically elderly	Underaccommodative
Intergroup divergence	Threatened identity (e.g., young seen as illegitimately superior)	Promote intergroup distinctiveness	Other's productive performance (e.g., 'hip'/colloquialisms)	Approximation (divergence)	Dissociation	Contra-accommodative

Source: N. Coupland, Coupland, Giles and Henwood, 1988, p. 22ff.

In a gerontological context this suggests that if contextual features trigger an elderly identity for older people in cross-generation encounters, they may assume or emphasize communicative characteristics or strategies they associate with elderly speakers. As with all the possibilities being aired here, we must expect considerable individual differences to intervene because there is a great diversity of social roles, responsibilities and experiences to be found within any community of older people. On the other hand, the process of self-stereotyping may be one by which a highly diverse population has potential to actually *acquire* a degree of homogeneity, and not least in response to the stereotype-driven assumptions and behaviours of the younger people they interact with.

Data we shall present in later chapters, in fact, demonstrate many different ways in which an elderly identity can be constructed for an older speaker through local selections made – for example, patterns of elicitation and topic-management – by a conversational partner (cf. also J. Coupland, Coupland and Grainger, in press). But it is also true that our society abounds with public displays of 'the elderly role', including the ageist representations of the elderly as stooping figures on British road-crossing signs (see chapter 1), the perceived association of the elderly with the handicapped (as labelled on certain seats on public transport); also, of course, stereotypic representations of the elderly in the media. To the extent that there is an enduring mythology of ageing and prefabricated roles, images and behaviours for 'the aged', it may be that styles of talk addressed to older speakers (including forms of overaccommodation) may not, in fact, need to construct elderly identity as much as simply trigger an identity package that is already available to them.

Intergroup Divergence

There are many means by which older speakers can symbolize or encode disapproval of, and dissatisfaction with, others' orientations to them. Sociolinguistic retaliation can be achieved in many ways, from overt commenting on another's ways of speaking or verbal aggressiveness to emphasizing cross-generational differences, what CAT refers to as 'intergroup divergence'. These reactive strategies are themselves not without problems, however. Aggressive responses again risk confirming negative elderly stereotypes of being grumpy and irritable.

Diverging from a younger conversationalist's interests, assumptions and topics – for example, raising themes of elderly experience and achievements, or denigrating the immaturity of youth-culture – may very well *increase* intergroup distance, even though it may have originated as a *refutation* of the partner's intergroup model.

These are the conceptual and analytic resources that we have been able to find in recent statements of communication accommodation theory and that we draw on in later chapters. In chapter 3 we consider in particular some of the ways in which the category of elderliness itself is represented and constructed in discourse. In line with this chapter's emphases, we argue that 'being elderly' can in many ways be an attribution that follows from how we present ourselves to others, but also from whether and how others accommodate to our self-presentations.

3

Formulating Age:
Discursive Dimensions of Age Identity

Sociolinguistics has established a substantial part of its recognized territory around the contrastive analysis of socio-demographic categories: socio-economic class groups, the sexes, regional or ethnic groups, and so on. While textbooks continue to reflect this interest, contemporary sociolinguistic research itself has become wary of invoking some of the traditionally conceived social categories. Despite its seminal impact on the field, the quantitative, social differentiation paradigm (cf. Labov, 1966; Trudgill, 1974) has frequently been criticized for its deterministic assumptions regarding social classification processes, treating socio-economic groupings and situational types as pre-ordained independent variables in correlational designs with limited explanatory potential (cf. N. Coupland, 1988; Smith, Giles and Hewstone, 1980).

The sex/gender issue thrives as a focus for contrastive, quantitative investigations, though there have been vigorous arguments put forward *against* the view that sex can be appropriately treated as a clear-cut and objective socio-demographic variable. For instance, Smith (1985) contends that individuals cannot be uncritically assumed to be prototypes of their sex-group, and that gender identity is, in fact, a matter of degree, with large individual differences in both femininity and masculinity (p. 165; cf. also, Kessler and McKenna, 1978). Similarly, a growing tradition of work on race and racism has challenged the assumed naturalness of ethnic categories as analytic units (cf. Husband, 1982). Potter and Litton (1985) pin-point the same general problem in the assumptions underlying research on social representations.

As we noted in chapter 1, sociolinguistic studies have almost entirely neglected older populations, and a major aim of this book is to promote sociolinguistic interest in an under-investigated social group, 'the elderly'. On the other hand, we recognize that category-based sociolinguistics has important deficiencies. Can these positions be reconciled? Our general position is that sociolinguistic research *can* justifiably sustain, and, in fact, needs to develop, its concern with socio-demographic categories and with the elderly in particular; but in doing this it must modify its assumptions about the *status* of categories themselves. We want to argue that studies need to focus on *processes* of *categorization*, on the premiss that categories are to a significant extent actively constructed by ingroup and outgroup members during communicative exchanges, and are thereby themselves quite directly amenable to sociolinguistic study. By implication, we believe that a trend in sociolinguistics to abandon social categories themselves would be an inappropriate reaction to well-founded criticisms.

The social constructivist approach we are endorsing is one that has been coherently argued in the socio-psychological literature (cf. P. Berger and Luckman, 1967; Gergen, 1985; Gergen and Davis, 1985; Shotter and Gergen, 1989). Recently, Potter and Wetherell (1987) have argued that discourse analysis can claim priority as the means of displaying social construction processes in action, their context-dependence and their variability. It is interesting, then, to note that at least one team of researchers, well known for earlier quantitative investigations, has independently reached a very similar position regarding the future of research in the language and sex roles area. West and Zimmerman (1985) conclude a review of that literature as follows: 'Where researchers have turned their attentions from gender as an isolated variable in sociolinguistic surveys to speech as a kind of action between humans of varying situational identities, we have developed a much richer understanding of the ways in which discourse helps construct the fabric of social life' (p. 119).

In this chapter we want to show the validity of Potter and Wetherell's general claim, and to parallel West and Zimmerman's priorities, through an analysis of how dimensions of *age identity* – inferable categorisations of speakers as elderly group- members in some specific respect – surface and are managed in a corpus of cross-generation and within-generation talk. We argue that 'elderliness' is in significant ways manufactured and modified in sequences of talk in which older speakers are involved, through the agency of elderly *and younger* speakers. We shall show that elderly identity can be a highly unstable phenomenon, reflecting the local circumstances in which it is produced. At the same time, this is not *at all* to undervalue the emotional or somatic implications of identity formations for the individuals concerned. On the contrary, as we argued in the first chapter, we assume that there are high stakes here for esteem, satisfaction and even health.

Themes of elderliness arise pervasively and in many different forms in talk between older and younger people, to the extent that old age can in itself be a substantial agenda for talk involving older people. This chapter provides a general overview of age-identity marking processes in one conversational data-set; here, too, we consider the implications for social attitudes to ageing and for intergenerational relations. The specific themes and processes that we identify are then examined in greater detail in following chapters. We start with an introductory discussion[1] of how age identity has been investigated in earlier traditions in social psychology.

Approaches to Age Identity Analysis

Within social psychology we find support for our emphasis on categorization processes in recent trends in the conceptualization of not only identity in general, but also of age identity in particular.

Direct concern with the notion of age identity began with research aimed at assessing the age at which people come to think of themselves, or are thought to become, old. Researchers often asked people simply to classify themselves as old or elderly as opposed to not old, middle-aged or young (for example, Tuckman and Lavell, 1957; Tuckman and Lorge, 1954). An important finding was that people tended to dissociate themselves from the category 'old' and judge themselves as younger than their age in years (Blau, 1956; Riley and Foner, 1968; Tuckman and Lorge, 1954; Zola, 1962), a phenomenon that became known as 'denial of ageing' (Bultena and Powers, 1978).

Since then, there has been more concern to investigate the meaning behind such age identifying or disidentifying statements (see, for example, Guptill, 1969; Mutran and Burke, 1979). Measuring the meaning or content of age identity as a static, intra-individual construct is, however, only one way of broaching the task of investigating people's self-concepts in old age. As Gordon and Gergen (1968) have pointed out, one may study the self as *process* as well as the self as structure. Studying the aged self as process is strongly advocated by symbolic interactionists (see, for example, Spence, 1986) and Meadian theorists (for example, Chappell and Orbach, 1986) who share a concern with the negotiated and constantly renegotiated nature of people's social and personal sense of identity – what Ainley and Redfoot (1982) have described as the 'essentially embodied nature' of age identity or 'identity-in-the-world'. Clearly, one approach to this task is to study the ways in which individuals introduce and formulate age-identifying statements, and modify them in relation to the actual or anticipated reactions of others, in sequences of talk. Potter and Wetherell's (1987) review arrives at this position as a general rationale for a discourse analytic perspective in social psychology as a whole.

The Interactive Study Data Context

Here (and in several later chapters) we focus initially on one particular data-set: a corpus of 40 videotaped interactions where pairs of volunteer subjects, women aged 70–87 and 30–40 years, took part in first-acquaintance conversations. When participants were recruited, they were simply told they were to converse with 'people of different ages'. Each pair of speakers, who had never met previously, were then asked to 'get to know one another'. They were left alone, knowing they were being videotaped, for eight minutes. Each pair was also recorded for a two-minute period after their 'get acquainted' session, unaware that cameras were still running, though these two subcontexts are not distinguished in analyses for this chapter.

The elderly women, most with (grossly characterized) upper-working-class backgrounds, were members of two day centres in Cardiff, Wales; most lived alone and were widowed. The younger women were mostly lower-middle-class and married, and were recruited through an advertisement in a local newspaper. Twenty of the dyads were intergenerational (purely for ease of reference we refer to them as young–old); 10 were peer-young and 10 peer-elderly. We recognize the risks involved in working with such gross labels, though later analyses are, in fact, sensitive to variations in age (however defined), circumstances, experiences and, indeed age identifications within the groups we now call 'old' or 'elderly' and 'young'. In fact it is precisely the fluid and contingent nature of categorization processes that we are intending to make clear.

According to the study design, therefore, each subject participated in two interactions, one within and one across generation. All relevant sequences were transcribed (using notation developed from that of Jefferson, as summarized in chapter 2, note 1 and explained in more detail in Atkinson and Heritage, 1984). Several short extracts from the data are reproduced below, and, more extensively later, as examples of the processes we discuss.

Because we do not make explicitly generalized claims here, the particular nature and constraints of the data we are using are not critical. On the other hand, we are interested in how age identities surface in interaction, and the open-ended task we set participants might itself have encouraged them to mark their generational identities. Relative age was, at least to some extent, made salient in the design of the study, as participating speakers were aware they would be talking to two differently aged people. Again, self-identification was to an extent required by the 'get to know one another' rubric. Our thinking was that the controlled contrast between inter- and intragenerational conversations, plus the guarantee that participants in the study were non-familiars, at least offered us a clearly defined experimental basis from which to work in this exploratory study. But, as we shall point out, what previous descriptions there are of young–old and peer–elderly discourse do, in fact, endorse our most general finding in this chapter: that the marking of elderly identities is pervasive in social contexts where older speakers are involved, and is achieved in diverse and complex ways.

Dimensions of Elderly Identity Marking

It is not possible to delimit absolutely the means by which older adults can signal, or come to be associated with, elderliness. Such associations may be highly indirect and result from participants or observers doing a good deal of inferential work to which we have no easy access. Also, we cannot expect uniformity across the generations or even individuals in what are taken to be central or peripheral attributes of elderliness. We can expect different traits to be subjectively associated with particular category labels in this semantic field: not only 'elderly', but also 'old', 'pensioner', 'retired', and many other terms (see pp. 15–16). For reasons like these, the taxonomy of elderly identity-marking processes we describe is necessarily very general, though, in fact, also rather conservative. We identify broad dimensions that can easily overlap one another and are certainly interrelated in continuous discourse. But we want to show that they constitute at least a significant portion of the means by which the older speakers in our data project or conversationally 'acquire' elderliness. First we outline the fundamental subcategories, with examples; we then consider the socio-psychological functions that age-identity marking can fulfil for elderly speakers and their conversation partners.

The six basic categories fall under two general headings: age-categorization processes and temporal framing processes.

Age-categorization Processes

This heading subsumes those discourse sequences through which an older speaker comes to be viewed (or is predictably viewable) as inhabiting an 'elderly' category. Either the category is explicitly defined as old age, or it implicitly (stereotypically/prototypically) characterizes old age.

Disclosure of chronological age   The first process involves identifying the individual (self or other) as elderly in terms of age in years. Disclosure of chronological age is quite frequent in the data (elderly speakers tell their age in 12 of the 20 intergenerational encounters); this might be surprising, at least in view of supposedly general taboos against the making of intimate disclosures in first-meetings with strangers (C. R. Berger and Bradac, 1982). There also appear to be folk norms of etiquette specifically precluding age- telling by women.

Telling age is arguably the most explicit means of self identifying as elderly, though people will, of course, differ in the age boundaries they set to the age category labels they use. A particularly interesting finding is that many of the chronological age disclosures in the data appear as expressed attributions for ill health, as in the fragment[2] from 12, where E2 says 'I'm I'm not very well these days too (.) I'm seventy last Octo[ber]', clearly implying she means her age to function as an account for her being unwell (see pp. 137–8).

Age-related category or role reference A second age-categorization process is the invoking of a category label itself (as a noun or some form of modifier) in reference to an individual or her peer group. We find a wide variety of particular category labels used, including 'old', 'elderly', 'pensioner' and 'geriatric'. Sometimes the category is invoked appositionally to a first-person pronoun reference, that is, self is co-identified as category member, as in the following fragment: 'I think us pensioners are very lucky really' (I29, E16). Sometimes the main propositional content of an utterance is to identify self with the category: (I4, E2) 'I'll have to pay for that myself and I'm a pensioner'; 'I'm great grandmother now for two' (I39, E19). Often, the elderly category is implied in making another disclosure rather than the topic of a disclosure in its own right, as in: 'well I've got two grandchildren and four great grandchildren [*laughs*]' (I26, E13). Focusing on succeeding generations in this way is by far the most frequent way in which elderly speakers refer to their generational role, and for some elderly people in the data, there is no shortage of triggers to a generational identity: E20 tells her young partner she has well over 50 grandchildren and between 20 and 30 great-grandchildren. Sometimes an elderly life position is invoked, though without a specific category label being used: 'you've got to make the best of it (.) especially at our age' (I20, E10); 'well of course when we get old we get little presents don't we?' (I35, E18).

There is of course a wide range of particular orientations to the age categories here. Very often 'old' is invoked as an outgroup category, even by speakers we are referring to as elderly. For example, in I20 E10 refers to 'Molly . . . an old lady' in identifying one friend among others at the day centre she attends. It appears to follow that she takes the general population of the day centre (for 'the elderly') to be *not* 'old'. Again, in I21, E12 tells her young conversation partner that 'some of the people at the day centre are quite confused . . . they're really geriatrics'. The term 'pensioner' on the other hand, as we have seen, is often tolerated in use as an ingroup category reference.

In general, the category is necessarily fuzzy-edged, for example because the pronoun 'we' in peer-elderly talk often refers ambiguously either to the two co-present participants alone or to members of the social group 'the elderly'. In this context any talk that is interpretable as an appeal to shared experience or consensus (and, by implication most of the discourse processes we discuss in the remainder of this taxonomy) will readily imply shared elderly category-membership.

Age identity in relation to health, decrement and death   To the extent that people associate later life with declining health (cf. the discussion of decremental myths in chapter 1), commentaries on one's own ill health (at least of specific types), declining abilities and eventual death can imply elderliness. As we shall show in chapters 4 and 5, we find high frequencies of 'painful' self-disclosure (PSD) by elderly speakers in the present data, both among their peers and intergenerationally. We define PSD as the revealing of a cluster of categories of personal and often intimate information on one's own ill health, bereavement, immobility, loneliness, and so on.

Very similarly, Taylor (1987) has analysed what he calls the 'production of frailty' in discourse. His data are audio-recorded conversations between elderly home owners and their student lodgers. Taylor, too, argues that elderly people habitually use frailty to construct elderly identity in the personal narratives they tell: 'Accomplished in and through discourse, an elderly identity of frailty orients communicators to illness and death and reflects the allocation of power within elderly/other relationships'.

The elderly speakers in our data very frequently comment on aspects of their own decline, infirmity or dependency, as they see it. For example, in I38, E20 says 'I cannot now I cannot concentrate to buy [presents for her grandchildren]'; in I18, E10 attributes her momentary loss of attention to her age: 'what was I going to say (.) oh god now it shows my age'. More generally, age (and, in the following fragment, chronological age) appears to be taken to provide an adequate account for frailty: 'and I'm I'm not very well these days too (.) I'm seventy last Octo[ber] . . . so I find I can't do it so good' (I2, E2).

Even when the ill-health, frailty or incapacity is not reported as a current state, elderly speakers often still *orient* to their own decrement in their talk. In this way they establish a life position along a decremental scale. For example, (I16, E7): 'I don't think I'm quite ready for anything like that yet' (referring to the Meals on Wheels catering service); and later: 'it's not so frightening going into a home [a residential home for the elderly] because they don't even know they're there themselves so when our time comes we know we're going to be like that'. Similarly, in I4, E1 anticipates her own increasing dependency and even, implicitly, her own death: 'I'm only hoping I can carry on because there's nothing like your own home'; and later: 'I pray I'll keep my faculties until I go'.

Overall, there are few overt references to death in the data. At one level this is not surprising given that speakers are first acquaintances in a relatively public speaking context. Still, other databases we have examined (with Romola Bucks) show that sensitive interviewers can induce many elderly people to talk extensively and openly to strangers about death, including their own (see also Nussbaum, Thompson and Robinson, 1989). In the present interactive data death is implicated in sequences where elderly speakers are appraising their lives retrospectively; expressions invoking a perspective on 'all my life' (for example, E5 in I10) are not uncommon. On one occasion, in a young–old conversation (I20), E10 reveals that her husband and her grandchildren's other grandparents are now dead, so that she is 'the only nanna'; as the younger woman comments, 'the only one now'. In sequences like these the end of the life span is tacitly but clearly invoked.

Even denial of infirmity, in the form of disclaimers and supposedly resisting stereotypes of decline with age, can implicate an ageing identity and so leave elderliness 'in the air' in elderly talk. For example, in I26, E14 says: 'well I'm always busy you know (.) they talk about old age and "you're lonely" (.) well believe me I'm never lonely and I'm never bored and I'm always busy doing something'; and in, I3, E1 says: 'well I lead quite a busy life although I'm eighty-six.'

Temporal Framing Processes

In addition to the more and less direct invocation of elderly categories in talk, we find various means by which elderly speakers in the data relate their personal experiences from distinctive temporal perspectives that come to mark them, again indirectly, as 'elderly'. This further set of possibilities again shows how older people's discourse can function to construct age identities, this time through narrative techniques that locate the narrator in a particular life-span position (cf. N. Coupland

and Nussbaum, in preparation). Under this second general heading, which is concerned in various ways with time past or the present in relation to the past, we want to recognize three subtypes.

Adding time-past perspective to current or recent-past states or topics In a series of studies, Boden and Bielby (1983, 1986) have shown that talk about the past frequently functions among peer-elderly pairs as a topic resource that informs talk about current states and circumstances. Their case is that 'among old people there is a broad recalling of the past in the context of the present which achieves for them a shared sense of meaning: this feature of talk is far less salient amongst young adults' (1983, p. 308). From our own data at this stage we want to make a simpler case: that the strategy of time-shifting – into the past, from focus on the present or recent past – predictably encodes an elderly identity for the speaker at that point in the discourse. Consider the following fragments:

I21, E12: I'm a widow nearly seventeen years ago;
I20, E10: I've been going there [to the day centre] for eleven years;
I22, E11: I wanted to see where he was buried and all after how many years (.) thirty odd years;
I10, E6:   I retired in 1974 I'd been nursing for forty-six years . . . came down to Cardiff in 1952 and I was at the CRI [hospital] until I retired . . . my mother died when she was forty-five in 1933.

In these examples the matter being reported is a state, activity or event that is current or linked to the relatively recent past. The elderly speaker nevertheless locates these topics within a clearly time-past frame, extending the report into time past.

All the above examples, in fact, use numerical markers of time past, and they can therefore easily encourage the sorts of inferences about elderly categorization that we discussed earlier. Some instances of what we are calling the time-past perspective category could therefore be equally considered as age categorization processes in terms of their identity consequences. A further example is provided in I6 when a young speaker (Y3) asks her elderly partner 'and what made you decide to move?'. (The older woman has recently moved from a large house to a small flat.) E3 replies: 'well (.) I spent all my time years ago in Radnor Street (.) I had 25 years of (.) marvellous (.) no worries or troubles (.) two nice children you know (1.0) and er and then the War

came of course didn't it (.) so um my son then he was er (.) getting on
for twenty he went and er (1.0) my goodness what I had after . . .'. What
follows is a protracted life-history narrative.

Self-association with the past   Talk about the distant past can, of
course, function as an elderly identity marker in its own right
(independently of the time-shifting strategy). It can certainly establish
an historical divide between an elderly speaker and a younger
speaker. This is particularly probable when older people come to
associate themselves with the past, a perspective that sometimes
involves overt self-*dis*sociation from the present. Older speakers
sometimes comment on how the past, for them, is a matter of places
or experiences that no longer exist:

I29, E15: of course I remember Llanedyrn when it was all country we used
           to go for walks and that before any of that was built;
I22, E11: I wouldn't recognise the place (.) it's years since I've been up this
           part of the city . . . years ago I used to come up here scrubbing
           floors;
I21, E12: you wouldn't know . . . don't know if you ever heard of it it was
           R D Jones' the Carlton (.) when I left school at sixteen I went
           straight there.

The second and third fragment above are interesting in showing
polarized patterns of dissociation. In the second, the speaker is
marking her own estrangement from newly developed areas of the
city; in the third, the elderly woman is marking the younger woman's
estrangement from time past ('you wouldn't know'). At times elderly
speakers present themselves as dislocated in quite fundamental ways
from contemporary life: in I34, E17 says: 'it's a good thing I suppose
for the younger ones but I'd like to see old Cardiff as it was . . .
I'm lost in my own city now . . . .'. In I32, E15 is just as explicit
in attributing her experience of disengagement to age-category
differences *per se*: 'I don't like it [the city centre] so much now . . . it's
a bit busy for an older person.' Markers of cultural estrangement, and
none is clearer than E11's reference to scrubbing floors in the
fragment from I22, also fall in this category. The very notion
of scrubbing floors, pretty much an outmoded domestic chore
reminiscent of the first part of this century, seems to invoke
elderliness and implicit change.

Recognizing historical, cultural or social change A third, and again overlapping, process in the temporal framing set is commenting on general social change (that is, not necessarily focusing on personal experiences, though it is, of course, within this sort of topic area that discourses of personal estrangement are likely to occur). We find that social change often provides an independent topic-agenda for intergenerational and peer-elderly talk. For example, in I14, Y7 remarks on patterns of language shift in Wales: 'your generation were speaking Welsh weren't they?' Economic circumstances provide another common theme. For example, E16 in I31 says: 'in those days you had to work hard to make ends meet because you had no money'; and, conversely, in I32, E15 remarks: 'we're lucky today because our parents didn't have a pension.' Sometimes elderly speakers make global assessments of times changing: for example, in I20, E9 says: 'but times are so different aren't they? . . . everything's fast isn't it? (.) you've got to sort of run with it.'

Relationships between Categories

The six subcategories above are an informal taxonomy of age identity-marking processes, at least as they surface in our data. We should repeat that the categories are in no sense pure and discriminable sets. Each could be further subdivided; fitting particular conversation sequences into each category is very much dependent on contextual factors, so each is fuzzy-edged. We are only providing a guide to the diversity of discourse processes that can be involved in marking elderliness in conversation. Also, there are differences in kind across the strategies listed. Borrowing terms from the work of Le Page and Tabouret-Keller (1985), we can say that some categories are relatively 'focused' in that they can be delimited relatively sharply. (The disclosure of chronological age is probably the most focused in this sense; in chapter 6 we give a more developed contextual account of the management of age disclosure in this and another data context). Others are highly 'diffuse' categories and less easy to differentiate – the temporal framing set as a whole is diffuse in this sense. Still, the taxonomy does highlight several key issues in the way elderly identity is conversationally 'managed' and allows us to consider some implications.

The various dimensions we have isolated do not only overlap but actually *conspire* in the construction of elderly identities. The themes of old age are in several ways *structurally interrelated* in the discourse sequences we are examining. We have referred to themes of change providing a context for expressions of dislocation – of the old from the contemporary world, or of the young from time past. As we shall see in analyses of the structure and distribution of painful self-disclosure sequences, the telling of age can function as a salient pre-context for the disclosure of own problematical circumstances. Conversely, ill health or its denial appear to establish a preference for age disclosure (in expressions of the type 'I'm doing well for eighty-five, and so on). In these ways age identity is best seen as, on the one hand, an intrinsically rhetorical projection and, on the other, as an inference to be drawn from the interplay of various age, health and other circumstantial or experiential reports.

Variable Identities

One major contribution that the discursive approach to social identity makes is that it demonstrates *variation* where consistency might otherwise be assumed. For example it would be wrong, and in fact perhaps ageist, to assume that an elderly identity uniformly designates an undesirable life circumstance. We have perhaps given the impression that the elderly identities being encoded in the interactive study data are predominantly negatively weighted. Overall this might be an accurate reflection, though it is vital to recognize extreme *affective variability* across particular instances.

For example, most of the invocations of elderly generational identities (described under 'Age-related category or role reference') – statuses and experiences of parenthood, grandparenthood and great-grandparenthood – project very positive social roles. Both elderly and young speakers construe these generational roles as functional for society as well as for the older person herself, her family and friends. An instance would be the following, where E9 expresses feelings of warmth and accomplishment that are endorsed by her younger recipient, Y10:

EXTRACT 3.1

E9: so the people that get older get older the younger
ones get older then you get closer don't you
Y10: that's very true I think yes (.) oh
E9: now my granddaughter's thirteen . . . but I see a lot of
them it's lovely yeah=
Y10: =yes it is nice I think it's nice you know you need
the children need grandparents

But there are other ways of projecting grandparenthood. In I39, E19 follows her disclosure that she has two great-grandchildren with the comment: 'makes you look old doesn't it?' E19 at least seems to have some reservations about the great-grandmother life position, and she perhaps finds the role at odds with her contextual age. Subtle details of prosody and non-verbal style, which are not easily captured in a conventional transcription, also allow humour and irony to sway the affective balance, so it is often unclear how elderly people are in fact construing their own elderliness behind the veils of impression management and social convention.

Being elderly can, as we have seen, be projected in positive ways or seemingly neutrally as 'the way we are'. Still, it is true that many attributions made in the data do indeed reflect old age as a handicap or a constraint. The fragments above show elderly speakers construing elderliness in terms of poverty, immobility, progressive ill health and dependency. Some of these construals are unmistakably pejorative, as in the use of the term *geriatric* to designate an incompetent out-group. When, in I35, E18 associates ageing with gift-getting – she says 'well of course when we get old we get little presents don't we?' when she has been appreciatively discussing Father Christmas's visit to the day centre – she is endorsing the stereotypical trappings of second childhood and the inverted-U model of ageing we discussed in chapter 1.

The data also show clear instances of variable age identity-projections within the same individual. When Potter and Wetherell (1987) advocate a discourse analytic perspective on social identity (and other key constructs in social psychology), they stress the inherent instability of identities, and indeed all social categories that are negotiated 'on-the-ground' (cf. Giles and Coupland, 1991a). Potter and Wetherell claim that 'social psychology not only tends to play down the issue of variation in areas crucially concerned with it, but . . . the procedures psychologists regularly use for dealing with discourse have, often inadvertently, acted as management strategies for suppressing variability' (p. 39). Certainly, age categorizations in our corpus can be variable in the way Potter and Wetherell suggest. Individual speakers are, for example, prone to making superficially inconsistent self- and other-categorizations at various points in their talk. For example, E9 (who was E10's conversation partner in the earlier fragment of I20, where E10 refers to 'Molly . . . an old lady') was ready to use the same category identification of Molly, but later identifies people who use the day centre as those who are 'old like me you know'.[3] Membership of the category 'old' is therefore at one level a token to be manipulated for immediate purposes in the discourse. A speaker is not uniformly 'old' or 'not old'; rather, she self-selects and self-projects in and out of the category, aligning herself momentarily with 'the old' in respect of some currently salient, desired (or at least tolerated) trait, and then setting herself outside the same group in relation to some other criterion.

The Interpersonal Contextualization of Identity

This fluidity of self- and other-identification may seem to deny the very essence of the concept of an identity, if we take it to be some relatively durable and significant personal alignment or self-appraisal. It might also seem to deny the ultimate significance of group identity to the individuals concerned. We think these are unjustified interpretations.

First, it would be wrong to regard the variation we find as erratic or random. The data above all suggest that age-identity marking is a *relative* process, with one's own or other person's elderliness being constructed *vis-à-vis* some other identity. Since the concepts 'old' and 'elderly' are, like a whole class of attributives in language, essentially gradeable qualities, it is not surprising that apparently the same categorization can be opted into and out of according to contextual demands. This does not need to imply that the self-concept correspondingly varies. When, in I21, E12 tells her young conversation partner that 'some of the people at the day centre are quite confused . . . they're really geriatrics', the term 'geriatric' is presumably intended derogatively of an out-group precisely to enhance the speaker's own identity.

The clearest cases of identities being negotiated relatively are when themes of competitiveness arise, often in peer-elderly encounters. In I26, E14 tells her partner she is 'very busy knitting for her two grandchildren'; E13's response (quoted above) is: 'well I've got two grandchildren and four great grandchildren [*laughs*].' This contrastive establishment of generational roles becomes clearly competitive when E14 in turn replies 'oh! you've done better than me'. The implications of 'doing better' here are interesting. On the one hand, a survival ethic is invoked, and the resisting of decrementing forces, forces against which individual life positions can be appraised. On the other hand, prominence is given to the relative positions of the two individuals, each acting as a life-span reference point to the other. Very similarly, as we shall see in chapter 6, age telling among elderly peers is often reciprocated, leading again to mutual life-position appraisals.

Again, there is evidence in the data that age-related roles in discourse can be fashioned, or certainly constrained, by interlocutors, their expectations and assumptions. In relation to ill health and the other personal topic areas we take to define painful self-disclosure (see chapter 4), for example, young speakers play a significant role in eliciting this information, directly or indirectly, from elderly speakers. Older people who are questioned quite specifically in this way about their health, family histories, the past, times changing, life at a day centre and so on will be obliged to an extent, if only by the global requirement of being cooperative, to answer appropriately. When they do this and engage in talk about these topics, they may easily reinforce their perceived elderliness. Also, in peer-elderly talk, elderly people will predictably be under some pressure to accommodate to the projected identities of their interlocutors – a case of the phenomenon we termed 'ideological matching' in chapter 2. In cases like these it seems appropriate to consider age identities, in context, to be *mutually* constructed to a considerable degree.

Negotiating Personal Identity

What might be the consequences of the processes we are discussing for older people's own self-concepts and identities? By whatever means the variability in age identification comes about in discourse, it seems plausible to argue that individuals have the opportunity, or perhaps the obligation, to actively negotiate *their own* identities here as part of a truly dynamic psychological process. For example, if a contrast is established between a speaker's own good health or mobility and her contextually older peers, the effect may be to deny a decrementing elderly identity while covertly invoking it as a possibility. In some cases, then, people who select and project themselves *out* of a stereotypically 'old' social group (when we have seen that several peers do indeed orient to their own decrement, present or anticipated) may be doing so strategically, following a partially conscious decision to resist dispreferred alternatives. The discourse sequences in which such self-presentations are embedded ('is my projected identity credible? credited? challenged? endorsed?') are likely to be key processes constituting the bottom line of people's self-appraisals. As we shall see in later chapters, elderly people's disclosures of troubles and age often appear to form part of well-rehearsed and even ritualistic sequences, with various predictable, aphoristic next moves such as complimenting or expressing surprise, denial or disbelief. Particularly in gerontological contexts, this is where we find evidence of the impact of rhetorical practices on identity and well-being, and the crux of the relationship between discourse and health.

Social Constuctivist Interpretations

Notwithstanding the variation we have pointed to, we find that elderly identities, along the multiple dimensions we have explored in this chapter, pervade the contexts of our interactive study data wherever elderly participants are involved. The sheer scale of this seems significant in its own right. It is, of course, true that age-identity markers and age-related disclosures will surface in talk particularly where age has become a salient dimension. And we might be tempted to think that age salience is a natural result of older and younger speakers coming into contact. We believe that this is an ageist assumption. In other intergroup contexts (in talk between the sexes, ethnic groups, the social classes, and so on), we would assume that speakers could *potentially* align as group members and mark this in their talk, but we would not assume this was inevitable or even predictable. Why should we assume that elderly category membership is more 'naturally' salient?

This raises the related question of whether participants themselves approach cross-generation conversations with the same assumptions. Are younger speakers prey to the expectation, which is still ultimately ageist, that their partner's being elderly makes elderliness available as a resource for their conversation, as a principle to guide their selection of topics and organization of conversational rights and obligations? In this chapter we have introduced some descriptive evidence that this might be so, though more detailed investigation (in later chapters and, of course, beyond the scope of this book) is needed.

Some might also argue the case that the life circumstances of the elderly, or, at least, those older people in the present study, make it inevitably the case that decrement and disadvantage should surface as themes of talk. Again, we think this position is unwarranted. The 20 elderly people in our interactive data are by no means a maximally disadvantaged group; all of them are reasonably mobile and enjoy at least moderately good health, and they all live pretty well independent lives in the community. As is probably the case across the life span, our life circumstances do tend to offer us predictable topics for talk. But this does not mean that it will be the age-salient dimensions of our experiences that will be most prominent, let alone the negative aspects of these, particularly in relatively public, self-monitored speaking contexts.

For these reasons, we need to explore more particular motivations or belief contexts that could underlie elderly people's predisposition to present themselves as elderly and/or deny their elderliness in first encounters like those we are studying. To end this chapter, it might be useful to anticipate some of the arguments we develop in later chapters in connection with much more detailed analyses. Goals that we can infer govern elderly people's age-identifying discourse include:

1 (minimally) to elicit engagement and a range of positive responses from an individual interlocutor, from praise ('I lead quite a busy life although I'm eighty-six') to sympathy ('I'm not very well these days too I'm seventy');

2 to stake a claim, at the intergroup level, for owed respect,

attention, interest or care and to revel in the heroism of old age
per se; or to redress stereotyped assumptions that these orientations
are always appropriate, and thereby earn respect and credit in
other dimensions;

3   to enact a set of relative evaluations, for example of the life
     position of an elderly speaker in relation to other elderly people
     (present or not) or to other reference individuals or groups;

4   to defuse a potentially threatening situation, perhaps simply the
     get-to-know-one another task requirement, through self-handi-
     capping (see the discussion of this strategy in chapter 2);

5   relatedly, to transfer age from the implicit to the explicit agenda,
     thereby defusing the threat imposed by uncertainty (Berger and
     Bradac, 1982);

6   to tap the existential function of talk: to try to come to terms with
     the balance between one's own chronological age and contextual
     age, and reduce one's own uncertainty about present states and
     future possibilities.

All of these motivations appear to have relevance as forces driving
age-identity management, in specific respects and at specific points,
to the data we are exploring. The discourse analysis perspective we
are adopting requires interpretations that reflect the sequencing and
local placement of individual conversational moves and strategies,
and it is at that very specific level that we are most confident in the
particular interpretations we offer. Having argued that age identity
needs to be seen as a discursive formation, we would not be happy to
pursue questions about absolute or primary socio-psychological
functions underlying the encoding of elderly identity in general.

Still, for many elderly people there does appear to be a range of
potentially *positive* functions served by what are predominantly
negatively loaded self characterizations and self disclosures in talk.
We can show how self projecting on some dimensions as 'elderly' can
establish a baseline for positive personal appraisal, express positive
and valued experiences of ageing, score points against competing
peers and also at times satisfy the conversational expectations of
others. More detailed analyses of these strategic possibilities could go
a long way towards offsetting the stereotypes that are available to label
elderly talk as 'egocentric', 'grumbling' and 'disengaged'.

With a greater awareness of the identity loading of elderly talk, the
caring and counselling professions could and should give far more

emphasis to styles and strategies of face-to-face interaction with older people. Training and other interventionist initiatives in the area of elderly communication (and we consider some particular instances in chapter 8) need to attend in much more detail to conversational options, for example, in considering ways of responding to elderly troubles-telling or life narratives (see also Coleman, 1989; Thorsheim and Roberts, 1990). Discourse analysis would appear to offer a way forward for theorists and practitioners in the evaluation of medical consultations, home-care assistance and less institutionalized types of social support. The malleability of age identities that we have pointed to offers good grounds for assuming that training and intervention based around sociolinguistic awareness might conceivably 'cut through' and improve support and counselling effectiveness and psychological well-being.

For inter-generational encounters as a whole, the so-called generation gap, the data we have introduced in this chapter help us to identify some potential routes to miscommunication, and the maintenance of the 'hard' intergroup boundaries that we considered in chapter 2 (see also Giles, 1979). The age identity projections of younger and older participants in the study differ fundamentally, despite some superficial similarities. The young women, like the older women, though far less regularly, comment on social change – for example, in talk of child-rearing experiences. There are certainly age-identity implications here ('we are mothers with shared experiences') but without the estrangement potential we noted between young and old. Elderly people's reflections on change are made very often in the presence of young interlocutors, who have, by definition, limited potential to share or match the elderly's historical experiences. On the other hand, if younger speakers reflect on change, their elderly interlocutors, of course, have equal potential.

Again, rhetorical sequences reflecting social or cultural change carry an intrinsically contrastive age-identifying potential. Young speakers in the data also occasionally rue the passing of time and their own accompanying 'decrement'. Y6 in I11 facetiously says she has 'passed the perfect physical age for having babies', which she considers to be 17.[4] She also feels she has passed what she calls 'the perfect mental age', 25. Very significantly, her self-deprecation, to a young peer, suggesting she is 'always falling asleep at the drop of a hat', is said flippantly, with laughter. In this respect, then, a dimension of age-identity signalling and sometimes even the same precise contents of talk are equally available to individuals across the lifespan, though with quite *different* particular identity consequences. (An older woman claiming she fell asleep 'at the drop of a hat' would be inviting attributions of far more literal decrement.)

Cross-generation talk does in these ways draw on different agendas, and different rhetorical possibilities or probabilities within shared agendas. Consequently, accommodative options in this context are likely to be severely curtailed, often with no preferable strategy readily available. As we have already suggested, there may be an inadequate experiential base for young interlocutors to draw upon in circumstances where a neutral option might otherwise be to match anecdotes, opinions or ideologies. Where the usual accommodative possibilities are not available, there is a risk of young people's discourse styles to the elderly involving overaccommodation (see chapter 2) and talk being modelled on fossilized, stereotyped construals of the old. 'Elderspeak', demeaning and de-individuating language, can surface in just these contexts, and, as part of this self-perpetuating process, generation-groups can come to be consolidated as culturally distinct formations. A discursive perspective on age identity can, at least, give us access to the means by which such dilemmas and disjunctions may arise, and then begin to offer us clues as to how we can resolve them.

4

'My Life in Your Hands': Processes of Intergenerational Self-disclosure

This chapter examines the interactional dynamics of one of the processes we listed in chapter 3 of age-identity formulation in talk: the telling of ill health, troubles and difficult life circumstances. We will therefore be illustrating, in one particular dimension, the fundamental theme of the volume: that examining conversational strategies, particularly in intergenerational contexts, is an appropriate route to understanding how older and younger group members align to one another, and hence to understanding social ageing itself. At the same time, we shall be asking what discourse analysis has to contribute to a long-established tradition of research in communication science – the study of self-disclosure and 'disclosiveness' (see Holtgraves, 1990), which has to date all but ignored matters of sequential organization and the detail of disclosure in action.

In chapter 5 we provide a more quantitatively based and interpretive account of intergenerational troubles-telling, building on the sequential analyses that we introduce here. To allow our own approach to be compared, and contrasted with existing research in the self-disclosure paradigm, the present chapter begins with a brief discussion of what is implied by this concept and an outline of alternative ways of approaching self-disclosure.

Perspectives on Self-disclosure

At the most general level self-disclosure can be viewed as a set of possibilities within what Goffman (1959) calls conversational 'information games'. If we construe social interaction as involving 'a potentially infinite cycle of concealment, discovery, false selection, and rediscovery' (p. 8), which happens in participants' knowledge of each other's probable monitoring of both parties' behaviour, it is appropriate to consider *why* personal and sometimes intimate information comes to be disclosed in the manner it does. What socio-psychological functions are being fulfilled during disclosive sequences? And what evaluative and attributional processes are likely to be at work in particular settings? That is, the full range of strategic and interpretive considerations that we introduced in chapter 2 as relevant to a discursive analysis of situated talk seem directly relevant to understanding self-disclosure. While self-disclosure seems to fit Goffman's specification of 'expressions given' during interaction, we think it is also useful to treat disclosure as part of the general management of identity in talk, and as the overt *and covert* presentation of self. So, self-disclosure needs to be treated also as part of what Goffman alternatively calls 'expressions given *off*'. Our focus in this chapter will certainly be on the strategic purposes that may underlie particular forms of disclosive talk, set against appraisals of what is supposedly normative for disclosive behaviour. As before, we ultimately want to trace the group-level implications of these discourse processes.

It is plausible that, within the limitations imposed by focusing on a relatively small data-set, patterns of self-disclosure can reveal generation-specific strategies for the management of intergenerational talk. Certainly, the self-disclosure literature (see Cozby, 1973, and Jourard, 1964 for early reviews) has frequently sought to distinguish social groups in terms of their overall propensity to disclose personal information. Findings suggest, for example, that women in general self-disclose more than men, and particularly in same-sex dyads (Cline, 1986), and that lonely people may 'overcompensate' in terms of self-disclosure (Solano, Batten and Parrish, 1982). Generalizations about situational constraints have also been attempted. Berger and Bradac (1982, p. 86) posit a set of regulative rules for self-disclosure in context; for example, 'Do not disclose intimate information to new acquaintances', 'Do not disclose negatively valenced information to new acquaintances', 'Do not disclose excessively', and the corollaries of all three.

This literature offers some preliminary competing hypotheses for the analysis of self-disclosure in our videotaped interactive study data (see chapter 3). We might anticipate relatively free self-disclosure here by the older participants by virtue of the sex and loneliness variables, but this prediction might be tempered by appreciating that the data context is a public one involving new acquaintances.

At the same time, we have several reservations about framing our own analyses in terms of the self-disclosure literature's predictions. First, we would argue that the existing literature is restricted to a contextually weak account of its phenomena, whereas our own data show that self-disclosure needs to be characterized as a complex of interactional processes attending particular contents of talk, sequentially organized and interpersonally managed. C. R. Berger and Bradac (1982), for example, quote Pearce and Sharp's (1973) definition of self-disclosure as 'the voluntary and intentional revelation of personal information which cannot be obtained from other sources' (p. 85). Our own data suggest that what is 'voluntary and intentional' is often difficult to determine, and that there are often *textual* as well as recipient-initiated pressures on speakers to self-reveal (see below).

Elementary semantics suggests that there are two distinct working definitions of the concept 'disclosure': as *content* (information disclosed) and as *process* (the making known of such information). Both are, we assume, important to the understanding of self-disclosure, though the *implementation* of disclosive sequences has been largely ignored to date. (The general information-biased perspective on communication that underlies this conception of self-disclosure has recently been critiqued by J. Brown and Rogers (1991), among others.) The detailed sequential mapping of what we shall define as 'painful' self-disclosures (PSD) in this chapter is required so that our interpretations of the intergroup significance of PSD management can reflect at least some of the complexity and subtlety of self-disclosure as process.

Second, the existing literature assumes that self-disclosure arises out of demographic differences (as we have seen above) or personality differences, with 'disclosiveness' sometimes seen as a personality type (Kelley, 1967; C. R. Berger and Bradac, 1982, p. 86). More ambitiously, we wish to involve an array of variables in our attempts to understand self-disclosure: life circumstances, identities, goals and norms for interaction, intergenerational stereotypes and, crucially, discourse strategies and patterns themselves. At least these factors need to be considered if we approach self-disclosure as a mode of facework (Goffman, 1955; P. Brown and Levinson, 1987) and as a dimension of intergroup accommodation (see chapter 2).

Third, we also assume that an integrated, interdisciplinary and 'triangulative' (cf. Stubbs, 1982) methodological approach to self-disclosure is required. That is, complementary to a distributional analysis of the frequencies of types of self-disclosure (ultimately needed to establish that there are identifiable intergroup differences to explain – see chapter 5), interpretive analyses of particular discourse sequences can help us understand the strategic management of self-disclosure. For example, what considerations of our own and other's positive and negative face, in Brown and Levinson's sense, are relevant to the making of PSDs in context? What accommodative intents may be operative?

'Painful' Self-disclosure

Our particular analytical focus is on the full set of sequences that incorporate painful self-disclosure[1] by either participant in each of the 40 interactions. The set of sequences is delimited somewhat arbitrarily by including only those 'core' disclosures that fall within a predetermined schema of topic categories:

1 *Reported bereavement*: Bereavement is disclosed in all three basic conditions of the study (elderly to young and young to elderly in the intergenerational context, elderly to elderly, and young to young, though by only two of the 20 younger participants in all). Bereavements disclosed are usually not recent, and it is, of course, significant that all but two of the elderly women are widows. Apart from the loss of husbands, loss of parents is disclosed (by one older and one younger participant), and loss of children. Several of the elderly women have lost middle-aged daughters, and some have lost babies as young women.

2 *Severe ill health*: Chronic or enduring ill health is disclosed by elderly to young, by elderly speakers to their peers and (in only one case) by young to young. The range of health problems in question includes: ongoing medical problems such as emphysema, arthritis, tinnitus, shingles, heart disease and ruptures; hospital

stays and operations (including hip replacements, mastectomy, anal polyps and colostomy), also worries about future hospitalization and recall of suffering during previous hospital stays; sensory decrement, including general problems with eyesight or hearing; and accidents, such as serious falls, where they have reportedly short- or long-term consequences to health.

3   *Immobility*: Immobility is disclosed only by elderly speakers (to younger participants and to peers). Predictably, these disclosures are often linked to disclosures of ill health, if not embedded within them. This category often takes the form of reporting inability to walk far enough to see friends or relatives, to go shopping or to get to the day centre without transport. Some people also report being unable to do things they once could do (housework and so on).

4   *Disengagement and loneliness*: These topics are disclosed by elderly to young, elderly to elderly and one young person to her older speaking-partner. Here we find reports of physical isolation and felt alienation from others and from previous social roles. Loneliness is often attributed to old friends losing touch, and families failing to visit as often as wished. Inability to fill time is usually accounted for by ill health.

5   *Others*: Diverse family, financial and social troubles make up the remainder; for example, own failed marriage and failed marriage of own child (where this has, in turn, caused the discloser emotional pain and practical problems). Others disclose troubles involved in coping with rearing young children after losing a husband and, in one instance, nursing a dying friend with little outside help.

We make no claims as to the intrinsic or actual painfulness of the states, events and histories being disclosed. We use the term as a convenient gloss for a diffuse category of reports that are plausibly but non-specifically painful, predictably in their occurrence and, perhaps, in their telling, though, of course, possibly only in our own conceptualization of them. We at least make the non-ageist assumption that experiences of, say, bereavement or ill health are predictably painful no matter how long ago they occurred.

The ground for the contextual account of PSD is laid in the consideration of sequential possibilities. An exhaustive analysis,[2] based on transcriptions, of all PSD sequences in the data has produced a taxonomy of strategies that the interactants (we shall refer to them as either disclosers of painful information or recipients of disclosure) variably employ in four different phases of disclosive sequences: pre-contexts (summarized in figure 4.1), disclosive modes (figure 4.2), recipient next-moves (figure 4.3) and closings (figure 4.4). The taxonomy outlines the principal procedural variables whose distribution across the 40 interactions will be reported and commented on in chapter 5.

Pre-contexts

The pre-context of any disclosure of painful experience is, strictly, unlimited and should ideally subsume the whole of participants'

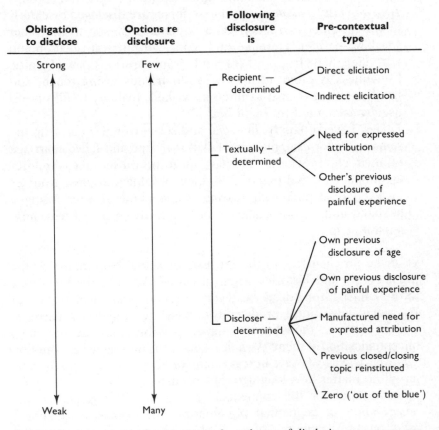

Figure 4.1 A taxonomy of strategies in four phases of disclosive sequences: pre-contexts

relational histories and certainly the whole history of the interaction in which they are engaged. Nevertheless, given our primary interest at this point in the interactional dynamics of self-disclosure, it is plausible that significant information will be available from examining the *local* contextualization of disclosive acts. The subcategorization of pre-contexts distinguishes three broad means by which subsequent disclosures are triggered.

Recipient-determined disclosures are elicitations of PSD by recipients. They may be *direct* elicitations, such as 'are you keeping well?' (Y14 to E14); 'do you sleep all right when you go to bed?' (Y6 to E6); 'is your husband still alive?' (Y3 to E3); and 'when were you widowed?' (Y12 to E12). All these particular questions are asked by younger of older interactants, and are considered to be direct elicitations because they invite, and to an extent require, predictably painful disclosure on particular topics. In this context a question such as 'is your husband still alive?' must be deemed by the questioner to risk eliciting troubles-telling. In this case, in fact, it triggers the response: 'no I lost him two years ago love worse luck (.) the world isn't the same place without him . . . ' (E9 to Y10). Such questioning strategies reflect an apparent assumption on the part of some young people that they are warranted in eliciting PSD from the elderly or, perhaps, that such elicitation is accommodative or even (*contra* C. R. Berger and Bradac) normative. The specificity, or 'closedness', of the particular question variably constrains the response options available to the discloser. But we see direct elicitations as imposing some considerable degree of obligation upon the discloser to disclose painful experiences, assuming these are there to be disclosed.

Indirect elicitations do not invite painful self-disclosure as much as enable it. The recipient asks a question about the discloser's family or life circumstances, and the response, which we judge in context not to be specifically foreseeable, is a PSD. For example, 'where are your family living now? are they all fairly close to you or are you quite spread out?' (Y11 to E11); 'have you got any family?' (Y13 to E13); 'do you have any family?' (Y15 to E15); and 'what made you decide to go [move house]?' (Y18 to E18). Though they may not invite PSD, elicitations in this subcategory *may* indirectly impute frailty, incapacity or misfortune.

On the other hand, there are many disclosive sequences where the discloser herself, to a greater or lesser extent, establishes the pre-context for her own disclosure. There is then a *discloser-determined* category, in which there is relatively little interpersonal obligation to disclose from among the PSD topics (or others), and relatively many options available. But before discussing subtypes within this category, we need to explore an intermediate category, at least in terms of the obligation and options scales proposed in the figure. These are *textually determined* disclosures, in which PSD seems contingent upon just-prior textual happenings more obviously than being determined by either participant. It is as if the text's own momentum generates a need – though obviously a need experienced by interactants and to be satisfied in and through their talk – for painful experiences to be disclosed.

On occasions, for example, a recipient (of the disclosure-to-be) makes an elicitation that has no apparent direct or indirect bearing upon painful experience. But an adequate and, we assume, truthful response that provides the information specifically requested is a PSD, or alternatively is a statement that itself requires a PSD as expressed attribution. Just before extract 4.1, E2 has said that she is currently knitting squares to make a blanket. Presumably seeing this as a relatively simple knitting task, Y2 (at lines 1 and 2) asks if she has ever knitted before.

EXTRACT 4.1 (from I2)

```
 1  Y2:                       are you have you just star have
 2        you ever kni knitted before?
 3  E2:  yes! I've made
                  [    ]
 4  Y2:        oh you used to knit did you?
 5  E2:  I've made myself cardigans and all=
 6  Y2:  =yes=
 7  E2:  =but my eyes are not so good see
 8  Y2:  so you want some something fairly simple is it?
           [
 9  E2:       I  I got (.) I should have my (.)
10        rupture done and I won't go in
11  Y2:  you've got a rupture in?
           [                     ]
12  E2:   I'm too nervous behind the navel
13  Y2:  ohh
           [ ]
14  E2:  and I'm too nervous to go in and have it done=
15  Y2:  =are you?=
```

16 E2: =you follow me?=
17 Y2: =is it is it painful?
              [   ]
18 E2:   so I won't go in and have it done
19 Y2: no
20 E2: *no* it doesn't affect me I just get a my legs get a
21   bit tired
22 Y2: [*nodding*] oh I see=
23 E2: =and of course I I do have suffered I've had a couple
24   of blackouts (.) lately
              [   ]
25 Y2: [*nodding*]   oh yes=

E2 answers emphatically 'yes', going on to say she has made 'cardigans and all' – relatively complex knitting tasks. This response opens up an attributional void: *why* does she now knit squares? The void is filled by the disclosure that her 'eyes are not so good'. In terms of obligations and options we would see there being some significant obligation to sustain the logic of the text in this way, though there is a greater range of options here than in, for example, responding to direct elicitations of the sort we discussed earlier. After all, the immediate requirements of textual coherence have been satisfied – an answer has been given – and it is, of course, true that not all implicational, attributional and contextual queries are satisfied in conversation anyway. Self-disclosure can be avoided in these instances by simple omission, while it can be avoided in the context of direct eliciting only by prevarication, falsification or tactical hedging.

An interlocutor's own previous disclosure is another type of textual determinant of disclosure, though different interpersonal goals are involved. Here we consider matched behaviours that appear to be central instances of communication accommodation, where participants engage in similar discourse activities, generally to enhance their own social attractiveness and/or to promote communication efficiency (see chapter 2). A preliminary analysis of the sort of closely sequenced, mutual self-disclosure that we find in extract 4.2 would suggest we have matched, convergent language strategies realizing psychological convergence. Before the transcribed extract, E2 has already disclosed that her husband has died.

EXTRACT 4.2 (from I4)

```
 1  E1:  my husband was with the Cardiff Corporation=
 2  E2:  =oh yes
              [     ]
 3  E1:          and er(.) he'd only retired three weeks he had to retire
                                                    [   ]
 4  E2:                                              oh
 5  E1:  at sixty-five you see
              [        ]
 6  E2:          my er husband went abroad and caught a germ abroad
                 [                                      ]
 7  E1:                          and er and       then
 8        I er found him dead in bed(.) and he'd only retired three weeks
 9        you see
10  E2:  oh they don't have no retirement isn't it awful
                 [                                    ]
11  E1:                          and he was looking so forward
12          to his retirement
            [                 ]
13  E2:  oh bless him
14  E1:  yes=
15  E2:  =what a shock for you
                      [   ]
16                          yes it was shock yes
17  E2:  oh its marvellous you're like you are isn't it
18  E1:  well(.) I'm eighty-six last May ((3 sylls)) [laughs]
                      [     ]
19  E2:                  oh god
```

At line 6 E2 is presumably beginning an account of the detailed circumstances of his death (he 'caught a germ abroad'). The transcript shows that this is embedded within, and probably offered to match, a disclosure by E1: 'he'd only retired three weeks', (line 3).

Following from the range of accommodation processes outlined in chapter 2, other interpretations are plausible too. In particular, the matching of self-disclosive acts need not be seen as psychologically convergent if there are reasons to claim that the participants are not attuning their communicative strategies to each other's wishes and needs. In extract 4.2 the significant criterion is whether E1 and E2 would evaluate their talk as attuned and complementary, or whether their disclosing is in a sense *combative*. The very fact of the two narratives overlapping, both formally (simultaneous speech) and functionally (interrupted narrative development) suggests that there is some competition to occupy the role of discloser. A more appropriate model of complementary talk at this point might show participants timing their contributions in ways that allowed narrative disclosures to develop and be responded to supportively (see below). For the moment, the significance of instances of matched troubles-telling, however, is that disclosure is itself a significant pre-context for disclosure, whether convergent or combative. This observation is in fact one of the most frequently stated conclusions from socio-psychological studies; Won-Doornink (1985) writes that 'the most frequently shown determinant of disclosure is disclosure itself' (p. 97; cf. also Ludwig, Franco and Malloy, 1986).

The decision to match disclosure is under the control of the second discloser herself. Certainly, we need to see 'other's previous disclosure' establishing own-disclosive options and obligations by virtue of the teller's perception of interactional propriety. This is a different social process from the previous subtype (need for expressed attribution), where disclosure is required as a part of the general pressure upon any one interactant to maintain coherence in her own talk. Our ranking of these two subtypes is intended to imply that there might (other considerations apart) be a greater degree of optionality in the matching case; but both subtypes can appropriately be labelled 'textually determined' because they arise primarily from immediately previous and specific textual happenings.

We are reticent to rank the five subtypes of the discloser-determined category in any precise order, because impressionistic rankings of degrees of obligation and ranges of options are too strongly influenced by particular contents and by subtleties of context; other things are predictable *un*equal. We also acknowledge that other criteria can equally well be addressed – for example sociocentric versus egocentric and legitimate versus illegitimate – to validate somewhat different rankings of strategies in figure 4.1. Our impressionistic ranking of the discloser-determined subcategory reflects the criterion of markedness; given no obligation and with an equally wide range of options, the pre-contextual types at the bottom of the figure are entirely unpredictable and most clearly non-normative in C. R. Berger and Bradac's (1982) terms.

The subtype listed last in figure 4.1 relates to disclosing painful experiences when there is a maximally unconstrained choice of topics and moves available, and seemingly no immediate obligation to disclose. These instances include one where virtually no contingent pre-context either exists or is manufactured; the PSD is made 'out of the blue'. In extract 4.3, where a lacuna develops, the speaker, from a potentially very wide range of new topic options, chooses to tell a painful experience.

EXTRACT 4.3 (from I20)

```
 1  E9:  you from Cardiff?
 2  E10: pardon?
 3  E9:  you from Cardiff?
 4  E10: yes I live in Llanedeyrn
 5  E9:  oh yes nice there
 6  E10: yes
          [    ]
 7  E9:  that's where we are now isn't it not far from there
 8  E10: no we're not
 9  E9:  no (heh)
          [  ]
10  E10:    ah    (5.0)
11  E9:  I get a bit tired walking now ((that))er false legs er
                                            [
12  E10:                                        where
13       have you been?
14  E9:  I've got two false hips(.) so I get tired walking transplants
          [                      ]
15  E10: [astonished] you got what?
16  E9:  yeah transplants
              [        ]
17  E10:      good gracious me!
                [  ]
18  E9:            yes marvellous isn't it
19  E10: oh dear
```

It is possible to interpret silence as itself a pre-context for disclosure and to argue that E9 may be motivated by a desire to resolve an apparent breakdown of the conversational flow. But a wide range of other topics and strategies could have been selected to achieve cooperative talk at this point.

Another discloser-determined pre-context, 'manufactured need for expressed attribution', also has a marked quality, although it does remain within the bounds of an ongoing topic. But here such topics

are developed with unexpected shifts in levels of intimacy or affect.
We find this in extract 4.4, where the topic of lunch at the day centre,
raised at line 1, is sustained to line 9 where it is linked to the
disclosure of the colostomy and its consequences.

EXTRACT 4.4 (from I3)

```
 1   E1:  every day(.) we have a nice meal(.) only sixty pence
                         [   ]
 2   Y1:               mm
 3   E1:  we pay(.) a cooked dinner=
               [       ]
 4   Y1:  ((3 sylls))
 5   Y1:  =mm=
 6   E1:  =sweet and a cup of tea(.) but I nev don't have the sweet(.) I
          only have um two cream crackers and a bit of cheese because it
          suits me (1.0) [voice almost at a whisper, hand in front of mouth]
          I don't broadcast this but I've lived with a colostomy for
          17 years you see(.) so
                     [    ]
11   Y1:            mm
12   E1:  I've got to be careful what I eat=
                       [    ]
13   Y1:                   yes
14   Y1:  =yes=
15   E1:  =well then they're(.) good in the centre they know that(.) and
          they'll er(.) give me a little bit of fish if there's anything
          with any onion in it
18   Y1:  mm
            [
19   E1:  they're very good=
20   Y1:  =mm mm
21   E1:  so er(.) [lowering voice again] really and at the time I just
          wanted to die
23   Y1:  mm
            [
24   E1:  and er well I didn't know what they were talking about
25   Y1:  mm
26   E1:  but er so anyway I'm pretty good lucky ((I can't say
                               [    ]
27   Y1:                      mm
28   E1:  anything could I good))
29   Y1:  no
```

The colostomy is the expressed attribution for E2's not eating the sweet and is therefore clearly contingent. We do not mean to imply that the pre-contextual information (in this case the general discussion of the day centre lunch) is offered expressly to preface planned disclosure; rather, that the discloser behaves *as if* the attribution is needed. In that sense the need is manufactured by the discloser herself rather than textually generated. On the other hand, disclosing the fact of a colostomy, markedly intimate, is likely to run counter to the recipient's expectations of E1's topic development and needs to be framed with an appropriate disclaimer. The ironic 'I don't broadcast this', in a context where there are known overhearers, is a rare acknowledgement of the infringement of Berger and Bradac's norms, but at the same time it highlights a preparedness knowingly to disregard them. Such a fragment suggests there is indeed a will to disclose and a general appreciation of interactional benefits accruing that offset recognized disadvantages. In fact, the general category of discloser-determined disclosures needs to be accounted for in those terms.

Where self-disclosures are coherent moves within a turn's textual development, relating with some degree of predictability to previous own-moves, we can identify further subtypes of the discloser-determined category, slightly higher on the obligations and options scales. Sub-types of this sort include elements of disclosive chains where the fact of a teller having disclosed on one topic establishes, although weakly, a relevance for a subsequent disclosure on a different topic by the same speaker. Extract 4.1 showed E2 disclosing her own failing eyesight at line 7 and Y2 pursuing this topic at line 8. E2's next PSD about her rupture (line 9) constructs a coherence within the discourse that depends on the perception of ill health as a topic bridge (our third subcategory in figure 4.1).

Coherence can also link, or be imposed across, non-adjacent moves, and so a fourth subtype is when tellers reinstate a closed or closing topic in a PSD. In extract 4.5, E5 and E6 appear to be closing a sequence on the topic of helping others. At line 12 E6 gives a summary or reformulation of E5's stated policy for helping others and E5's next move has the force of a generalized evaluation of her own just-endorsed position. To that extent, 'that's the answer' predicts the closing of the 'helping others' topic. E5's reinstating of the topic provides a context for reporting that she nursed a friend who was dying of cancer, in a way that is entirely topically coherent with what has gone before. But the coherence has been re-established at E5's own instigation and the PSD is afforded a relevance by discursive choices the teller herself has made.

EXTRACT 4.5 (from I10)

```
 1   E5:  =it's been my interest to (.) give collect and do (.) and
                                                 [   ]
 2   E6:                                         quite
 3   E5:  even(.) take the shirt off my back if they wanted it=
                                          [   ]
 4   E6:                                  yes
 5   E6:  =I know=
 6   E5:  =knowing they want something=
 7   E6:  =yes=
 8   E5:  =and that you're
 9   E6:  yes=
10   E5:  =ready to help them
                      [        ]
11   E6:              lovely
12   E6:  you have compassion
13   E5:  that's the answer
14   E6:  mm=
15   E5:  =now I nursed a friend for f nine weeks day and
16        night with cancer=
17   E6:  [sympathetically] =oh=
18   E5:  =on my own=
19   E6:  =yes=
20   E5:  now and then visitors used to come for five minutes
21        ten minutes=
22   E6:  =yes
23   E5:  but I never changed my suit . . .
```

Talk about own age, the final subcategory needed to account for the data, is another seemingly coherent pre-context for disclosure of painful experience. In extract 4.6 E3 has told her age at line 1 which appears to elicit Y3's complimenting expression of surprise. The compliment is accepted but specifically (in fact it is specified non-verbally) in relation to E3's facial appearance; she then contrasts her own mobility problems, caused by thrombosis, with this. Elderly people's telling of their age seems to carry some intrinsic potential as a PSD pre-context because age in years can be used as a baseline for appraising own state of health (see chapter 6). The trade-off between age and health is overtly recognized in E3's framing of her age-telling: '. . . you wouldn't believe it' (line 1). She is apparently well for her age or, conversely, can claim to appear younger than her age because she is apparently well.

EXTRACT 4.6 (from I6)

```
 1   E3:  you wouldn't believe it I'm eighty-seven
 2   Y3:  wh eighty-seven good heavens you don't look eighty-seven
 3   E3:  [gasps and laughs] well not up here [holds hand up to face]
                            [        ]   [                          ]
 4   Y3:              [laughs]      I hope I look like you when I'm
 5        eighty-seven                                           [
 6   E3:                                                    not up
 7        not up here(.) I'm not [holding hand up against face]
 8   Y3:  ooh
 9   E3:  [much more seriously] but it's this [lays hand on leg] [
                                                                [   ]
10   Y3:  aah
11   E3:  ((2 sylls)) thrombosis ((1 syll))
                      [                             ]
12   Y3:          so how did you get here today?
13   E3:  [petulantly] oh! in the car that gentleman brought me
                                            [    ]
14   Y3:                                     oh
15   Y3:  well that's kind isn't it
                        [
16   E3:                    yes wasn't it nice I thought it
17        was very nice                [
18   Y3:                                yes(.) aah(.) so what
19        made you come today?
```


Modes of Disclosure

The various types of pre-context we find in the data have already led us to suggest that, as interactional events, PSDs may arise from quite different social motivations, may be marked or unmarked events in the unfolding of a conversational text, and therefore are likely to have quite different communicative and socio-psychological consequences. The justification for listing types of pre-context at some length is that the nature of a self-disclosure itself is in significant respects determined in relation to factors in its interactional history. On the other hand, disclosers may encode their disclosures (whatever their contexts) in what may be significantly different ways, selecting options from several subsystems that we set out in figure 4.2 under the general heading of 'modes of disclosure'.

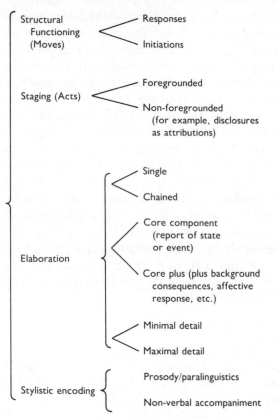

Figure 4.2   A taxonomy of strategies in four phases of disclosive sequences: modes of disclosure

In terms of their function in the structure of an interaction, we have already seen that acts of telling may be initiating moves in conversational exchanges (in the general sense of Coulthard and Montgomery, 1982). Others are clearly responses to initiations by recipients. For example, 'I should have my (.) *rup*ture done and I won't go in' (E2 in extract 4.1, lines 9–10) is disclosure as initiation; 'but my *eyes* are not so good see' (also E2 in the same extract, line 7) is disclosure as part of a move responding to Y2's 'oh you *used* to knit did you?' (line 4). This gross structural distinction merely restates our earlier observation that PSDs may differ in terms of options and obligations, since we can reasonably assume that responses are essentially predicted moves while initiations are essentially predicting moves (again, see Coulthard and Montgomery, 1982, p. 111).

A more sensitive analysis allows us to distinguish self-disclosures that, as individual communicative acts, are more or less textually foregrounded. Figure 4.2 presents this range of options under the heading 'staging', a term we borrow from P. Brown and Yule's (1983) discussion of thematization processes above the sentence level (p. 134). Just as syntactic components may be thematized or foregrounded, so communicative acts themselves can be rendered more or less prominent by their relations to other acts. Again, in our earlier discussion of PSDs as (occasionally) expressed attributions, we recognized the parenthetic nature of some disclosures (such as extract 4.1, line 7 'but my eyes are not so good see'). Within the staging alternatives, such instances can clearly be seen as non-foregrounded by comparison with focused accounts of painful states or events, such as E3's disclosure of her thrombosis (extract 4.6, lines 6–11). A uniquely non-foregrounded disclosive act occurs in extract 4.7 (lines 13 and 15) when E12 tells of her emphysema and osteoarthritis precisely as an attempt to support a claim that she is not 'miserable and moaning' (line 7).

EXTRACT 4.7 (from I21)

```
 1  E12  you know(.) yes(.) mm [breathes] I think you see when you're
 2        getting older at this age you (2.0) there's lots of things can make
 3        us a bit miserable but [breathes] we have a look on the bright side
 4        and
                         [                                    ]
 5  Y12:                      [agreeing] oh yes mm
 6  Y12:  yes
 7  E12:  nobody wants you when you're miserable and moaning
                         [   ]                      [        ]
 8  Y12:                  mm                         mm
 9  E12:  and groaning . . .
10  E12:  =it applies all ages really doesn't it you know=
                         [     ][      ]
11  Y12:                  yes    yes
12  Y12:  =certainly=
```

13 E12: =because I can't breathe I've got [*breathes*] emphysema and I'm
    [   ]   [   ]   [   ]
14 Y12: mm   mm   mm
15 E12: full of [*breathes*] osteoarthritis and what have you but erm
             [   ]   [   ]
16 Y12:   mm   mm
17 E12: [*breathes*] thank goodness the old brain-box is still going

The remaining subcategorizations of disclosure modes all have to do with the extent to which disclosive acts are elaborated in their telling. In the data we find three co-occurring sets of alternatives in the elaboration system. These have to do with syntagmatic elaboration at progressively more delicate levels. Simply in terms of the topics being disclosed we can distinguish single from chained disclosures. A speaker makes a single disclosure when she reveals one of the topic subtypes (as listed earlier). Chained disclosures arise when a previous own disclosure functions as a pre-context for disclosing another topic; for example, again, the chain of PSDs in extract 4.1: sensory decrement (eyesight), ongoing medical problem (rupture) and an apparently unrelated further instance of the ill-health subtype (blackouts). With any PSD, a speaker may restrict herself to what we wish to call a core component: the reporting or naming of the painful state or event and no more than this, such as the references to emphysema and osteoarthritis in extract 4.7. Alternatively, she may report some or a good deal of contextual information in addition to this, such as outlining the consequences of colostomy (extract 4.4, line 12, 'I've got to be careful what I eat') and affective response (lines 21 and 22, 'and at the time I just wanted to die'). A final dimension of elaboration relates to the amount of detail a teller provides within each component, core or otherwise. An instance of elaboration at this level occurs when E2, in the text following on from extract 4.1, details the cause of her blackouts and the side-effects of the drugs prescribed, that is, giddiness, inability to walk and loose bowels.

Finally, it is, of course, the case that modes of disclosure can be subcategorized by their stylistic encoding. At prosodic, paralinguistic, and non-verbal levels such variables as speech rate and intensity, whispering and laughter, serious or smiling facial expression, posture and orientation will significantly colour the making of a disclosure and will probably also have variable interpersonal consequences. We might expect there to be a systematic correlation between stylistic choices made here and the intrinsic intimacy, recency, 'painfulness' or in some other sense the salience of the disclosure's context. However, modes of disclosing in the data are sometimes interesting in particular because of the unpredictable, marked covariance of content and style. When E2, in the elaborated sequence just discussed, is describing the most unpleasant side-effects she is suffering, she accompanies the account with expansive gestures, a generally animated non-verbal style, laughter, smiling and the prosodics of levity. To the extent that seeming incongruities of this sort regularly occur, they can be significant clues to the presentational function of PSDs. Possible interpretations here are that E2 is compensating stylistically for what she may perceive to be embarrassingly intimate self-disclosures; more interestingly, that she is 'smiling through' her adversity and seeking to gain face through telling face-threatening troubles in a controlled and cheerful manner. Jefferson (1984b, p.367) suggests laughter in troubles talk shows troubles-resistivity in the teller, indicating she is in a position to 'take it lightly'. In any event, the style of a self-disclosure needs to be taken into account in interpreting its functioning as facework (as we do in chapter 5).

Next Moves

Our reason for taxonomising recipient next-moves is to identify discourse processes that may allow us to capture the problematical nature, at least in potential, of PSDs in the data. Also, in later chapters we shall be assessing the contribution made by recipients to the development of PSD sequences, which gives information, for example, about cross-generational differences in strategies of active listening and social support. For these reasons, it is important to see recipient next-moves and closing moves (the fourth phase of the taxonomy) as integral elements of the organization of disclosive sequences. On the one hand, recipients' next-moves provide implicit or explicit commentaries upon the PSDs they follow and help us assess their interactional significance. On the other hand, they play a central role in enabling or inhibiting further disclosive talk within the same or a new PSD sequence. This last function is used to rank, again impressionistically, the processes we list in figure 4.3.

Figure 4.3 distinguishes minimal moves from full moves. Minimal moves are brief verbal or at least vocal utterances, which may also

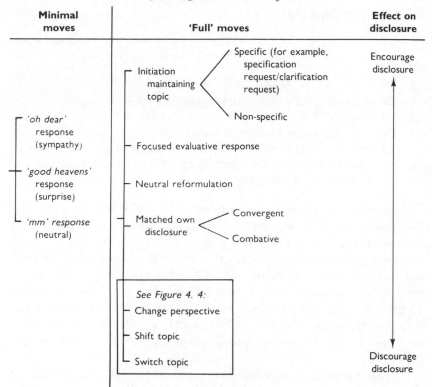

Figure 4.3 A taxonomy of strategies in four phases of disclosive sequences: recipient next-moves

occur as back-channel utterances overlapping acts of telling themselves. The effective force of these moves is unclear from their transcribed forms and depends heavily on their non-verbal and prosodic and paralinguistic realizations. But some moves that we label 'oh dear' responses may be taken to encode sympathy, at least in their unmarked realizations; they can be distinguished from more affectively neutral responses (for example 'mm') and expressions of surprise or shock (for example 'good heavens!'). Most commonly, such utterances occur at the beginning of full next-moves of the sort we shall consider. Their most significant function in interactive terms, however, seems to be when they occur as isolates in place of full moves, as in extract 4.8, where Y9's 'oh yes yes mm oh well' and 'um', punctuated by pauses of increasing length, suggest she does not readily find an appropriate full next-move.

EXTRACT 4.8 (from I18)

```
1   E8:   =because when I was a widow you see after eleven years I had three
2         little children you see to bring up I worked very hard I
                            [  ]
3   Y9:                    mm
4   E8:   done everything cook er parlour maid everything I done
5   Y9:   mm hm
6   E8:   well I had to get a living you see=
7   Y9:   =oh yes yes (1.0) mm (2.0) oh well (3.0) um(.) I was going to say
8         I'm I've started working again I've got a little daughter and I've
9         just started back to work
```

Y9's minimal responses are all neutral, in the sense we have just discussed, and the closest instance in our data to a zero response. It is not unreasonable to suppose (though see chapter 7) that the seven- or eight-second sequence transcribed as line 7 is problematical for both participants, and particularly for Y9, who eventually shifts topic, making an initiation on a non-painful theme. More typically, recipients elect from a range of moves that, in their most basic functioning, sustain the flow of talk, signal an affective or evaluative response to the disclosure, and develop conversation more or less coherently.

As positive support, recipients may, with a full move, initiate talk on the topic of the disclosure being made. They will often make topic-specific initiations, for example, requesting specification of a medical condition described ('you've got a rupture in?', in extract 4.1, line 11), requesting clarification ('you got what?', in extract 4.3, line 15) and asking a teller to evaluate a condition she has described ('is it is it painful?', in extract 4.1, line 17). These new initiations impose (or reimpose) an obligation to disclose painful experiences, in line with our 'direct elicitation' subcategory of pre-contexts. An alternative is for a recipient to make a non-specific initiation, which again establishes, or re-establishes, a relevance for disclosive talk. In extract 4.9, Y5's 'were you?' offers a general possibility of further talk on E5's being a war widow, information that she goes on to elicit more specifically (at line 5) when E5 does not take up the offer beyond a neutral 'yes' in line 4.

EXTRACT 4.9 (from I9)

```
1   E5:   I was a war-widow at the age of twenty-eight=
```

```
2   Y5:  =were you?=
         [         ]
3   E5:  ((2 syll))
4   E5:  =yes
5   Y5:  and you've been widowed since then you've never remarried=
                                          [                         ]
6   E5:                                   I've been widowed
7        =never married no=
8   Y5:  =how old were you when you left school?
9   E5:  I was at school until I was sixteen I went to Canton
         High School
```

Non specific initiations of this sort can generally be distinguished from the minimal back-channel moves previously discussed, though classification here depends on subtleties of speech-timing (overlapped or non-overlapped speech) and prosody.

A broad category of moves labelled 'focused evaluative response' – always involving positive evaluations in our data – expresses recipients' sympathetic or empathetic orientation to the states or events recounted, and, by implication, to the disclosing of them. For that reason, we tentatively rank this category towards the 'encourage' end of the disclosure scale in figure 4.3. The responses are 'focused' since they evaluate the particular experiences related. In extract 4.2, at line 15, E2 ventures that E1's husband's death was a 'shock' for her; in extract 4.10 at line 11, Y11 notes that E11's bringing up five children alone 'couldn't have been easy'.

EXTRACT 4.10 (from I22)

```
1   E11:                          and when I got married
2        unfortunately my husband after I'd(.) had five children I
3        decided I'd had enough of him although [breathes] I didn't
4        want (1.0) I wanted my children to have a father
5        but er(.) I thought well he's no good to me he's
6        no good to the children because he was to used(.)
7        beat me around and so forth [breathes] so out he
                                    [        ]
8   Y11: [sympathetically]     oh dear
9   E11: went! [breathes] so I brought up the five of them on my
10        own
11  Y11: oh that couldn't have been easy
                              [    ]
12  E11:                       see
```

13 Y11: ((2 sylls))
               [   ]
14 E11: never knew where he was never had any(.)
15   [*breathes*] support from him 'til about three years ago [*breathes*]
16   and I wanted to go my daughter went off to Australia so
17   I wanted to go out to visit [*breathes*] but I had no pension
18 Y11: oh yes yes
19 E11: and er I wanted my daughter ((and)) well it must be sorted out
20   mum ((be)) you know I=
21 Y11: =yes
22 E11: which I did and to my surprise I had a little bit of money from . . .

As in both the quoted instances, moves in this category can often make an original contribution to the disclosed topic itself, as recipients evaluatively rework the account in terms of the discloser's own hardships or difficulties, thereby to an extent sharing in the reconstruction of the painful states or events.

The previous two categories share the characteristic of broadly reinforcing disclosure. This means they are strategies that carry the possibility of escalating disclosive talk; one might say the 'risk' of doing this, to the extent that responding to PSD is problematical in some dimension. The most obvious problem at this juncture for recipients is that of response-finding. If there is a risk of escalation, it will also be a risk from the teller's perspective if responses to an extent oblige her to engage in self-disclosive behaviours she finds difficult. On the other hand (and again from both participants' perspectives), several of the response alternatives to be considered are in danger of trivializing PSD accounts or signalling disinterest. For these reasons, it would be surprising if recipients did not on occasions seek a form of 'safe ground' in responding neutrally, hoping to avoid the pitfalls of either extreme. In our data, however, few next-moves deserve to be labelled 'safe' in this sense. The category we call 'neutral reformulation' (see figure 4.3) best fits this rubric, though even here we find attempts to reformulate aspects of a trouble that seem unsatisfactory in themselves.

In extract 4.11, while E2 is disclosing the side-effects of her course of treatment, Y2 produces a range of response types, including moves (at lines 11 and 13–14) that do little beyond restating the teller's own comments and decisions.

EXTRACT 4.11 (from I2)

```
 1  E2:  . . . I'm on(.) capsules(.) too much my blood's
 2       too mu too thin=
 3  Y2:  =too too thin is it? . . .
 4  E2:  I've left them I I shouldn't have left them off but I
 5       have(.) left them off=
 6  Y2:  =mm=
 7  E2:  =for a week and I'm fine
 8  Y2:  yes
 9  E2:  well there's after-effects after them see . . .
10  E2:  . . . I going to see him and tell him now=
11  Y2:  =tell him that you're having side-effects . . .
12  E2:  so that's what I'm going to tell him when I see him
                                            [          ]
13  Y2:                                          oh it's just as
14       well isn't it to stop them and tell him
```

Such moves are clearly accommodative in signalling attention and understanding, and in being congruent responses to the difficulty reported – line 11, indeed, functions as an utterance-completor to E2's line 10 – though they fall short of positively eliciting further disclosure or making focused positive evaluations. The responses are therefore relatively neutral in respect of encouraging or discouraging disclosure (though, again, speech rate, non-verbal accompaniment, etc. are highly relevant to the analysis), but they are accommodative as attuned discourse management strategies (see chapter 2).

The remaining options available to recipients within this third phase of the analysis are covered elsewhere in our discussion. The possibility of a recipient matching a PSD with one of her own, either convergently or combatively, is one we considered in the earlier account of pre-contextual options. The three remaining possibilities, changing perspective and shifting or switching topic, tend to both discourage more self-disclosure (as their prospective function) and advance an ongoing disclosure (as their synchronic function). For these reasons, these three options can appropriately be discussed in our fourth and final phase, moves towards closing.

Moves towards Closing

The closing of a disclosive sequence, like the closing of a conversation (according to Schegloff and Sacks's (1973) well-known account) is typically a complex interactional process, needing to be achieved rather than merely happening. This perspective does not allow us to taxonomize closings themselves, but rather the moves that either or both participants in our data employ as elements of their negotiation of closings. Taxonomized moves will frequently not achieve a close, and we often find multiple moves of the same or different subcategories being produced by one or both interactants. We interpret the structural and functional complexity we find in this phase again as evidence of the potentially problematical nature of PSD sequences themselves, and of the heavy responsibility that the management of such sequences can impose on participants.

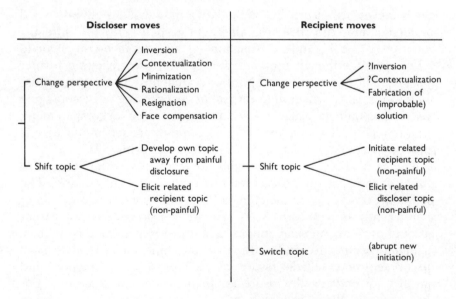

Figure 4.4   A taxonomy of strategies in four phases of disclosive sequences: moves towards closing

Figure 4.4 lists moves realized by tellers and recipients separately, and it is interesting to note the different ranges of strategies employed by people in these different interactional roles. Also, we shall suggest that even those strategies that are identically labelled in the two columns of the figure can carry subtly different interactional forces. Within both columns we can distinguish between moves that refer back to painful information disclosed and seek to modify it by changing perspective, and moves that, on the other hand, develop conversation away from painful topics by shifting or switching topic. In the case of discloser-managed topic shifts, a previous disclosure is, by definition, closed. Recipient-managed shifts or switches may or may not achieve a close.

Various subcategories of disclosers' moves (those we call inversion, contextualization, face compensation and minimization) and all subcategories of recipients' moves that change the perspective on a disclosure (inversion and contextualization again, plus fabrication of an improbable solution) function to 'lighten' a disclosure and to effect a change of key (in the sense of Hymes, 1972). The inversion strategies are attempts to reinterpret disclosed information in a positive light, to look on the bright side or make light of the trouble (cf. Jefferson, 1984b).

In I 23 (the source of extract 4.12) E11 has told of her loneliness, which is caused by having moved to a flat at the top of a hill, inaccessible to her friends and former neighbours. She moves to close the sequence by describing the positive aspects of her new home, 'it's healthy and there's plenty to see and you're near the shops'. A discloser is fully at liberty, and perhaps even under some obligation, to invert her own painful disclosure in this way since it is clearly her own analysis of her life circumstances that is at issue. When a recipient attempts an inversion move, there is an inherent risk of imposing an inappropriately revised account of an experience already reported as painful. In I 18, an elderly woman (E10) had disclosed that her husband died after 11 years of marriage and that she has lived alone in a non-native country ever since. Her younger conversation partner (Y9) then offers 'yes (1.0) ah well (.) still I mean it's nice that you're settled here (.) ((2 syllables))'. In this case, the inversion is hardly apposite, because there is no obvious 'bright side' to the reported life experience.

A more general strategy for changing perspective on a disclosure is the locating of a painful state or event in its broader context. The lighter key is achieved by focusing on a more global account of the discloser's life circumstances, as in extract 4.12, where E12 (at line 6) redefines the significance of her mobility problem (lines 1 and 3).

Like others, she has the day centre to go to, which can offer ambulance transport and which exists largely to provide the sociable environment her immobility would otherwise preclude.

EXTRACT 4.12 (from I23)

```
1 E12: yes [breathes] well I can't walk far because(.) I'm full of
                                  [          ]
2 E11:                                   no
3 E12: arthritis [laughs]
              [    ]
4 E11:        [laughs]
5 E12: but er(.) wh what else(.) can we expect something
6      that(.) we're lucky that we've got the day centre to go to
            [   ]                              [           ]
7 E11:        oh I                          oh yes(.) oh
8      I think they're marvellous places
```

On another occasion, in I 40, a younger recipient (Y20) offers what is in its context a virtually identical contextualization move, 'so this is really good for you isn't it then to be able to go somewhere like this'. The move is made in response to a disclosure by an elderly conversation partner (E20) of having been widowed for 21 years. This contextualization attempt may be appropriate at one level (the centre offers genuine social support for many who live alone) but it makes possibly unwarranted assumptions about the elderly person's particular circumstances and needs; it arguably patronizes through assuming a knowledge of what is good for the teller.

The third subcategory of recipient moves termed 'fabrication of improbable solution' shares with inversion and contextualization the inherent problem of ignorance, a necessarily inferior awareness of the topic disclosed. On one occasion, in I 10, E5 has been reporting the acrimonious break-up of her son's marriage, divorce and its painful consequences to all concerned. E6 responds 'perhaps they'll go back together', which is unlikely in terms of the account given and is in any case not relevant to what has already passed – E5 has already commented that 'the children . . . are very badly affected'.[3]

Disclosers have the further options of face compensation and minimization, still within the general set of strategies that 'lighten' disclosures to some extent. We find instances of disclosers compensating for the face-threatening PSDs they have made (see the extended discussion of PSD as facework in chapter 5) by counter-balancing them with self-reports that build positive face. In I 2, E2 concludes a PSD on the theme of her own immobility by saying 'so I I find I can't do it so good'. Her next turn is: 'so I but I do all my own work', said assertively and cheerfully. The effect of the move is ultimately similar to that of the contextualization strategies we discussed above, though the immediate function of such face-compensation moves is to contrast one particular report with another, rather than to set a painful experience in the context of its broader significance. With minimizing strategies, disclosers seek quite simply to retract elements of their previous disclosure, to redefine their own painful experience as less painful than they earlier reported it. For instance, in I 15 a younger speaker (Y7) has reported having just been told she has osteoarthritis in her hip. She is a sports teacher and plays squash for her county, so that her sporting and career prospects are seriously in jeopardy. Yet when her speaking partner (Y8) suggests 'it must have come as quite a shock', Y7 says 'yes (.) well no it'll go (.) apparently these things come ((and go))'. We have no access to how valid Y7 perceives this self-assessment to be, but it does contradict her earlier account; certainly, it marks a transition from Y7's self-disclosure to her initiation of talk on a new (other-related) topic.

The two final perspective-changing strategies that disclosers use are moves that terminate disclosures without alleviating their projected painfulness to any significant extent. A discloser may offer a rationalization of how her painful circumstances have come to be, for example, when E16, in I 31, suggests that her grandchildren do not visit her because they are 'interested in their jobs I suppose'. This is clearly a move towards closing, since E16 has shifted from revealing to accounting, and to accounting in a spirit of apparent acceptance. Her 'I suppose' might suggest she doubts the validity of the account and, perhaps, that it is only the interactional difficulty in this passage of talk that is at all likely to be resolved.

Exclusively in peer-elderly encounters, we find a move towards closing that is simply the expression of resignation. In extract 4.12, E12's first move to close after her disclosure of being full of arthritis is 'oh wh what else (.) can we expect'. As in our earlier discussion of talk about age as a relevant pre-context for PSD, the fact of being elderly itself seems to provide, for some disclosers, something of an account, and we have seen that accounting for PSDs can also be a strategy for closing them. On the other hand, this last retrospective closing move stands out from all others in not clearly offering a means of recovering from PSD. And 'recovery' seems a more appropriate concept here than 'repair', since the reported painful experiences, and, indeed, the interactional 'damage' that might be done in their reporting, can in no meaningful sense be made good.

As in previous phases of the analysis, we do not mean to imply that the strategies we list are mutually exclusive and cannot co-occur. In fact, the 'change perspective' subtypes often preface the various means of topic development and change listed in the two lower quadrants of figure 4.4. Since there is a normative requirement for coherent topical development in conversation, it is not surprising that the strategies we find in our data generally involve progressive topic shifts away from the reported painful experience. Once again, either participant can take the initiative for developing a topic, and a discloser may steer her own topic away from painful disclosure. An example is in extract 4.10, where E11 continues her life narrative, a compilation of reports of painful happenings, towards an account of good fortune in the last line of the extract. While the younger interlocutor, as we have seen, has provided responses to some of the self-disclosures made, responsibility for terminating the run of disclosive sequences as a whole is assumed by the teller herself within the flow of the narrative. The effect here is to routinize PSD in that no ultimate response from the recipient is required or even allowed. And it is the same effect that E14 achieves in lines 8 and 10 of extract 4.13. The topic shift is again coherent in that her question about Y14's children being in school (at line 10) develops from E14's short reference (at line 8) to her own children. In the structure of the discourse topic shift is achieved this time through an elicitation on a related recipient-topic with no predictable painful associations. Once again, however, we see how a discloser can manage a PSD in a way that requires minimal or no contribution towards closure from her recipient, however emotionally taxing the sequence may be in other respects.

EXTRACT 4.13 (from I28)

1 E14: have you got any children?
2 Y14: yes
3 E14: oh you have=
4 Y14: =yes(.) four of them [*laughs*]

```
 5 E14: (exclaims) four! oh dear you've done mind er (2.0) oh that's nice
 6       I I think to have a family
 7 Y14: mm
 8 E14: we'd have had four if they'd lived but we er got two
        and we lost two
 9 Y14: [sympathetically] ohh(.) yes=
10 E14: =[louder] they're all in school are they?
11 Y14: um one is sixteen yes and thirteen and then I've got a nine-year-
12       old
```

When shifting to a non-painful topic is achieved by a recipient of
PSD, the same options exist of initiating (on a self-related topic) and
eliciting (on a discloser-related topic). We find initiation in this sense
in extract 4.8, line 7, where Y9 takes up E8's topic of working while
bringing up children (lines 1, 2 and 4). Development by means of an
elicitation can be seen in extract 4.6, where Y3 (at line 12) advances
E3's topic of her thrombosis of the leg through a question about how
she travelled to the university. In both instances recipients very
resourcefully balance the closing of disclosive talk and the requirement
to talk topically, though in neither case do participants' contributions
appear fully attuned or complementary. Y9's initiation is topically
contingent but grossly mismatched in its emotional content. Y3's 'so
how did you get here today?' may be heard to dismiss the essence of E3's
disclosure, her thrombosis, in favour of the practical consequences it
may or may not have had for her on this particular occasion. We are
again drawn to see recipient moves towards closing as inherently
problematical for one or, possibly, both parties to PSD discourse.

One fragment in our data challenges our earlier assumption that
closure needs to be achieved interactionally.

EXTRACT 4.14 (from I13)

```
1 E7: because I'm not Welsh you see I was evac I was an evacuee (2.0) I
2      was evacuated from London               [     ]
3 E8:                                               ahh
4 E7: (1.0) and erm (1.5) I had twins well I lost one I lost a little boy
5      (1.5) and I had the(.) daughter I I'm almost sure it was
6      Llandough I went to but I'm not (1.0)
                        [ ]
7 E8:                   mm
```

    8   E7:   not sure
               [   ]
    9   E8:   if you pass my bag I could comb my hair
   10   E7:   mm?
   11   E8:   pass my bag I could comb my hair
               (2.5)
   12   E7:   you you *want* it?

In extract 4.14, E7 has disclosed the death of her baby son (line 4).
Neither she nor her elderly interlocutor produces any of the moves
towards closing we have discussed, and the topic is switched abruptly
by E8 at line 9. As an exhaustive listing of the strategies that show up
in our 40 conversations, the taxonomy needs to list this move type,
though it raises a host of questions about attentiveness, task
perception and norms of talk. But another possibility is that disclosive
talk may feature so repeatedly in the experience of some elderly
people that topic switches like that of E8 may be less markedly
counterattuned than they would otherwise appear.

Overview

In the next chapter we attempt a general interpretation of the patterns
of PSD management we find in the data based on numerical
overviews of their distribution by age-group (of teller and recipient)
and over time. The present chapter has defined the basic parameters
of PSD discourse to make this a feasible enterprise. At the same time,
the analyses we have presented so far do support some important
theoretical conclusions. First, we are in a position to challenge non-
interactional *definitions of self-disclosure itself.* We saw earlier in the
chapter that C. R. Berger and Bradac, for instance, endorse Pearce
and Sharp's conceptualization of self-disclosure as the voluntary
revelation of personal information not available from other sources.
Our data show not only that many acts of self-disclosure are, directly
or indirectly, elicited by the interlocutor, but also that some are
engendered by textual processes in their own right. There are clearly
interactional moments where the will to disclose (or not to do so) may
be overridden by the sequential pressures and requirements of talk

itself. Again, even within our broad category of discloser-determined disclosures, some speakers may voluntarily disclose, seeming to have manufactured contexts for their own acts of telling, which can make them seem other than voluntary. In general, then, we prefer to see self-disclosure as a complex of discourse behaviours through which the transmission of personal (and, in our case, intimate and painful) information is negotiated relative to considerations of interactional cooperation, interpersonal accommodation, textual coherence and self-presentational intent.

Second, the analysis above has derived concepts that can be combined to offer a rich definition of *disclosiveness*. At the beginning of the chapter, we commented that in the socio-psychological literature disclosiveness is typically seen as a personality trait, though we would again argue that interactional management needs to be central to its definition (cf. Holtgraves, 1990). Disclosiveness may be more than a propensity to produce very intimate information very frequently. An interactional focus suggests more particular criteria. Disclosive talk is better defined as talk that shows elaborated acts of disclosure (in the senses defined above: chained, contextually full, and detailed); disclosing when there are few or no interactional obligations to disclose and when multiple alternatives are available (for example, manufacturing pre-contexts for disclosures, with 'out of the blue' disclosures as a limiting case); perhaps also, not enabling a speaking partner to make self-disclosures. Correspondingly, our data suggest that processes of disclosing cannot be dissociated from processes of eliciting and responding. Does apparently disclosive behaviour reflect 'interrogative' behaviour[4] by recipients and/or their preparedness to sustain and endorse particular acts of telling or self-disclosure in general?

Finally, the chapter has raised questions about the interactional *consequences* of disclosing personal, painful experiences. We have raised the possibility that responding to PSD generally entails a responsibility for recipients and can be problematical. We have suggested that encoding responses can be problematical because of competing, and even contradictory, goals and constraints. Responding to PSD involves plausible uncertainties about what is accommodative, attuned talk at that point, and invokes folk theories about what is therapeutic or beneficial behaviour (cf. Cohen, Sherrod and Clark, 1986; Dunkel-Shetter and Wortman, 1982). Figure 4.3 suggested that next moves to PSDs may be inherently unsatisfactory, with recipients forced into making one of a set of dispreferable moves – an accommodative dilemma of the sort we discussed in chapter 2. Undesirable alternatives include (a) the aggressive or seemingly dismissive discouraging strategies of shifting or even switching topic; (b) the potentially overaccommodative sympathy or empathy strategies; (c) a bland and perhaps disinterested neutrality; and (d) signalling interest and involvement, which risks sustaining and even escalating PSD. When recipients move to close, there are sometimes discontinuities or implausibilties in their attempts to console disclosers or lighten the conversational key.

The intergenerational significance of self-disclosure processes and the status of PSD as 'problematical' are issues we consider in the following chapters. For the moment, we hope to have highlighted self-disclosure as a complex social *process*. While there are likely to be significant determinants of disclosive talk to be found in socio-historical and circumstantial dimensions of people's lives across the life-span, and while disclosure may satisfy some general emotional or therapeutic needs, we must recognize that it still needs to be achieved in real-time interaction. Sequential considerations are not merely the fine detail or the periphery of socio-psychological processes; they are the actual means by which they are experienced, refined and perpetuated. For this reason, explanatory theorizing will need, at its centre, to model self-disclosure in discourse, as the realization of strategic intentions within a framework of contextual possibilities.

5

Troubles-telling, Facework and Age Identity

The template of staging alternatives available to disclosers and recipients of what we have been calling PSD offers some particular opportunities for contrastive analysis of younger and older participants' contributions to PSD management in the interactive study corpus. Numerical information can then add to the mainly sequential observations we have made this far about PSD processes. In this chapter we begin by presenting a distributional account of PSD sequences in the data, first in gross terms, then in relation to more specific sequential and stylistic characteristics of self-disclosure exchanges. Then we interpret the patterns of self-disclosure in the data, using concepts derived from theories of facework and interpersonal accommodation.

A starting point is provided by the observation that disclosing intimate, personal experiences is a category of what P. Brown and Levinson (1987) call 'face-threatening acts' (FTAs), threatening to both the discloser's and the recipient's faces. The conversational work done by both participants when they take part in PSD sequences can be adequately explained only in these terms, though there are complexities and some contradictions involved. We want to suggest that specific ways of encoding PSDs fall within the rubric of underaccommodative discourse, and some patterns of response to PSD appear overaccommodative, in the senses of these terms that we introduced in chapter 2.

Having stressed the need to view self-disclosure as process, we are aware that there is an epistemological tension between qualitative and quantitative approaches to our source data. In terms of PSD, the data cannot be adequately characterized *solely* by quantitative means. In fact, even attempting to do this risks compromising our commitment to a dynamic account of interactional processes and to particular features of the development of individual encounters. On the other hand, because we want to explain PSD as a behavioural dimension in our data and present it as a potentially significant intergenerational dimension in other contexts, our interpretations can usefully be strengthened by at least a reasonably precise overview of its distribution. Because the data demand a context-sensitive, interpretive account, we believe that numerical analyses will ultimately misrepresent the procedural complexity and contextual uniqueness of individual instances. It also forces us to adopt far more of a homogeneous perspective on our study participants – as 'elderly' or 'young' – than is warranted. On the other hand, we need to account for the probability that there are broad and perhaps generalizable trends in the use of PSD, and we think that to ignore these would limit our understanding of PSD as a generational, and intergenerational, phenomenon.

So, it is a matter of fine judgement where the distributional analysis should start and end. What follows is a compromise. We shall give a cumulative interpretation of the distribution of PSD, starting with quite gross overviews of the proportions of undifferentiated PSD discourse found in the data.

The Distribution of PSD across the Interactive Study Contexts

The study was designed to give access to certain contextual variables: (a) the three demographic combinations of conversations as intergenerational, peer-elderly and peer-young; (b) the camera-on/camera-off conditions (first eight minutes and last two minutes, respectively); (c) relational development over time (for analytical purposes, each encounter is subdivided into five two-minute segments). Across each of these conditions there is predictable variation in PSD behaviour, predicted either by informal stereotypes of elderly talk and/or by research-derived conclusions about normative self-disclosive behaviour (cf. chapter 4). Our interpretations of the intergenerational functioning of PSD will need to account for any strong trends that emerge across these contextual dimensions.

At the most general level we first need to demonstrate the

distribution of PSD as a mode of talk, for which purpose we need a gross index. We have taken *the sequence* as the unit of analysis, delimited as talk in the topic areas we defined earlier as painful self-disclosure. Of the pre-context alternatives (see figure 4.1), only direct and indirect elicitations can appropriately be considered part of the disclosive sequence. Recipients' next-moves and the whole range of closing strategies up to the point where talk (through switching or shifting) opens on non-painful topics are also included in the distributional analysis of sequences. The sequence is a relatively robust unit for quantification, because it does not require us to distinguish between individual topics (for example, loneliness and bereavement, or ill health and immobility) that often co-occur and where the much-discussed indeterminacy of topic boundaries (cf. Levinson, 1983) would otherwise be a problem.

Tables 5.1, 5.2 and 5.3 report the proportions (in percentages) of talk within each two-minute segment of each encounter realizing PSD sequences in intergenerational, peer-elderly and peer-young contexts respectively.[1] Note, then, that the structural unity of a sequence is not respected here (single or multiple sequences, complete or partial, occur in individual segments), because sequences do of course often span the boundaries between time segments. The percentages merely represent the proportion of a two-minute segment of talk devoted to PSD by either or both participants. All cells in table 5.1 identify talk on topics relating to the elderly participant's reported painful experiences and states, except where the letter Y appears within a cell. In those instances the disclosure relates to the younger participant's painful experience or state. (On one occasion, the elderly and the young participant both generate PSD in the same segment: in I25, minutes 9–10). In table 5.2, all PSD is, of course, by elderly speakers; in table 5.3 it is by younger speakers.

Abstracting from the three tables, we can arrive at a simple summary of the proportions of talk devoted to PSD by the elderly and young respectively across the data as a whole. In table 5.4 the figures shown for the elderly are averaged values of elderly PSD within both the peer-elderly context (10 interactions) and their contributions in the intergenerational context (20 interactions); those for the younger group are derived correspondingly.

Tables 5.1–5.4 support the following observations on PSD in the data:[2]

Table 5.1 Proportions of talk in 20 intergenerational encounters devoted to PSD sequences

Interaction	Minutes: camera-on				Minutes: camera-off
	1–2	3–4	5–6	7–8	9–10
2	17.5	25.0	100.0	27.5	0.0
3	0.0	0.0	0.0	0.0	42.5
5	0.0	0.0	0.0	5.0	0.0
6	90.0	100.0	19.5	61.5	15.0
9	75.0	32.0	0.0	40.0	0.0
12	18.5	0.0	0.0	40.0	58.5
14	0.0	0.0	0.0	0.0	0.0
16	2.5	67.5	0.0	0.0	0.0
18	0.0	32.5	37.5	5.0	0.0
19	0.0	7.5	0.0	0.0	25.0
21	45.0	0.0	0.0	81.5	0.0
22	0.0	12.5	48.5	62.5	45.0
25	0.0	(Y)26.5	0.0	0.0	35.0 (E:25, Y:10)
28	6.0	22.5	0.0	15.0	22.5
31	0.0	0.0	63.5	50.0	0.0
32	0.0	0.0	2.5	21.0	0.0
33	56.5	10.0	0.0	0.0	5.0
34	(Y)5.0	0.0	0.0	0.0	0.0
38	5.0	0.0	0.0	0.0	0.0
40	25.0	18.5	5.0	0.0	5.0
Mean of elderly	17.1	16.4	13.8	20.5	12.2
Mean of young	0.3	1.3	0.0	0.0	0.5
Overall	17.4	17.7	13.8	20.5	12.7

Mean % of PSD of intergenerational contexts: 16.4

1 PSD is a recurring but variable component of talk produced in this context. In fact, of the 40 encounters, PSD occurs in 33; where it occurs, it accounts for between 1 per cent and 57 per cent of speaking time (mean 13.7 per cent).

2 PSD is, at least in terms of its frequency, a major component of encounters involving at least one elderly participant, where it

occupies far more time (approximately 16 per cent) than in peer-young encounters (approximately 6 per cent); half the peer-young encounters, but only 7 per cent of the encounters involving at least one elderly participant, have no PSD.

3 In the cross-generation encounters almost the whole of PSD is talk about the elderly's (and not the young's – less than 3 per cent) painful experiences.

4 Elderly PSD is sustained at approximately the same levels of frequency across peer and intergenerational contexts (independently, then, of whether one or two elderly participants contribute personal painful information).

5 Young PSD is more frequent in the peer context than intergenerationally, where it is minimal.

6 There are no clear trends as to PSD's development in the course of interactions or across camera-on versus camera-off conditions. This means there is no evidence of a regular increase in PSD when interactants are told the camera is switched off; in fact, the lowest mean proportions of PSD occur in the camera-off

Table 5.2 Proportions of talk in 10 peer-elderly encounters devoted to PSD sequences

Interaction	Minutes: camera-on				Minutes: camera-off
	1–2	3–4	5–6	7–8	9–10
4	0.0	0.0	7.5	87.5	60.0
7	0.0	20.0	30.5	27.5	0.0
10	0.0	42.5	43.5	98.5	0.0
13	87.5	62.5	23.5	5.0	0.0
20	41.0	0.0	0.0	0.0	65.0
23	0.0	30.0	0.0	17.5	0.0
26	0.0	0.0	24.5	0.0	0.0
29	0.0	0.0	0.0	0.0	0.0
35	7.5	10.0	10.0	0.0	0.0
39	0.0	0.0	0.0	25.0	0.0
Mean	13.6	16.5	14.0	26.1	12.5

Mean % of PSD in peer-elderly contexts: 16.5

Table 5.3 Proportions of talk in 10 peer-young encounters devoted to PSD sequences

Interaction	Minutes: camera-on				Minutes: camera-off
	1–2	3–4	5–6	7–8	9–10
1	0.0	30.0	12.5	40.0	0.0
8	0.0	21.5	0.0	0.0	0.0
11	0.0	0.0	0.0	0.0	0.0
15	20.0	30.0	37.0	0.0	0.0
17	0.0	0.0	0.0	0.0	0.0
24	0.0	0.0	0.0	37.5	0.0
27	0.0	0.0	0.0	0.0	0.0
30	0.0	5.0	0.0	0.0	77.5
36	0.0	0.0	0.0	0.0	0.0
37	0.0	0.0	0.0	0.0	0.0
Mean	2.0	8.7	5.0	7.8	7.8

Mean % of PSD in peer-young contexts: 6.3

condition when elderly interactants are involved. A clear majority of encounters (28 of the 40) have no PSD in the camera off condition.

Corresponding to 2 and 3 above, we would expect the ranges of painful topics (in the defined sense) on which speakers disclosed to be far greater in the elderly-to-young and elderly-to-elderly contexts than those where the young are disclosing. On the basis of a detailed mapping of topics throughout the PSD data (see table 5.5), we find

Table 5.4 Proportions of talk devoted to PSD sequences by elderly, by young and overall

	Intergenerational context (20 encounters)	Peer context (10 encounters)	Overall
Elderly PSD	16.0	16.5	16.3
Young PSD	0.4	6.3	3.4

Table 5.5 Distribution of topics (simple, summed occurrences) of PSDs across the four demographic contexts of the study

PSD topics	E→E	E→Y	Y→E	Y→Y
Bereavement				
of husband	10	12	0	0
of parent(s)/sibling	3	3	1	0
of son/daughter (as adults)	1	1	0	0
of son/daughter (as child)	1	2	0	1
of friend	1	0	0	0
Ill health				
ongoing medical problems	9	12	1	2
hospital stays/operations	5	5	0	0
sensory decrement	0	2	0	0
physical decrement	0	3	0	0
of another (e.g. dependant)	3	4	0	2
problems in childbirth	0	0	0	3
Immobility	2	3	0	0
Loneliness	1	4	0	0
Disengagement				
estranged family	0	4	1	0
lost former activities	0	2	0	0
Others				
own divorce	0	1	1	0
raising children alone	1	2	0	0
child's divorce	1	2	0	0
nursing dying friend	1	0	0	0
financial difficulties	0	2	0	0
redundancy from work	0	0	0	1
fear of violence	1	1	0	0

that the elderly's range of painful topics is indeed greater than the young's. There are several PSD topics that appear uniquely 'elderly' in the data, such as death of husband, sensory decrement, immobility, loneliness, lost former activities, financial difficulties, fear of violence, while only two (being made redundant from work and childbirth difficulties) emerge as unique to the young as a topic of PSD. Bereavement and own ill-health are the most frequent painful topics disclosed on.

These initial accounts of PSD in the data leave many central issues unresolved. They do suggest there may be grounds for considering the elderly speakers in the data to be behaving 'disclosively'. The fact that the elderly have, quite simply, more painful information to disclose and, indeed, that several of the topics listed in table 5.4 relate more specifically to the old than to the young (experiences of bereavement, certain subcategories of ill health, and immobility as probabilistically – though not at all inevitably – associated with ageing, and loneliness as a predictable consequence of some of the above) is, of course, a fundamental consideration. But it is not in itself adequate to account for the fact of disclosing such experiences in this context.

Elderly PSD seems to be a 'public' as well as a 'private' phenomenon, judging from its prevalence early on in encounters and its not increasing in the camera off condition. But the distributional findings can tell us little in themselves about the contextualization of PSD, about the means by which PSD tends to come about (and not come about) in different interpersonal circumstances. And these are the considerations that should allow us to interpret the social significance (attitudinal, evaluative and attributional) of PSD as a meaningful intergenerational discourse practice. In other words, we now need to shift the distributional analysis from a static one back in the direction of the dynamic, textual considerations introduced in chapter 4, seeing disclosures of painful experience as arising in very different discourse contexts, being sustained and sometimes resisted by participants, and being closed by various complex means.

The taxonomy introduced in the last chapter gives the basis for doing this, though there are again limitations on its use for quantitative analysis. At one extreme, it is clearly impossible to characterize all aspects of the development of all PSDs through a coding scheme. Alternatives specified in the four phases of the taxonomy are not always independent, and certain listed options are not always clearly available to participants (because of previous structural choices made in the histories of particular PSDs). Most obviously, there would be little to be gained from a distributional overview of next-moves (figure 4.3), since these clearly relate to and derive their interactional force, from their relations to previous (disclosive) moves.

More generally, the taxonomy exists mainly to draw attention to the strategic diversity of moves open to participants in negotiating PSD sequences, and it cannot be assumed that particular discourse moves in particular sequences can always be unambiguously labelled. On the other hand (and as in the discussion of the broad distributional analyses above), we will lose generalizations if some of the more feasibly countable dimensions of the taxonomy are not quantified. In what follows we shall work towards an understanding of PSD in the data by reporting occurrence frequencies of several of the alternative strategies and moves the taxonomy has specified, but qualify these through (necessarily selective) discourse analyses. These can revive the complexities and issues that surfaced in the previous chapter's discussion, and which counting procedures inevitably regularise and even suppress.

The Distribution of Pre-contexts

A fundamental question is whether the older participants in the study are behaving disclosively in some more particular respect than simply featuring frequently in PSD talk. What distributional evidence is there to suggest PSD is a mode of talk that accords with or satisfies a need or a will? Reviewing the pre-contexts of PSD is suggestive. In extract 5.1, for example, E3's disclosure on the loss of her husband comes about as a response to Y3's direct elicitation 'so is your husband still alive now?'

EXTRACT 5.1

```
1   Y3:  so is your husband still alive now?
2   E3:  no
3   Y3:  no?
4   E3:  I lost him=
5   Y3:  =aah
6   E3:  twenty-four years ago=
7   Y3:  [sympathetically] =oh dear
```

In extract 5.2, E7 is apparently more disclosive since the PSD (developed beyond the reproduced fragment below) arises 'out of the blue'. Y8 and E7 are discussing E7's visits to a day centre, when E7 raises the topic of her visit to a medical specialist and her impending admission to hospital. The reference to hospitalization is in no sense incoherent, but (we assume) will leave the recipient to construct non-obvious implicatures between 'going to the day centre' (which is a social, not a medical or caring, institution) and the new topic.

EXTRACT 5.2

```
 1   E7:  . . . I go to a day centre
                              [
 2   Y8:                      oh is that in Llanedeyrn?
 3   E7:  in er (.) Llanedeyrn
 4   Y8:  yeah
 5   E7:  oh I wouldn't know what to do without it
              [  ]
 6   Y8:     mm
 7   Y8:  is it good?
 8   E7:  no er (.) Tuesday I see the er specialist (.) and
 9        I'm going into hospital Monday (2.0) well they
10        wanted wheels on wheels or whatever you call them
11        I don't know little parcels of (.) nonsense
12   Y8:  mm
13   E7:  well I don't think I'm quite ready for anything
14        like that yet
```

The remaining possibility listed in figure 4.1 was for textual determination of PSD, which we took to subsume either convergent matching of an interlocutor's own previous PSD or divulging painful information to satisfy some clear coherence requirement. This second subtype was exemplified in the previous chapter (transcribed as extract 4.1 and discussed further below) when an elderly speaker (E2) disclosed her poor eyesight in explanation of having said she is knitting squares to make a blanket instead of doing more complex knitting tasks.

Table 5.6 presents an overview of the pre−contexts to all PSDs in the data (that is, individual self-disclosure cores, as previously characterized), using the categories from figure 4.1.

Abstracting from table 5.6, we find that, across all participant contexts of the study, more than half the PSDs made (52 per cent) are determined interactionally by disclosers themselves, in the defined

Table 5.6 Distribution of pre-contextual categories across participant contexts

Pre-contexts	E→Y	Y→E	E→E	Y→Y
Recipient-determined				
direct	11	0	3	1
indirect	12	2	2	1
Textually-determined				
need for expressed attribution	9	0	4	3
other's previous PSD	0	1	8	2
Discloser-determined				
own previous disclosure of age	2	1	1	0
own previous PSD	9	0	5	0
manufactured need for expressed attribution	20	0	14	2
previous closed/closing topic reinstituted	2	0	2	0
zero/out-of-the-blue	3	0	2	0
Total	68	4	41	9

sense, rather than being directly or indirectly elicited (26 per cent) or being textually generated (22 per cent).

But we have already seen that most PSD in the data is by elderly speakers, so that it is more particularly apposite to look at (again from the table) the relative distribution of pre-contextual types where the elderly disclose. (Young PSD occurs so infrequently that entries in individual cells by pre-contextual type are unreliably small.)

Table 5.7 Summary of the percentage distribution of pre-contextual types across elderly PSDs

Pre-contexts	E→Y	E→E	Overall
Recipient-determined	34%	12%	26%
Textually-determined	13%	29%	19%
Discloser-determined	53%	59%	55%

It seems that elderly speakers play a substantial part in determining their own painful self-disclosive talk in the data, whether conversing with younger (53 per cent) or older (59 per cent) partners. Younger speakers, however, play a more consistent role (34 per cent) in eliciting PSD from the elderly than elderly speakers do of their peers (12 per cent). In these peer-elderly contexts PSDs that are not discloser-determined are brought about more by textual determination (29 per cent), which here reflects older speakers' propensity to match PSDs (under the 'other's previous PSD' category in figure 4.1).

The Distribution of Disclosive Mode Variables

The taxonomy identified several variables that characterize the telling of a PSD (under the heading of 'mode' in figure 4.2). Disclosive mode, while inadequately treated in the self-disclosure literature, is likely to be interactionally highly significant and a key variable in the isolation of disclosive behaviour. We are far from having exhaustively characterized the complex, multiple dimensions of PSD mode. There are again sequential considerations here (to do with the structural composition of any one disclosure), considerations of genre (relating to the use of narrative, reporting, listing or other formats in the telling), as well as many encoding variables (prosodic or paralinguistic, non-verbal). Also, the interactional impact of a PSD will be sensitive to how these individual variables interact. For example, some PSDs in the data appear to infringe what we assume to be the normative co-occurrence restrictions among variables of the sort we have listed, where painful experiences (including loneliness, chronic illness, immobility) are disclosed in a matter-of-fact, even apparently light-hearted prosodic (high speech rate, wide intonation range), para-linguistic (laughter) and non-verbal (smiling, animated) style.

Despite these limitations, it has been feasible to quantify the distribution of a few of the most salient modal variables, with particular reference to the degree of *elaboration* shown in the telling of PSDs across the participant-contexts, and their thematic prominence or foregrounding. Our decision to quantify these variables reflects (a) the relative ease with which they can be coded and (b) the light they

Table 5.8 Distribution of subcategories of disclosive modes across participant contexts

Modes	Numerical distribution				Percentage distribution	
	E→Y (68)	Y→E (4)	E→E (41)	Y→Y (9)	All elderly	All young
Foregrounded	57	2	36	6	85%	62%
Non-foregrounded	11	2	5	3	15%	38%
Single	50	4	30	9	73%	100%
Chained	18	0	11	0	27%	0%
Core	27	3	18	0	41%	23%
Core plus	41	1	23	9	59%	77%

may shed upon the interactional weight or salience of PSDs across the different contexts.

Table 5.8 summarizes the distribution of the three selected two-term variables across the contexts of the study. The table again aggregates older speakers' PSDs and (separately) young speakers' PSDs, taking means across intergenerational and peer contexts; it shows some suggestive differences. By the criterion of mode, and in relation to young speakers' PSDs, elderly people's PSDs in the data are more frequently foregrounded, and more frequently elaborated through chaining (encoding multiple disclosures in sequence) – indeed, chaining of PSDs is here an exclusively elderly phenomenon.[3] On the other hand, in terms of their internal complexity (whether disclosures are developed beyond their simple core elements), elderly disclosures are more frequently cores alone than young disclosures are.[4] This last finding reflects elderly speakers' occasional willingness to introduce personal painful topics and leave them undeveloped without offering details of background, affective response or consequences. Extract 5.3 (a portion of extract 4.1 shows a PSD sequence on the topic of E2's failing eyesight operating as pre-context to a chained, further PSD on the subject of her rupture.

EXTRACT 5.3

1 Y2: . . . are you have you just star have
2   you ever knitted before?

```
 3  E2:  yes! I've made
                      [
 4  Y2:                        oh you used to knit did you?
 5  E2:  I've made myself cardigans and all=
 6  Y2:  =yes=
 7  E2:  =but my eyes are not so good see
 8  Y2:  so you want something fairly simple is it?
                 [                                      ]
            I I got (.) I should have my (.)
10          rupture done and I won't go in
11  Y2:  you've got a rupture in?
            [                    ]
12  E2:  I'm too nervous      behind the navel
```

In quite a different way, simple, core disclosures by elderly speakers can come about as attempts to minimally satisfy coherence requirements when PSDs are directly or indirectly elicited, as in the following:

EXTRACT 5.4

```
 1  Y6:  . . . are you on your own?
 2  E6:  er (.) yes
 3  Y6:  do you have
            [
 4  E6:  I have no family now (.) and erm (.) go I go to
 5          the community centre
```

The Distribution of Moves towards Closing

The taxonomy in figure 4.4 identified highly variable and overlapping strategies available to disclosers and recipients to move painful self-disclosive sequences towards closure. The category labelled 'change perspective' subsumes several discourse functions in this area (though a different precise set for disclosers and recipients). The unifying force of the category of acts is that they seek to realign PSD talk, usually towards some more positive self- or other-presentation. This realignment can be a matter of redressing the probable loss of face involved in disclosing painful information through playing down (minimization in figure 4.4) the ultimate significance of a misfortune or difficulty, or 'inverting' the PSD – moving to close by focusing finally on the more positive facets of an otherwise painful circumstance. In extract 5.5, E16, on the other hand, is content to rationalize, or provide an account for, her grandchildren's infrequent visits.

EXTRACT 5.5

1 Y16: . . . any grandchildren?
2 E16: yes I've got a couple of grandchildren they live erm
3   (.) there's two of them live (2.0) in Cathays but I
4   never see them
5 Y16: [*quietly*] mm (1.5) oh that's a shame=
6 E16: =well they they're (.) well as I say the young ones
7   just don't bother they're (.) interested in their
8   jobs I suppose that's it

A distributional overview of the degrees of responsibility taken for the management of PSD closings can again help the interpretation, though it can only partially represent the dynamics of this process. Table 5.9 summarizes the frequencies of *first* moves made by either participant towards closing PSD sequences, with these moves assigned to the subcategories of closing strategies listed in figure 4.4. By virtue of the restrictions this involves, we do not claim that table 5.9 characterizes the means by which PSD sequences *are actually* closed across the data; only that the first move (in itself possibly successful or unsuccessful) towards closure was of a recognizable sort and made by one and not the other participant. On the other hand, we would argue that *some* interactional significance attaches to this variable, if only because the first move towards closing a PSD may betray a felt responsibility for closing and offer a clue to the degree of problematicality associated with a PSD. It may also suggest how participants are, at least initially and overtly, glossing or recontextualizing the preceding elements of the sequence, and how they (variously) propose to 'resume normal business' after troubles-talk (cf. Jefferson, 1984a).

Summarizing the broadest findings from this analysis, we find that moves towards closing the PSDs of older participants overall are shared in roughly equal proportions by disclosers (52 per cent) and recipients (45 per cent); moves towards closing young PSDs overall (though recall that there are only 13 such sequences in total) tend to

Table 5.9 Distribution of (first) closing strategies across participant contexts

	E→Y	Y→E	E→E	Y→Y
Discloser moves				
Change perspective				
Inversion	4	0	1	0
Contextualization	9	0	4	0
Miminization	1	0	0	1
Rationalization	2	0	1	0
Resignation	1	0	0	0
Face-compensation	1	0	0	0
Shift topic				
Devel own topic away from PSD	12	1	8	7
Elicit on related recipient topic (non-painful)	2	0	1	1
Initiate on related discloser topic (painful) (chaining)	7	0	3	0
Recipient moves				
Change perspective				
Inversion	1	0	2	0
Contextualization	4	0	4	0
Fabrication of (improbable) solution	0	0	1	0
Shift topic				
Initiate on related recipient topic (non-painful)	4	2	3	0
Elicit on related discloser topic (non-painful)	18	1	0	0
Initiate on related recipient topic (painful) (matching)	0	0	11	0
Switch topic	0	0	1	0
Externally imposed				
Interaction ended	2	0	1	0

be made by disclosers themselves (76 per cent) rather than by recipients (23 per cent). *All* of the nine peer-young PSDs are discloser-closed, while more than half (54 per cent) of the peer-elderly PSDs are recipient-closed. By far the most common strategy for the young recipients in the intergenerational context of the data is to elicit related but non-painful discloser topics, though the elderly amongst themselves never do this. The elderly's most frequent strategy in responding to other elderly's PSDs is to match a painful self-disclosure with another from their own experience.

The evidence from this phase of the distributional data is that young recipients of elderly PSD do significantly more conversational work towards closing PSD talk in general than elderly recipients do. The young PSD sequences, despite their small numbers, suggest that moving first to close own PSD is habitual at least among young peers. Lee and Jefferson's (1980) account of troubles-telling implicitly endorses this finding in that what they term the 'close implicature' (including in their textual examples only *tellers'* optimistic projections, invocations of the *status quo*, and so on) is an integral part of the fundamental template ordering of troubles-telling sequences (see the Appendix). Elderly conversationalists in our data are almost as likely to let their interlocutors make a first move to close, and, when in the role of recipients, will close an ongoing PSD sequence by initiating another of their own almost as often as they change topic or perspective in other, non-painful directions. This general pattern complements the findings from the pre-contexts analytical phase, again showing an elderly commitment (relative to the younger participants) to PSD – its introduction into ongoing discourse, its elaboration in the telling and its sustaining (with the elderly both as tellers and as recipients).

Discussion

The frequency data give us a rather better understanding of the apparent counter-normativity of elderly PSD: disclosing what is in some sense 'negatively valenced' personal information to strangers in an apparently public context. The quantitative differences between younger and older people, particularly relating to self-initiated PSD, are therefore the principal focus of this final section. But it is also important to note the characteristics of the tabulated data. In many cases, mean figures showing intergroup sociolinguistic differences camouflage quite extreme variability across and within individual speakers or dyads. For example, there are peer-elderly dyads where there is minimal or no PSD (see I5, I14, I29 and I38 in tables 5.1, 5.2 and 5.3). Some peer-young dyads do contain PSD talk (see I1, I15, I24 and I30). There is considerable variation in both the proportion (compare I5 and I6) and the placement (compare, say, I3 and I33) of elderly PSD. These facts temper any simple interpretations in terms of group behaviours. Still, the patterns of PSD management we have been able to trace in the data do cross-refer interestingly to the intergenerational accommodation processes we introduced in chapter 2. The discussion also invokes explanatory concepts from Brown and Levinson's (1987) work on strategic face-management.

Let us first consider a familiar possible interpretation of cross-generational PSD in terms of decrement. In chapter 1 we examined research designs and findings in linguistic gerontology and pointed to a paradox: that research questions often impose a diachronic and degenerative perspective on synchronic age differences in speech, language or communication. All too often, patterns of elderly usage that differ from (observed or normative) younger adult models are attributed to decrement and cognitive deficiency. Researchers seem to be too tolerant generally of deficit explanations of elderly talk. In this tradition it would be possible to construe elderly PSD as norm-violating talk, socially unsophisticated, egocentric and too concerned with the past. Indeed, in detailed post-encounter interviews that we conducted with participants in the interactive study several of the younger speakers did complain that their elderly partners had shown little interest in them. So we should not dismiss this cluster of evaluations of elderly PSD. Possible perceptions of it as underaccommodative (in the terms of accommodation theory) will be a key element in understanding the intergenerational management of PSD. On the other hand, there are more compelling *positive, functional* explanations for elderly PSD.

In the interviews some younger PSD-recipients, in fact, evaluate elderly PSD very positively as accommodative on the dimension of intimacy ('she seems very warm'; 'she opened herself to me'). Also it is likely that some young recipients find elderly disclosiveness consistent with the stereotypes they already hold. Those who perceive the old to be behaving in entirely predictable, role-consistent ways will presumably judge PSD to be less interpersonally underaccommodative, though the extent to which they experience it as less problematical is an open question. The substantial number of instances in our data (see table 5.6) where young people, directly or indirectly, elicit troubles-related information from elderly speakers suggests there is indeed some regular expectation on their part that painful self-disclosure is available to them as a resource to first-acquaintance conversation. These findings suggest that some of the younger people's discourse behaviours here are themselves potentially *over*accommodative. There is certainly a class of eliciting moves made by the young here that would not normally be thought appropriate between young conversationalists; for example, 'do you sleep alright when you get to bed?'; 'is your husband still alive?' Older people who might share our perception of these elicitations might then think they show too much familiarity and are patronizing, badly attuned to their own wants and needs.

Moving away from deficit orientations, what more positive functions can PSD fulfil? P. Brown and Levinson's (1978, 1987) politeness model gives a basis for reading the quality of social relationships (1978, p.64); they characterize facework strategies as a significant component mediating communicative intention and language style. PSD options and phases certainly involve the bilateral negotiation of face, and Brown and Levinson's basic concepts can very appropriately be applied.[5] PSD is clearly face-threatening in at least two general senses. Acts of disclosing painful experiences predictably threaten the discloser's positive face (the wish or need to be well regarded); at the same time, they predictably threaten the recipient's negative face (the wish or need to avoid imposition or encroachment). In this second respect problems for some PSD recipients are predictable , posing considerable accommodative dilemmas. In chapter 4 we noted how responses to PSD are a catalogue of moves, *all* of which are arguably dispreferable. For example, stemming the flow of sympathy or empathy can signal a dismissive attitude, while sustaining these orientations risks perpetuating and even escalating PSDs. Threatening own face (in disclosing) is a strategy that is more likely to be adopted where there are counterbalancing considerations – either some form of face-promotion (see Penman, 1990) or the satisfaction of some identity need.

The life-circumstances of the elderly people in our study might themselves offer a rudimentary explanation. It is quite plausible that elderly disclosers of painful information are using a mode of talk that is far more readily available to them and relatively more routine to them than to younger people. We noted above that several of the topic categories defining our category of painful experiences were probabilistically associated with old age, and that the requirements of the experimental setting (the 'get to know one another' instruction) might have led to different patterns of self-disclosure. It is possible that what we have considered painful life events and states are central to the elderly group's (more so than the young group's) own identities – to their own conceptualizations of what is knowable about themselves. We are far from claiming that painful self-disclosure is purely routine for the old (an ageist stereotype), but it is certainly the case that the option of editing out negatively valenced personal information will present itself more frequently to the old than to the young. We have grounds for seeing intergenerational conversations, once again then, as *intercultural* encounters (cf. Giles and Coupland, 1991a). Future research on the varying beliefs and values of different age-groups would be valuable to help substantiate this claim.

The socio-demographic circumstances of the elderly people in our study – they are in many cases rather immobile, widowed or lonely – are also the starting point for an analysis of facework. The finding that the elderly speakers most frequently determine the fact of their own painful self-disclosing (cf. table 5.6) forces us to look for some interactional pay-off; indeed, some element of *positive* face, that is, paradoxically, being earned through what is ostensibly face-threatening communication. Simply at the level of conversational *engagement*, it is clear that PSDs can offer the short-term benefit to a discloser's positive face of having 'newsworthy' information to reveal. It is interesting that several PSD sequences are elaborated (see figure 4.4) as sometimes quite lengthy conversational narratives, and that some have a rehearsed quality.

But the disclosure of personal, painful information might be seen to be more profoundly functional for disclosers as intrinsically *therapeutic* (cf. folk beliefs about 'talking through your troubles' or 'getting it off your chest'). (In chapter 7 we report some group-discussion data that shows that some elderly people do overtly recognize the importance of talk, for them, as 'therapy'.) Our point is that a prevalence of 'problematical' circumstances will at least cause the old (and, of course, others) to recontextualize the threat to face that PSD carries. Perhaps it is even the threat value of PSDs that allows them to be perceived as potentially cathartic self-revelations.

In line with our discussion in chapter 3, PSD clearly functions in the negotiation of age identity, and this leads to an interpretation in terms of *self-stereotyping* (see chapter 2). Because age is a moderately salient dimension in our experimental setting, older people's self-presentations in intergenerational settings may be modified towards stereotypical 'elderly' portrayals, stylistically or in the selective reporting of social circumstances. So, PSD is in part a process of convergence *not* to any aspect of the young's own discourse, but to a social expectation or stereotype of how elderly talk does, or even should, proceed. This process can also operate among elderly peers (we have found high levels of PSD in that context, too), where interpersonal linguistic convergence would be a confirming strategy. These considerations of socially expected disclosure will be another means by which the threat value of PSD is lessened or neutralized. Older speakers might even find some positive value in presenting themselves in ways that reduce interactional uncertainty (C. R. Berger, 1979; C. R. Berger and Bradac, 1982) both within and across generations, and offer a dimension of solidarity in peer talk. Two important general observations on facework follow from the discussion this far. The threshold levels of perceived threat to positive face are apparently variable; what seems 'intrinsically' face-threatening may well be construed differently by different social groups. Threat to face seems able to be mitigated or overridden by considerations of social identity.

The paradigm of *self-handicapping* (see chapter 2) is also suggestive. By frequently referring to present and past painful events and states, elderly people may, rather paradoxically, be seeking to obviate a variety of negative attributions by the young about the elderly's capacities, motives and behaviours. The elderly may well be pursuing a hidden agenda (perhaps of elderly 'heroicism'), creatively setting positive competences and qualities against a backdrop of problems and disadvantage. Several of the moves towards closing PSD sequences that we have glossed as contextualization achieve this comparison explicitly in the discourse. They transform the negativity of a PSD into some appreciable positive quality, either through focusing on it selectively or, sometimes by outright denial: 'I can't breathe I've got [breathes] emphysema and I'm full of [breathes] osteo- arthritis and what have you but erm [breathes] thank goodness the old brain-box is still going [laughs].' PSDs can be encoded in non-foregrounded verbal or non-verbal (facial, prosodic) ways that deny their 'intrinsic' problematicality. It might even be the case that the fact of doing highly disclosive talk itself implies that the speaker perceives either a low threat value or that overriding facework considerations exist.

The multiple layering of face strategies that our analysis implies is not addressed by P. Brown and Levinson (1987), though it is a commonplace of discourse analysis that speech acts enter complex hierarchies of signification that make it impossible to attach unique functional labels to individual utterances (cf. Sinclair and Coulthard, 1975; N. Coupland, Grainger and Coupland, 1988). This hierarchical perspective allows us to interpret (positive) face-threatening acts at a primary level as doing face-*promoting* strategic work at a secondary or 'deeper' level. The self-handicapping interpretation can therefore be recast in facework terms as positive face being creatively *promoted through* doing PSDs as face-threatening acts. Self-handicapping suggests itself as a general explanation for elderly PSD, though it accounts most directly for PSDs that arise through elderly speakers either reinstituting PSD talk on a closed topic or self-disclosing 'out of the blue' (cf. table 5.6). We see these individuals as putting their own counter-normativity to work in the interests of positive face. There are occasions when, in a single PSD sequence, an elderly speaker will overtly endorse norms of PSD avoidance *and* infringe them: the emphysema and arthritis disclosure just cited is, in fact, prefaced by: 'nobody wants you when you're miserable and moaning and groaning . . . because . . . ' (see extract 4.7). The same paradox can be represented implicitly: 'I don't broadcast this but I've lived with a colostomy for 17 years you see . . . ' (extract 4.4). The paradox here is fundamental. Such creative constructions of positive face not only compensate for their face-threatening potential, but are fundamentally dependent on it for their effect.

The convergent matching of PSDs (which is frequent in peer-elderly contexts of the data) adds a dimension of *social comparison* (Festinger, 1954; Suls and Miller, 1977) and even social competition, where individuals vie for positive face through self-handicapping. PSD sequences seem well-suited to determining whether peers are, or can claim to be, 'better or worse off' than oneself. Quite possibly then, comparative or competitive PSDs function to validate the self and increase self-esteem (Goethals, 1986). Possibly too, the predominance of elderly over young self-disclosure protects older people from social comparisons with the young, highlighting their disadvantage relative to the young's abilities and few problems. From this perspective the need for reassurance and favourable feedback become crucial concerns.

Consolidating several of the previous observations and speculations, we would want to argue that PSD discourse can fulfil an *existential* function for the elderly (see also chapter 4). Berger and Bradac's (1982) theory of uncertainty reduction demonstrates that the desire to increase predictability is a fundamental drive in interpersonal communication. They argue that strategies of uncertainty reduction are employed throughout the development and decline of relationships. So, participants in initial encounters, like those in the present study, are concerned with reducing uncertainty and, at first, with predicting others' attributes, needs and concerns. Subsequent predictions will be made about the state of the relationship itself (Baxter and Wilmot, 1984), and perhaps about its decline (Duck, 1982). But uncertainty reduction must also function at the *intra*-individual level. People in later life, and no doubt others perhaps including the terminally ill, will be drawn to question their own life positions and they will use social encounters, perhaps especially new encounters, as a platform for making these appraisals. There will be prospective appraising, conjecture about what is left to endure or enjoy and about the energy investment needed to pursue any future worthwhile goals. Retrospectively, elderly people are likely to review their significant life events, good and bad. From this point of view it is easy to see elderly PSD as a focal, predominantly retrospective, process of self-appraisal that is significant intra-individually as well as interpersonally. So, younger people's tendency to provide high levels of affective support to elderly PSD will provide significant new data to the self-appraisal process. Empathetic support to PSD, designed as some form of 'therapy', may, in fact, only confirm some elderly people's conclusions about their hard-lived lives.

To go beyond these interpretations, and particularly to tease out the probable longer term consequences for intergenerational relations, we need a new analytic perspective, one that gives us more direct access to older and younger people's own evaluations and formulations of talk. This is what we embark on in chapter 7. For the moment, purely from the analysis of cross-generation talk itself, older people's disclosure of painful experiences seems to be a prototype of intercultural communication, at one level unexceptional and at another ridden with potential misalignments and dissatisfactions, in the long if not the short, term. The counselling style we have seen younger participants adopting is undoubtedly tolerable to many of the elderly, and there may be some satisfaction to be derived from the intimacy of PSD, perhaps even from the difficult experience of responding to it. Elderly disclosers may air grievances and educate their younger conversation partners in the ways of the old; but there are clear suggestions in the data that their role opportunities and the identities they are able to adopt are constrained by the intergroup framing of the exchanges. Still, how 'problematical' or 'miscommunicative' these processes deserve to be labelled remains to be explored.

Before turning to these questions in the group-discussion contexts of chapter 7, we consider one final set of self disclosure processes that are still very relevant to the management of age identities in talk: age-telling and its organization as a cross-generation phenomenon.

6

Telling Age in Later Life:
A Strategic Analysis

Variably, at different points in the life span, taboos and normative prescriptions are associated with both seeking and providing information about age. Personal experience (in the absence of empirical studies) suggests that children and adolescents are often asked to tell their age by distant relatives or new acquaintances, or have this information revealed for them by parents or guardians. Inquiring about age in these contexts, to the extent that it is more than ritualized, seems to be a way of signalling engagement and perhaps nurturance by well-meaning adults who are interested in following the growth and development of the young. In the middle years of life, age in years, and perhaps all discussion of own age, drops out of unmarked, everyday usage. Here it seems to feature predominantly in mock-denigrating remarks about the passing of time and references to the unwanted arrival of birthdays, all commercially promoted through the greetings-card industry.[1] So, age-talk finds its place among the broad spread of ageist constructions (in Western society at least) that we have considered at various points in earlier chapters.

Facetiously or not, many middle-aged adults represent their own ageing with a mixture of fear, reticence and regret. This and the teasing and chiding of middle-aged people on their birthdays, when they give up their favourite sport and so on, undoubtedly form part of the *interactional* means by which negative images of ageing and the elderly are reproduced. The crass images that tend to surface on these occasions amount to a check-list of the negative elderly stereotypes that have been uncovered by socio-psychological research: frailty, sexual inactivity, incompetence, grouchiness, unsociability and so on (cf. Braithwaite, 1986 and the language attitude studies reviewed in chapter 1). Within this calendar-marking tradition and the discourses we associate with it, personal life spans are portrayed as incremented scales with natural boundaries that are bench-marks to decremental decline: physical, social and socio-psychological (cf. Branco and Williamson, 1982). Decade-boundaries seem to have a particular salience in this respect, as do transitions from one generational category to another (parent to grandparent, for example).

On the other hand, in later life age in years resurfaces from its underground life. The data we draw on in this chapter, from two audio-recorded contexts, confirm the *prevalence* of disclosing chronological age (DCA) among at least some elderly groups. Given the pejorative associations of advancing age among younger groups, we are again led to ask about the social functioning of this further dimension of self-disclosure: why might age-telling by older people be not only tolerated but positively construed on occasions? And we address the question again through a contextual focus, examining the discourse sequences and routines through which age disclosure is managed. As we suggested in chapter 4, age-telling proves to be a particularly salient interactional dimension for the manipulation of age identity; more particularly, we shall explore the various elderly identifications, in context, that DCA can encode.

As in chapters 3, 4 and 5, we shall use data from the video-recorded interactive study corpus to illustrate several of the sequential processes we consider. This allows us to cross-refer to some of the other dimensions of the same data-set that we have previously discussed. But we also examine a secondary corpus here: a series of interviews with a further 40 elderly people (34 women and 6 men, aged 68–87 years). This population is a different set of volunteers from one of the two day centres attended by the 20 elderly females who took part in the primary interactive study. In these interviews three researchers asked a series of questions on the subject of experiences of health care (the questions are detailed below). We use this second source here mainly to support the distributional evidence from the first study in another dialogic setting. Brief transcribed fragments from this second corpus are attributed to speakers identified once again by fictionalized initials. Although exploring DCA in two settings gives us some confidence in the generality of the phenomena we are investigating, we are, of course, aware (here and throughout the volume) that we are dealing with specific populations and social circumstances, and, not least, with a culturally specific group. In keeping with our general aims in this book, we hope others may be tempted to research similar sociolinguistic questions in culturally more diverse settings.

Age Disclosure: Distributional Overviews

We begin with quantitative overviews simply to establish that elderly age-telling is a robust generational phenomenon. In the primary interactive data intergenerational conversations are the preferred contexts for DCA (15 disclosures in 20 interactions), most by older speakers (12, or 60 per cent of possible elderly DCAs to young interlocutors). Each of the three young DCAs in the intergenerational condition is made after (though not immediately after) an elderly DCA. In two cases (I14 and I19), the young person comes to disclose her age through herself having asked her elderly interlocutor how old her daughter or son is and then saying that she is a similar age; that is, the young person aligns with the succeeding generation. In one other case (I25) E13 asks Y13 her age and comments 'you're like one of my granddaughters', again aligning on a generational basis. DCA hardly occurs among the peer-elderly dyads, and in the two interactions (four disclosures) where it does, there is a possibly significant age difference between interlocutors (86 and 70 years; 77 and 66 years). The older woman discloses her age first and the younger woman reciprocates this disclosure within the same discourse sequence. Some dyads that our initial experimental design considers to be 'peer-elderly' contexts can therefore achieve an intergenerational salience, no less than the young–old dyads. Of the peer-young DCAs (five disclosures in three interactions), two pairs (in I11 and I37) are again matched in immediate sequence.

We considered several encoding variables in DCAs, distinguishing *stative* formats (reporting age as a state: 'I am X years') from *progressive* formats (age reported as a developmental process). The progressive type can be further divided into either *prospective* ('I'm going on X years') or *retrospective* ('I was X years in May') types. Another encoding distinction is between reporting age in precise years and locating age in relation to decade boundaries. Although these possibilities offer subtly different formulations of own age and are suggestive of different evaluative stances, we have not pursued this dimension of variability systematically in the present study. No distributional trends in encoding styles are apparent across the conditions of the controlled conditions of the study.

Given the small numbers in the interactive data set, it is useful to compare patterns of DCA in the secondary interview corpus. In 32 of the 40 interviews (80 per cent), elderly interviewees disclosed their chronological age. In six of the others, too, own age is referred to quite overtly without being specified as age in years (see the discussion of age categorization processes in chapter 3); for example, (VH) 'otherwise I can't grumble at all like (.) well not for my age'; (GM) 'oh well I mean to say you can expect it at my time of life'. DCAs were spontaneous to the extent that questions asked did not request this information (although an age category is made salient in the fourth question).[2] The first move made by interviewers was a supposedly phatic opening: 'How are you?', uniformly with primary stress on the final syllable; eight DCAs were made in responses to this opening. The second was 'How is your health generally?', with a supplementary question, if needed: 'Are you receiving treatment for any health problems at the moment?'; 16 DCAs were made in this phase of the questioning. The third was 'Do you see your GP (general practitioner) often? Are you seeing him/her at the moment?'; two DCAs. The fourth and final scripted question was 'Do you think doctors generally provide good health care for elderly people?'; only four further DCAs were elicited here. The remaining two DCAs in the supplementary corpus emerged in later, unscripted follow-up questions.

Therefore, DCA is not only frequent in the supplementary corpus, but it tends to occur early in the interviews and particularly in response to a direct invitation to appraise own health. In fact, the above distribution might suggest that the explicit or implicit thematization of health (if health is taken by the elderly respondents to be implicated in an otherwise phatic 'How are you?', cf. chapter 2) establishes a relevance for DCA. This relationship is explored in detail in the following qualitative analyses. Overall, the supplementary corpus confirms the pattern that emerges from the interactive study: that DCA is a regular feature of the talk of at least some groups of elderly people, particularly in cross-generational contexts.

Strategies of Age Disclosure

Without exploring the contextualization of elderly DCAs in the data, the simple frequency of instances might be taken as evidence that age in years has lost its pejorative associations when older people tell age. The importance of a discourse analytic perspective here, focusing on the staging of disclosive sequences, is that it immediately shows that DCA is, in fact, involved in complex, diverse and even contradictory presentational acts, where old age is neither wholly negatively nor wholly positively construed. The general position we adopt in this section, then, is that age in years is most appropriately seen as an *identity token*. We conceive of DCA as a 'counter', whose value is determined to a significant extent by its placement and timing in an interaction and which is 'played' in the pursuance of particular strategic ends. In adopting this position and as in the case of the troubles-telling processes discussed in earlier chapters, we are clearly rejecting the assumption that DCA acts merely to reveal one among many items of personal information, however much the term 'self-disclosure' seems to imply this. 'Mere' self-revelation *may* on occasions be the extent of its interactional significance (see below), but we find own age to be intimately related, in its telling, with other themes, and in particular issues of health and decrement.

In fact, many DCAs in the interactive data encapsulate a normative view of old age as decremental. So, in extract 6.1, E2 discloses her age (at line 11) in the context of identifying her own frailty:

EXTRACT 6.1 (from I2)

```
 1  E2: but today they don't want to know you
 2  Y2: mm=
 3  E2: I have a (.) nephew living up at the top of the road
 4  Y2: yes
 5  E2: but I don't see=
 6  Y2: =you don't see him?
                         [
 7  E2:                       ((don't want to know you)) (.) not
 8      unless I run up there
 9  Y2: yes=
10  E2: =and I'm I'm not very well these days too (.) I'm
```

11   seventy last Octob=
12   Y2:   =*were* you?=
13   E2:   =this October=
14   Y2:   =ah
15   E2:   so I I find I can't *do* it so good
              [   ]   [
16   Y2:   yes   you don't want to over*do*
17   things ((do you?))

The statement 'I'm seventy . . . this October so I find I can't do it so good' presupposes that there is a natural, socially agreed relationship between ageing and immobility, and so age in years is offered as a rationalizing *account* (see Cody and McLaughlin, 1990; Potter and Wetherell, 1987, ch. 4) of E2's frailty. Whereas in our speculations about middle age we suggested that advancing years could project incompetence or debilitation, we see that in later life acknowledged frailty can, in fact, be somewhat offset through self-presenting as chronologically old. In terms of social attribution theory, age functions here as a category-based, stable, uncontrollable and external attribution (Hewstone, 1989).

This accounting pattern in the management of DCA is very common in both data- sets. In the supplementary corpus, worsening health (reported in response to the health-appraisal question) is often directly attributed to chronological age, for example:

  SM: as well as I can be . . . I'll tell you first I'm
        going on ninety;
  CH: oh no very good (.) well I'm almost eighty and I can't
        expect much;
  MM: not on top of the world but . . . when you come to eighty-three
        years of age you can't expect to be like a spring
        chicken can you?;
  GT: I haven't been too well . . . because . . . of course I'm
        getting on now I'll be eighty next year.

One interviewee in the corpus reponds to the interviewer's 'how is your health generally would you say?' as follows: (GJ) [sighing] 'well my dear (.) well you haven't asked me how old I am', implying she cannot even attempt an appraisal of her own health independently of considerations of immutable age. The accounting can be done defensively, and even aggressively, projecting frailty or ill health as a moral right to be explicitly conceded by a recipient, rather than expressed as resignation. BD, for example, says that 'at eighty-four? I've got a right to be [a bit stiff] don't you think?'. Mitigation and reproach in this way seem to define a significant dimension of the attributional significance of these accounting episodes. In a small but still worrying number of instances the ill health being accounted for by age is reportedly an attribution made by medical practitioners (see Greene, Adelman, Charon and Hoffman, 1986); for example, (FM) 'as soon as you've got something wrong with you they say "'how old are you? . . . oh well you can't expect much more at your age" (.) they're not interested as far as I'm concerned (.) in my experience once you get to seventy . . . they put it down to your age whatever it is . . . I don't think it's *right*.'

On the other hand, several elderly individuals invoke the normative age and ill health association specifically to *differentiate* themselves from it.

EXTRACT 6.2 (from I3)

```
 1  Y1:  . . . I'm just a housewife now . . . well not just
 2        is it really? (.) because my children are at school
                        [    ]
 3  E1:       [laughing]  yes
 4  E1:  mm (1.0) oh well that's nice isn't it?
 5  Y1:  yes=
 6  E1:  =mm (1.5) well I lead quite a busy life although
 7        I'm eighty-six I'm not young [laughs]
                                 [
 8  Y1:                          gosh you don't look it!
 9  E1:  I was eighty-six last May
            [
10  Y1:         goodness you certainly don't look that . . .
```

In extract 6.2, E1 aligns herself with the younger woman's active lifestyle ('well I lead quite a busy life'), despite her age ('although I'm eighty-six I'm not young'). The expression 'good for one's age' has conventionalized precisely this association in everyday usage. E1 refuses to align herself with the perceived norm for 86, in the perception of her interlocutor and perhaps even in her self-categorization (Turner, 1986). Likewise, WJ (in the interview data) comes to a positive self-appraisal in relation to her age: 'I'm eighty so

I haven't done bad'; LD similarly: 'mind I'm gone eighty I'm going eighty-one . . . and I think I'm pretty good'. The tactic here is quite explicitly to promote own face, and it may be designed to impact dynamically, to procure confirmatory reactions about the disclosure's health status (see below).

DCA in the 'accounting' pattern mitigates the negative associations of actual frailty by appealing to decremental ageing as an extenuating circumstance – another form of self-handicapping, then. In the second, *disjunctive* usage, DCA allows the discloser to claim credit *against* normative expectations of frailty that are not in fact (or supposedly not) realized. Strategically, therefore, for the elderly people concerned, disclosing age carries very different identity potentials in the two formulations. But at the same time accounting and disjunctive patterns find their meanings in a single set of underlying assumptions about the assumed nature of ageing itself in our culture; that is, the socio-physical norm of decrement. In both cases chronological age is verbally established as one pole of a relational evaluation, the other pole being the subjectively experienced life position or what we earlier referred to (following A. M. Rubin and Rubin, 1982) as contextual age. Ageing is dually represented: first in chronological terms, as predictable, even ineluctable progression along an incremented scale; second in contextual terms, as a far less predictable ebbing and flowing, reflecting the arrival and passing of particular somatic, experiential and emotional circumstances (for example, illness, bereavement or institutionalization).

The relative positioning of the two indicators is certainly *negotiable*. First, it is clear that contextual age is an essentially subjective, global appraisal. Evaluating 'how one is' in ageing is open to moment-to-moment redefinition, depending not only on changing circumstances but also on the shifting salience of particular contributing factors and social comparisons (Goethals, 1986). There is a real sense in which we cannot know 'how we are', and if we did know, we would predictably be unable to represent this knowledge in any coherent, packaged formulation to others. Indeed, the responses to health-appraisal questions (some were quoted above) themselves have an overtly negotiative quality, often qualified or hedged, and appealing to particular standards of judgement. As Jefferson (1985) has noted, too, they often function as 'glosses' to be 'unpackaged' in subsequent exchanges.

We might model chronological and contextual age as two indicators advancing (since decline is the unmarked trend in the contextual dimension too) in parallel along a single graduated life-span template. If so, then in the cases we have considered DCA can be seen to be involved in negotiating the precise relationship between the two indicators. We can speculate that, in a broadly ageist attitudinal climate, for most adult individuals on most occasions there will be a preference to retard progress in both chronological and contextual dimensions, and that, given the inevitability of time passing, there will be a preference for contextual age to 'lag behind' chronological age (cf. Montpare and Lachman, 1989).

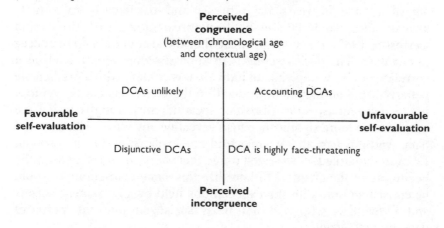

Figure 6.1 Subjective correlates of DCA management

Extrapolating from this simple schematization, it would appear that there are two orthogonal, underlying dimensions (see figure 6.1). The first is a simple evaluative dimension, reflecting the positivity-negativity of a person's self-appraised contextual ageing. The intersecting dimension is congruity-incongruity, capturing the degree to which the individual perceives her or his chronological and contextual life positions to be in or out of phase. In one configuration, then, we may be more socially active or healthy than we anticipated (positive incongruent, modelled in the lower left quadrant of the figure). In another, we may be immobile to an extent that we would, stereotypically, attribute to our chronological age (negative congruent, the upper right quadrant). Mapping discourse patterns of DCA management on to the figure, we find that it is just these two quadrants (upper right and lower left) that are filled out by the instances that appear in our data. The accounting pattern is generally consistent with a subjective profile in which the individual's decrement is congruent with her or his age. Disjunctive formats always build on a perceived or claimed discrepancy between old age and *positive* contextual age.

Figure 6.1 invites us to consider two further possibilities. Negative incongruent configurations would recognize one's contextual age to be running 'in advance of' one's chronological years: 'I'm bad for my age' would be the implicit force of a DCA made in these circumstances. Clearly, such a self-presentation with no available appeal to age in years for redress, and particularly to a first-acquaintance, would be a highly face-threatening act (P. Brown and Levinson, 1987); it is not surprising that such sequences do not occur in our data. The positive congruent context seems very unlikely as a correlate of DCA, implying an individual is content with a predictable pattern of life development. Indeed, in these circumstances, age may not be a salient aspect of a broader social identity, and disclosing age may have no more significance than revealing any other piece of social data. And it is here that we may find one explanation for the rarity of DCA in unmarked *middle*-aged usage that we commented upon at the beginning of the chapter. In later life this same configuration would be consistent only with the expectations held by a non-ageist society and individuals who had not been socialized into the norm of decremental ageing.

Response Options

A crucial further consideration, here as in relation to PSD management, is that life-positional evaluations are not made unilaterally. In the evaluative process the judgements that are most pertinent to subjects themselves may in fact be the judgements of others, which further justifies the perspective on how age identities are *discursively* managed. Discourse offers speakers the possibility of cognitively side-stepping their own awareness of decrement, and even of reconstructing age identities in new projections to new audiences. In just this way we are demonstrably sensitive to others' comments about our own chronological and contextual ageing, and probably in particular to the dimensions of positivity-negativity and congruence-incongruence that we have just considered (for example, 'you haven't aged at all'; 'only forty and you're balding').

In the extracts we have already examined, younger people can be seen providing diverse modes of support to elderly self-projections. In extract 6.1, Y2 elects to endorse the elderly person's presented frailty: she says 'you don't want to overdo things ((do you?))'. In extract 6.2, Y1's effusive responses – 'gosh you don't *look* it . . . goodness you certainly don't look that . . . ' – seem to be *required* if E1's disjunctive inference (that she is contextually younger than 86) is to be credited. In extract 6.3, Y13 does even more explicit consolidatory work in response to E13's DCA:

EXTRACT 6.3 (from I25)

```
 1 Y13: have you got any family?
 2 E13: I have a daughter
 3 Y13: does she does she live in Cardiff?
             [         ]              [
 4 E13:         she              she's living in Pencoed
 5       near Bridgend . . .
 6       she comes up every Tuesday and er (.) we go shopping
 7       and have a run around you know
 8 Y13: you haven't got any grandchildren
                   .[    ]
 9 E13:        she
10       yes I have er [laughs] I have [coughs] two grandchildren
              [         ]
11 Y13:      [laughs]
12 E13: and I have four great-grandchildren [laughs]
                          [        ]        [
13 Y13:                 [gasps]          [laughs]
14 Y13: oh! nice yes (.) you don't look that old [laughs]
          [           ]                          [
15 E13: they're lovely                        [laughs]
16       oh yes
17 Y13: [quietly] oh dear
18 E13: well I'm seventy-seven
19 Y13: [high pitch] really?
20 E13: yes [laughs]
          [
21 Y13:     I thought you were sort of 60 I just assumed
                                      [
22 E13:                             did you oh
```

23   that's nice
24 Y13: yeah yeah it's funny most people I know who are
25   seventy-seven aren't [*gasps*]dashing in and out of day
26   centres(.) oh that's nice (.) oh

At lines 10–12, where E13 is telling she has grandchildren and great-grandchildren, the stylistic key signalled by accompanying laughter seems interactionally significant. E13 laughs presumably because she thinks Y13 will think that having great-grandchildren is surprising. Y13 duly gasps (at line 13), and verbalizes the disjunction between her interlocutor's appearance and her generational role: she (line 14) compliments E13 that she doesn't 'look that old'. The DCA (line 18) will predictably elicit another disjunctive comment, this time establishing distance between E13's just-reported chronological age and (over lines 21–26) her physical mobility. It is interesting that it is the *younger* speaker here who introduces the ageist theme[3] of normal decrement (her assumptions about immobility at age 77) as a basis for a disjunctive response: she deems E13 'good for her age' ('I thought you were sort of sixty'). Surprise at age is encoded verbally in lines 14 ('oh!') and 19 ('really?'), and prosodically throughout the responses.

Such compliments and gifts of praise find their force as attempts to mitigate or deny an interlocutor's supposedly predictable decrement, sometimes insistently and in highly particular respects.

EXTRACT 6.4 (from I33)
[*Y18 has been telling how her mother's house has been burgled.*]

 1 Y18: . . . and *that's* made her nervous you know I think once
 2   something like that
                        [
 3 E18:   *yes* (.) of course (.) how
 4   old is *she?*
 5 Y18: she's seventy-two
 6 E18: I'm seventy-*eight*
 7 Y18: [*astonished*] *are* you?
 8 E18: *yes*
 9 Y18: [*gasps*] gosh you're *mar*vellous aren't you?
10 E18: [*laughing slightly*] I don't know
11 Y18: oh *gosh* you are I'd never have thought (.) you've got
12   lovely *skin* [*puts hands up to cheeks, forward lunge,
        laughs*] you *have* haven't you?
13 E18: [*puts hands up to cheeks, forward lunge, laughs*] oh I

14   don't know [*laughs*]
15 Y18: [*emphatically*] oh you *have*=
16 E18: =yeah
17 Y18: my mother (.) looks the same *sort* as you
                                       [
18 E18:   does she?
                                       [
19 Y18:   she she looks
                                       [
20 E18:   yes yes
21 Y18: *younger* than her age and she's got a great outlook on
22   life . . .

In extract 6.4, Y18 (at lines 11–12) compliments E18, saying she has 'lovely skin', and goes on to give an explicit rationale. She classifies her elderly interlocutor alongside her own mother, who she says 'looks younger than her age'. The compliment is constructed from a physiognomic observation, but also from the categorizing of E18 as a member of a favoured (in fact, atypical and, to that extent, disjunctive) social group, and from the intimate association with the compliment-giver's own mother. It is the older woman in this sequence who has initial responsibility for introducing the theme of chronological age, and she of course volunteers hers, perhaps seeking some expression of surprise at age. When this surprise materializes (lines 7 and 9), E18's downplaying of the compliment (line 10) appears to escalate praise giving in both scope and intensity, producing the intimate touching behaviour and mother references.

Sustained supportive recipiency to DCA of this sort may, of course, be rewarding to an elderly person's age identity, just as the intimacy it involves may be at some level emotionally bolstering (Krause, 1986). Still, from a broader perspective, it appears that inviting interlocutors to participate in age-identity appraisals can simultaneously incur potentially heavy costs as well as benefits to elderly disclosers. Y18's extended accounting for her assessment by making the particular and insistent reference to E18's 'lovely skin' and her global personal appraisals of her interlocutor would certainly be taken as counter-normative and intrusive in most first-acquaintance encounters. Though DCA appears to legitimize and even to require, such orientations to elderly disclosers, and though there is certainly no textual evidence of E18 disfavouring them here, we would argue that elderly role opportunities are being constrained and generational stereotypes confirmed.

Paradoxically, then, such 'supportive' responses to DCA may themselves play some part in threatening older people's negative face and the positive identities that DCA recipients are presumably seeking to build. It would also be wrong to equate short-term 'supportive' conversational responses with longer-term experienced social support. Certainly there are many cases where accommodation in face-to-face contexts will realize *low* levels of social support (for example, when a recipient, in fact, endorses some undesirable or unhealthy stance or practice). Recent theoretical work has begun to model the many complexities of 'supportiveness' in health and caring contexts (see Williams, Giles, Coupland, Dalby and Manasse, 1990).

Responses to DCA in our data seem to find a particular salience in the lexical item 'marvellous' (for example, in extract 6.4, line 9; extract 6.5, lines 3 and 10; extract 6.6, line 18; and very frequently elsewhere). It is used as if to identify a global attribute of people ('you are marvellous!'), though its referent is conventionally a little more specific: the person's health or well-being. Its force is to give credit and, of course, to compliment, but also to convey suprise. Its meaning is implicitly relative. It evaluates well-being in relation to circumstances – either ill fortune, ill health or old age – and is therefore directly apposite in this context. On the other hand, in our view, 'marvellous' often smacks of residualism, implying that individuals have endured their unfortunate lot (which is therefore made salient) with noteworthy and unusual success thus far. In its own right the term captures the disjunctive attribution we have discussed above, casting the subject as a fugitive from 'normally' decremental ageing. Arguably, therefore, it plays some small part in alienating and fossilizing the elderly, however well the compliment might be received in face-to-face encounters.

The conventionality of the term's association with age and health evaluations allows it to act in its own right as a trigger for DCA.

EXTRACT 6.5 (from I4)
[*E1 has been telling E2 how she found her husband dead in bed only three weeks after his retirement.*]

1 E2: *what* a *shock* for you!

               [

2 E1:			yes it *was* a shock yes
3 E2: oh it's *mar*vellous you're like you are isn't it

4 E1: well (.) I'm eighty-six last May ((3 sylls.)) [*laughs*]
                                    [   ]
5 E2:   oh god
6 E2: you can give me a few years
7 E1: so I'm not a youngster really
                    [
8 E2:   just gone seventy
9 E1: mm I was eighty-six last May
                [
10 E2:   [*quietly*] *mar*vellous [*tuts*]

In extract 6.5, line 3, E2 is being sympathetic about the shock E1 has suffered and says it is 'marvellous' she is as she is. The sense of 'marvellous' is already relative here; E2 is giving a global positive assessment of E1's state of well-being in relation to the particular loss she has suffered, the death of her husband. E1's DCA at line 4, following directly from E2's 'marvellous', extends the basis of the relative assessment. She is 'marvellous' more generally than E2 has recognized – in relation to her chronological life-position as a whole. She adds another standard of comparison and, of course, thereby accepts the compliment, endorsing and even developing its basis, implicitly indulging in self-congratulation.

More generally in the peer-elderly context, there is far less likelihood of elderly DCA sequences conforming to ritualistic patterns of disclosure and complimenting.

EXTRACT 6.6 (from I20)

1 E9: but times are so *diff*erent aren't they?
2 E10: yes
        [
3 E9: aah (.) ev it's er (.) everything's *fast* isn't it?
4   . . . you know you've got to sort of (.) run *with* it like
5   haven't you eh ((haven't you))
              [
6 E10:   oh *yeah* you've got to make the best of it
                            [   ]
7 E9:   [*nodding*] yes
8 E10: especially at our age=
9 E9: =that's right yeah
10 E10: I'm seventy-seven

11 E9: [*gasps*] oh that's *good* anyway isn't it?
                    [   ]
12 E10:   yes
13 E9: I'm sixty-six [*laughs, disbelieving expression*]
14 E10: [*surprised*] you're sixty-six? oh I'm a lot older
15   than you

                                    [
16 E9:   yes
17   I (.) I go to the centre and there's some there er
18   (.) ninety-four and they're *mar*vellous

In extract 6.6, E9 and E10 are commenting on social changes that
they have to accommodate. E10 moves to consolidate their shared
experiences in a group-categorization spanning both individuals
('*especially at our age*', line 8), which E9 appears to accept (line 9). It is
E10 who discloses her age first – she is 77. The response elicited
indeed conveys surprise, though mildly, and it is tempered by E9's
'anyway' (line 11). At this point there may be some obligation upon
E9 to disclose her age reciprocally, though in doing this she
necessarily dissociates herself from the common age-category E10
has invoked. One interpretation at this point is that E10 is sensitive to
this as face-threatening and goes on record to retract her earlier
assumption: ('oh I'm a lot older than you', lines 14–15). E9 then finds
a means of reuniting E10 and herself, despite the 11 years divide
between them, by referring to an outgroup who are uncontroversially
old and, more importantly, a couple of decades old*er* than E10
('there's some there er (.) *ninety-four*'). It seems to be safe for E9 to
use the 'marvellous' evaluation of this outgroup, when to have used it
to E10 would have been to widen the divide between them in
contradiction of E10's claim. Alternatively (since we don't have
privileged access to motives), it may be that E10 has scored an
exquisite victory over E9 in that having affiliated herself with E9 as
age compatriots, when it turns out that E9 is 11 years younger, her
surprise displays that the difference in age is not detectable from any
difference in appearance. By either analysis, we see that the strategic
possibilities of peer-elderly DCA can differ radically from intergenerational concerns, opening up quite different agendas for the
negotiation of face and identity that need to be pursued in greater
detail than has been possible here.

Overview

We hope to have shown the generally negotiative character of elderly age-disclosure and its centrality to the age-identity paradigm we have tried to develop through the book. Social identities are born, refashioned and lost in the exchanges we have examined. For the most part, we have focused on the ritualistic, identity-bolstering function of DCA in intergenerational contexts. But the limitations and pitfalls of DCA and would-be positive support have also become apparent. It would not be surprising if, as we conjectured in relation to the painful self-disclosure data in earlier chapters, the predictability of elderly DCA reflects some people's need in later life to continually reappraise their age identities, perhaps to regain valued ground from one context of talk to another. In elderly-to-elderly talk, though it is not common there, DCA can trigger threatening social comparisons among a highly differentiated group.

The analyses we have presented point to several gaps in our understanding of age-management strategies generally. It would be important to trace (as we have done in the case of troubles-telling) alternative pre-contexts to age disclosure and the means by which elderly people variously engineer opportunities to disclose age or respond to contextual pressures to disclose. Other data-sets would give a contrastive focus on DCA management by younger people (to the extent they *do* disclose age) and, of course, other particular groups of 'elderly' people. A developmental focus on the disclosability of own-age would add significantly to our general understanding. Certainly, there is an important dimension of cross-cultural and cross-situational variability to expose. Research could also explore why and how women *and men* conceal or falsely report their age.

The main value of our exploratory analyses in this chapter is to have given a justification for treating elderly DCA as functional and strategic. That is, though the task-requirement in the interactive study was, to an extent, to disclose, we needed to account for the uneven distribution of DCA across elderly and young groups; also for the sheer pervasiveness of elderly DCA in both environments. In the interview corpus, though we have ourselves argued that health and well-being enter a predictable relationship with considerations of age, interviewees were not asked to divulge their ages at any point. Hence, the relationship of health to chronological age is one established *by elderly interviewees themselves* in the data.

What particularly seems to distinguish elderly age-related discourse is precisely the multiple-layering of identity and face considerations that surfaced in our discussions of PSD. In the middle years of life many would see disclosing age as an act that threatens a discloser's face – both negative and positive. During face-to-face interaction in later life more directly face-threatening circumstances can be apparent to interlocutors, either through other categories of disclosure or inferentially on stereotypical grounds. Under these conditions the token of disclosing age may be played, as we have seen, to contextualize and so redress the more salient threat to face. Given that many elderly people's chronological ages will be in advance of their contextual circumstances (they will be 'good for their ages' or 'well-preserved'), the token then needs to be played to claim the credit that they may feel is due, and to promote positive face.

Still, we have also seen that face *loss* can simultaneously be incurred during DCA sequences. First, the elderly discloser openly accepts whatever negative associations old age in itself stereotypically connotes. Then again, motivated self-disclosure, be it of age or of troublesome life events, risks being construed as egocentricity. And we have already seen that this construal is readily accommodated within the stereotype of elderly talk. Most strikingly, DCA appears to invite, in response, behaviours that are otherwise counter-normative. In particular, as we noted earlier, the making of overt judgements and evaluations of others on the basis of appearance is clearly tabooed in first-encounters between young and middle-aged adults (cf. C. R. Berger and Bradac, 1982), except perhaps in signalling aggression or sexual intent. In whatever context, these are processes that necessarily threaten negative face. So self-disclosure, as we argued earlier, paradoxically entails threats to the elderly identity it is designed to protect or enhance. Further risks are incurred in the assumption that some positive response will, in fact, be forthcoming. In the controlled setting of the interactive study, and among our compliant participants, age disclosers have presumably experienced far less significant risks in this regard than in day-to-day encounters. Even where supportive feedback is obtained, there is no guarantee that the negotiative attempts by disclosers have been appreciated by recipients adequately, if at all. There seems to be ample potential for DCAs to be misattributed and for elderly stereotypes to be confirmed.

The most significant contextual consideration for the present discussion is probably the disparity of social embeddedness of the younger and older people we have seen interacting. It is therefore easy to see the scarce resource of new first acquaintances, as it certainly is for the older populations in our data, being employed by elderly people partly as a touchstone for evaluating where they stand developmentally and for modifying this self-conception if necessary. Age disclosure, as we have begun to characterise it here, therefore seems to offer one further coherent set of interactional possibilities to enact this negotiation of one's status as an ageing individual as a facet of one's own projectable self.

7

Intergenerational Talk: Consonance or Conflict?

In interpreting the patterns of across- and within-generation talk we have examined so far, we have stressed group-level considerations. More than this, we have at many points suggested that, at least potentially, younger and older people may find themselves conversing across a cultural divide, predisposed by their predictably varying social experiences, social attitudes and priorities for interaction. The contextual model of interaction, a developed form of communication accommodation theory, that we endorsed in chapter 2 made explicit reference to the 'belief states' of speakers and acknowledged that these are both influenced by and themselves influence macrocontextual factors. We have speculated about forms of potential miscommunication that arise in and through intergenerational talk; our discussion of under- and overaccommodation processes specifically addressed relational 'problems' of this sort.

We have cited empirical studies, from outside the language research area and within it, to support this general line of interpretation. There is ample evidence that age-prejudicial beliefs exist in Western society (for example, Kite and Johnson, 1988), that they do sometimes influence people's perceptions of social competence and affect younger people's behaviour towards the elderly (see chapter 1). Interestingly far less research has examined older people's beliefs and perceptions of young people and their attitudes and behaviours. At the same time, there is the irony that we have commented on the high degree of 'procedural fit' that characterizes much of the intergenerational talk we have been describing. We have even suggested that, in relation to the management of PSD and age-telling sequences, older and younger contributions to talk appear packaged and to that extent 'ritualistic'. In this chapter we review these apparently competing interpretations and argue that there need be no tension between them. We shall introduce some data that show that an 'intergroup' (Giles and Coupland, 1991a) framing of social encounters and its potential for 'miscommunication' (N. Coupland, Giles and Wiemann, 1991) can not only coexist with but actually *build* on locally 'well-attuned' patterns of interaction.

At this point the micro-analysis of situated talk, which we have proposed in earlier chapters as a valuable resource for understanding cross-generation relations, needs to be complemented by studies that focus more directly on the *attitudinal* contexts in which such talk proceeds. As we also argued in chapter 1, there is no single 'correct' methodology for analysing social relationships. In this chapter we maintain our perspective on discourse processes and talk-in-context, but specifically in examining data from young adults' (women in their 30s) discussions *about* intergenerational talk. We ask whether interpretive analysis not only of the overt content of these discussions, but also of how they are enacted and organized and of what they presuppose might give us information about how cross-generation encounters are construed by younger people as intergroup events. We focus on how themes of ageing are interwoven into these young women's discussions and evaluations of older women's troubles-telling. First, we return to the principal interactive corpus to assess its general character in terms of discourse attuning.

Intergenerational Goal Consonance

Our distributional analyses of PSD sequences in chapter 5 suggested that troubles-telling in cross-generation talk comes about through *complementary* discourse strategies. We showed how older speakers might, by several criteria, justifiably be said to be being disclosive in these interactions. But young participants also elicited PSD from their elderly interlocutors to a considerable extent: 34 per cent of instances, contrasting with elderly speakers eliciting only 12 per cent of instances from their peers. This is modest evidence of younger people sharing responsibility for engendering elderly speakers' PSD. The two processes (self-disclosure by older speakers and PSD-elicitation by the young) are, of course, not in competition. Young people's eliciting role will predispose and perhaps require particular disclosive acts, but more generally it will legitimize elderly disclosive behaviour. Conversely, disclosive talk by older people will establish interactional norms that legitimize eliciting behaviour.

But this complementary pattern does not mean that the younger group's goals here are purely to accommodate the elderly's wishes or norms established in particular interactions. The qualitative focus we adopted was revealing, and we found instances of young women's eliciting behaviours that presupposed interrogatory rights they would certainly not have had in peer-young conversations (and which may not, of course, be endorsed by particular elderly conversationalists either). We suggested that elicitations like 'is your husband still alive?' (in a context where there is no on-going PSD talk) and 'do you sleep alright when you get to bed?' (when previous talk has been on the general theme of reading habits) were intrusive questions in first-encounter conversations. We argued that they imposed obligations on elderly interlocutors either to disclose or to prevaricate. Less direct elicitations also enabled painful self-disclosures (for example, 'where are your family living now? are they all fairly close to you or are you quite spread out?'). These, too, could therefore be seen as potential threats to the equilibrium of discourse, and threats that are often tolerated by young elicitors.

The younger women as recipients showed a clear tendency to attune their responses to elderly PSD and, for that matter, age-telling. They signalled interest and engagement and in that way often sustained disclosiveness. Although several options were open to them as makers of next-moves to PSD, as figure 4.3 described, younger speakers in the data were rarely able to express shared experiences and, of course, could not match generational ingroup accounts. For example, signalling surprise at an elderly PSD, which itself marks engagement, was a frequent young recipients' next-move. If we assume that elderly speakers' disclosures were made at least partly because of the need for interactive engagement and the benefits to identity this in turn brings, expressions of surprise have to be seen as a valuable endorsement of the newsworthiness of the telling. If the telling is somehow cathartic, surprise is presumably therapeutic.

EXTRACT 7.1 (from I6)

1 E3: [*sighing*] and um anyway they had a house then in Bristol (.)
2   Bristol (.) had their own house there (.) but things didn't

3   seem to go (1.0) very well you know (1.0) and er (.) one day

4   he came home (.) and he said um (.) she's gone (2.0) with

5   two little kids ((and))

            [   ]

6 Y3:   *[quietly]* oh dear and how *old* were *they?*

7 E3: well the one was in his arms she he was about um twelve months old

                                                      [

8 Y3:   she left

9   the children? she left the ch

                [ ]

10 E3:   yes

11 E3: twelve month old

12 Y3: mm

13 E3: and the little the little girl was (.) four and a half

                                            [

14 Y3:   good

15   heavens above! and *where* did she go?

16 E3: she went back home to her mother=

17 Y3: =*[tutting]* oh dear *left* the children

In extract 7.1, Y3's high-rise intonation contour on the last two syllables of 'she left the children?' (lines 8–9), as well as her 'good heavens above!' (lines 14–15) are part of an extensive repertoire of sustaining and attuning recipient-moves the young employ. Sympathy is encoded, either verbally ('oh dear' at line 17 of the extract; cf. elsewhere: 'ah there's sad yeah' [I33]; 'oh that's a shame' [I10]; and so on) or prosodically and facially or posturally at appropriate points. Sometimes the affective response is focused on particular items of content isolated through selected reformulation of what the discloser has said: in extract 7.1, '*[tutting]* oh dear left the children' (line 17); or through explicit evaluative glosses: in I22, 'oh that couldn't have been easy'. Initiations maintaining the topic of an ongoing PSD are also common as young next-moves. In extract 7.1, 'and how old were they?' (line 6); and 'and where did she go?' (line 15) explicitly require the teller to elaborate the content of her PSD. Some of very many further instances are 'is he still there [in a mental institution]?' (I6); 'how long ago were you widowed?' (I21); and the following sequence:

EXTRACT 7.2 (from I16)

1 E8: I'm dreading (.) tomorrow and (.) Sunday

2   Y8: oh you're it's just Monday to Friday that you go (.) oh
              [
3   E7:   so it's (.) everything's getting me
4   ((down)) and I'm going into hospital on Monday
5   Y8: oh are you?
6   E7: and I'm a little bit erm
7   Y8: bit worried (.) how long are you going to be in hospital?

Overall, the various contributions we have shown the young participants making intergenerationally justify labelling them as *facilitators* (Holmes, 1984), and particularly facilitators of elderly PSD. Their quite frequent role in eliciting PSD runs contrary to what C. R. Berger and Bradac (1982) suppose is normative for interrogative behaviour among new acquaintances. These authors conclude that 'it appears that interrogative strategies that are impersonal, i.e. non-intimate and de-individuated, are more acceptable initially than are highly personal strategies' (p. 82). Our data also deny Berger and Bradac's later claim that 'highly personal internally focused strategies are likely to inhibit self-revelation' (p. 82). This is not the case when our elderly speakers are questioned on aspects of their personal states and experience.

In their role supporting ongoing PSDs, the young speakers are making contributions that Coates (1986, p. 115) and others have considered prototypically female in intersex encounters, providing, above all, solidarity and support to interlocutors. In the sex-roles literature this conversational orientation has been considered a powerless role, but we are reticent to classify the young speakers as globally powerless relative to the older speakers here. While in terms of amounts of talk and personal focus the elderly do very clearly dominate, the younger speakers are dominant in the domain of discourse management, through their eliciting behaviour and in directing the conversational 'flow'. To that extent the intergenerational conversations are very much like interviews, in the chat show or talk show mould, rather than selection interviews, with younger people enabling and sustaining extended spoken performances by elderly participants.

This analysis is, in fact, supported by the elderly-to-elderly PSD talk in the data. Elderly recipients of elderly PSD are often aligning with their interlocutors in their next-moves along a dimension of *group* identity, rather than in respect of the particular (interindividual) topic being disclosed upon. The elderly responses to PSD often appeal to shared experiences of ageing. While this might appear a wholly solidary strategy under the predictions of accommodation theory, we, in fact, find that it can also *inhibit* the development of particular PSD sequences, as for example in extract 7.3.

EXTRACT 7.3 (from I7)

```
 1  E3: but [sighing] it's (.) it's just erm (.) I don't get out
                                    [
 2  E4:                                just can't do
 3      the things we used to do=
 4  E3: =I I (.) couldn't do it love no
                                 [
 5  E4:                          I can't walk like I used to
                                                       [
 6  E3:                                                 well
 7      no and I got a stick now this thing
                        [
 8  E4:                   well I haven't got a stick=
 9  E3: =no=
10  E4: =but I can't go up=
11  E3: =no=
12  E4: =I walked from our Derby and Joan club [social club for elderly
        people] yesterday to go
                        [   ] [   ]
13  E3:                  yes     yes
14  E4: home=
15  E3: =yes
        [
16  E4:    and I had to stop three or four times on the way
                                         [
17  E3:                                    that's right yes
18      you're you're short of breath
                        [         ]
19  E4:                  it's like a   (.) with my breathing=
                                  [        ]
20  E3:                            I do
21  E3: =yes
        [
22  E4:  and also=
23  E3: =yes=
```

24 E4: =my legs don't seem too (.) dainty
                     [
25 E3:   no of course they don't we're all the
26   same

E4's particular disclosure of immobility 'I can't walk like I used to' (line 5) is overlapped by E3's 'well no and I got a stick now . . . ' (lines 6–7). Reporting the shared experience of mobility problems does not offset the fact that E3's self-reference cuts across her partner's self-disclosure. The effect is far from positively accommodative. Also, the fact of generalizing these experiences explicitly to the group ('no of course they don't we're all the same', lines 25–26) is depersonalizing. It seems that E4 has not been allowed to develop her particular disclosure of immobility and breathing difficulties as fully as she might have wished. As an ingroup member, E3 can short-circuit the disclosure by contextualizing and rationalizing it (see chapter 4) with a move towards closing the disclosure.

In extract 7.4 this ingroup convergence option for elderly peers builds on what is, in fact, a very locally shared experience.

EXTRACT 7.4 (from I20)

1 E9: [*puts on glasses*] oh that's better I don't like the light
2   (.) I never had anything wrong with my eyes before
3 E10: well well
4 E9: yeah till about six months ago and then it came (.) er
5   conjunctivitis? it's like er a lot of irritation
                     [   ]
6 E10:   [*sympathetically*]   ah   ah   dear god
7 E9: yeah never mind (.) it'll go I expect [*laughing*] one day
                                       [
8 E10:   I get a lot
9   of noise in my ear=
10 E9: =oh that's with our age as well
         [
11 E10:   have you got (.) have you got that?
                          [
12 E9:   I   get   that yes
13 E10: you get it?
14 E9: [*emphatically*] yes see you can't they can't do a thing with
15   that=

16 E10: =that that's right (.) that's what the doctor s

　　　　　[

17　E9:　　　　　　　yeah it's just like a lot of er (.) buzzing

18　　　and (.) blocked you know ears are blocked

E9 too is a sufferer from tinnitus, the focus of the PSD she receives. She chooses to frame the expression of solidarity again in group terms: she responds with 'oh that's with our age as well' (line 10).

There is clearly a strong potential sense of shared difficult circumstances in the joint experience of being elderly and all that this can suggest in terms of experiencing bereavement, social disenfranchisement, possibly degenerating own health and so on. But it is perhaps surprising that sharing such experiences, and in many cases the will to disclose them, does not, on the whole, lead elderly speakers to promote the telling of particular sequences, for example in next moves to PSDs. PSD discourse in *general* may well not be inhibited by elderly responses, though the benefits to elderly disclosers in terms of positive face that we have discussed in previous chapters cannot easily accrue. The phenomenon of combative matching of PSDs that we identified earlier (chapter 2), in fact, suggests that the *telling* function can override *recipiency* concerns altogether for elderly conversationalists at times. We might say that much elderly PSD seems best suited for *non*-elderly audiences, and can fully achieve its face-promoting function only in the intergroup context.

Problematicality

At this point we need to address the question of *why* younger people adopt such a facilitative orientation to elderly PSD, when there seems to be an intrinsically painful element, in one or more dimension, to *receiving* negatively valenced, intimate self-disclosures among new acquaintances. We have already argued that, in Brown and Levinson's (1987) terms, painful self-disclosure predictably threatens a recipient's negative face: her rights to unviolated personal space. Simultaneously, the discloser threatens her own positive face, her desire to be approved of or thought well of, by indulging in counter-normative self-disclosive behaviour.

At the most basic level the emotional loading of many of the disclosures we have considered 'painful' inevitably intrudes on recipients' negative face-rights in this context. Beyond this, young recipients of elderly speakers' PSD are forced into selecting among response-options (see figure 4.3), *all* of which bear potential face threats in their own right. If a recipient discourages ongoing painful disclosure (perhaps by selecting a pre-closing move, or shifting topic to non-painful self- or other-topics), there is an immediate threat to her positive face. The discloser may find her strategy underaccommodative, socially or even morally deficient: the discloser thinks the recipient is not resourceful or courageous enough to be a recipient of PSD, and perhaps not as courageous as the discloser herself is being in exposing her own face. If a recipient chooses the options that encourage disclosure (for example, through eliciting further information or through supportive back-channelling in the way we have seen younger people most typically doing), she accepts the prospective threat to her own negative face: she may have her emotional space invaded once again. And, of course, there will be a recurring positive face threat in the need to encode further responses.

This is the basis of a potentially intractable accommodative dilemma of the sort we sketched in chapter 2. It would not be surprising if the competing considerations of face resulted in no desirable or even tolerable response option presenting itself to some recipients on some occasions. The lack of relevant shared experience we have pointed to compounds this problem; younger people cannot resort to group-solidarity marking as older listeners, of course, can. It is therefore most surprising how *rarely* the flow of discourse reflects these predictable problems.

EXTRACT 7.5 (from I18)

```
 1  E8: =because when I was a widow you see after eleven years
 2       I had three little children you see to bring up I worked
                              [     ]
 3  Y9:                         mm
 4  E8: very hard I done everything *cook* er parlourmaid *ev*erything
 5       I done
 6  Y9: mhm
 7  E8: well I had to get a living you see=
 8  Y9: =oh yes yes (1.0) mm (2.0) oh well (3.0) um (.) I was going
 9       to say I'm I've started working again I've got a little
10       daughter and I've just started back to work
```

A sequence like the one in extract 7.5 (which we discussed earlier as extract 4.8) suggests that the young recipient *does* experience some problems in maintaining the flow of talk. But the young population in our data seems generally highly socially skilled in this respect and such instances are very rare. We have very little textual evidence of 'problems', therefore, although some responses to disclosures do seem to have an intrinsic inadequacy that we suspect is perceived by recipients themselves. In I40 the older speaker (E20) has said she has been widowed for 21 years and now attends a day centre. Y20 offers what we have termed a 'contextualization' move (see figure 4.4): 'so this is really good for you isn't it then to be able to go somewhere like this'. The contextualization, even if it is in itself appropriate, makes unwarranted assumptions about the elderly interlocutor's particular circumstances and needs. Appreciating this (if she does) will be uncomfortable for the young speaker who is nevertheless trying to reinterpret disclosed information in a positive light, to 'look on the bright side' in Jefferson's (1984b, p. 363) sense.

Up to this point, then, we have no coherent explanation for young people's tolerating of, and, from quantitative and qualitative evidence, their *goal* of generating, interactional sequences that carry threats to both participants. Expecting that the answer is to be found in group predispositions and beliefs, we turn now to a new data-set, the evaluative study.

Intergenerational Dissonance

A further data-set was gathered[1] as an attempt to expose some of the attributional and evaluative processes that might underlie the strategies of PSD management and recipiency we have already witnessed. An evaluative study was designed in which young women, very similar in age and background to the younger group in the interactive study, listened to 16 diverse audio extracts (each of approximately half a minute) chosen from intergenerational encounters in the videotaped study. Details of the design and procedures used in the interactive study were made clear to the groups of listeners before they heard the extracts. Nine of the extracts were from PSD sequences, randomly chosen and representing disclosures on topics of ill health, bereavement and loneliness. The remaining seven were again randomly chosen from non-painful sequences of elderly disclosure, including some clearly positive reports (talking proudly about children and grandchildren or current social activities) and some expressions of dissatisfaction or of current difficult (but still not painful in our defined sense) circumstances. The listeners were asked to imagine themselves in the roles of the younger women they heard on tape, and to describe their thoughts and feelings, what influenced them most and what was most problematical for them as supposedly the younger persons involved. A set of prepared questions was used to elicit otherwise free discussion among small groups of women on these issues and on the theme of elderly PSD in general. Discussions in 11 groups (involving a total of 43 women) were audio-recorded and transcribed.

The study does not, of course, give direct access to motivational and evaluative processes at work in the interactive study. The probable gaps between individuals' experiences in the two studies, the immediate versus the reflective contexts, the dyad versus the group contexts and the predictable face considerations in the young evaluators' public presentations of their apparent reactions to the PSD stimuli all preclude this. On the other hand, we thought that discourse on the theme of elderly PSD was open to analyses not different in kind from those we used in the original study. While it would have been wrong to have confidence in the overtly simple judgements expressed in the group discussions, a further interpretive analysis could give a sense of the kinds of attributions of elderly self-disclosure that young people would express in either accepting or denying its problematical nature. Therefore we were interested in how beliefs and goals *vis-à-vis* older people are represented in a specific context of talk, and in how they might be consolidated and constructed in discourse. Arguably, the group discussions as constituted would predispose intergroup formulations, giving us access to how generational stereotypes can mediate responses to, and plans for, intergenerational talk. Also, the real-time, reflective process that we would be tapping into might itself be crucial to the formation and perpetuation of intergroup attitudes.

The discussion in the previous section raised the possibility that PSD recipiency may be 'problematical' in several overlapping dimensions. We suggested that PSD in our interactive study imposed some *affective* load upon recipients, who may experience discomfort or embarrassment, frustration or, perhaps even boredom. The discourse analyses showed little evidence of *procedural* or sequential difficulty, which we would take to be represented by recipients showing difficulty in finding any plausible next move to PSD. Again, we hypothesized that the accommodative dilemma of responding to PSD might constitute a *strategic* difficulty: a next move may be found, though it would fail to satisfy recipients' own appraisal of what would constitute a desirable or at least adequate strategy at that point in the discourse. In our explorations of the evaluative group-discussion data, we were initially interested in whether participants would overtly recognize any categories of problem to be associated with PSD recipiency and, if so, which. Evidence of perceived problems in interactions with the elderly would, of course, have important repercussions in their own right, not least on younger people's willingness to take part in meaningful interactions with them (cf. Notarius and Herrick, 1988).

In fact, there is again *little* overt recognition in the group discussions of specific problems directly associated with receiving PSD. There are certainly references to procedural difficulties, but only very rarely of the sort anticipated. VB in DG6[2] and DB in DG10 do comment on the limited range of options open to recipients of PSD, by observing that there is often no option but to give sympathy or to change the subject (which is itself acknowledged to be difficult to achieve). More often, experienced procedural problems are said to take the form of expressed dissatisfaction with the recipient roles of the elderly speakers in the extracts, that they were interrupting and inattentive listeners (see, for example, extracts 7.6 and 7.7).

EXTRACT 7.6 (from DG6)

```
1   R:  what was it about the snippets of conversation that you found
2       the most problematic?
3  VB:  um (.) the fact that the older person interrupted you all
4       the time (.) whatever you
                      [    ]
5   R:              mhm
6  VB:  you said (.) she wasn't really listening (.) she had her own
7       mind her own thoughts and she was just preparing the next
8       thing she was going to tell you didn't really listen to the
9       question
```

EXTRACT 7.7 (from DG7)

```
1 HO: oh when they didn't stop and listen to you and they just sort
2       of carried on with what they were saying all the time when you
3       were trying to say something and they would just . . . continue
4       and sort of butt in before you'd finished your question
5       completely
                                          [           ]
6 DR:                                          yeah
                                          [
7  R:                                          yeah
8 HC: taking it on to a different tack um that's difficult
```

Several other discussants raise the problem of powerlessness, being unable to control the developments of topics or themes in intergenerational conversation. PE and GR in DG4 suggest that sudden changes of topic (as when an elderly speaker in the stimulus recordings chains a PSD on the subject of an abdominal rupture to one on her failing eyesight) are difficult to respond to. HC in DG7 comments that 'it is hard to get a conversation to where you want it to go' with older people.

There is, of course, an affective dimension to each of the procedurally focused complaints above, but specific affective consequences are mentioned very rarely. RT in DG10 responds to a disclosure on loneliness as follows: 'she just came across as if she wanted to moan to somebody and that was really embarrassing'. RT and KM in the same discussion ascribe this to a conscious intent on the part of some elderly people: they are 'trying to make you feel sorry for them in some way'. But most recognition of the affective impact of PSD is generalized into a discourse of sadness and sympathy for elderly people, living and having lived difficult lives. In extract 7.8, for example, LJ expresses a global response to the condition of being elderly.

EXTRACT 7.8 (from DG10)

```
1  R: right (.) what . . . did you find influenced you most?
2 LJ:  . . . um (1.0) you know if they're having problems with health
3       and this sort of thing then it affects you I think very
4       definitely it does to me anyway (.) um (.) if they're feeling
5       lonely and depressed then that oh that hurts me very strongly
                                              [   ]
6  R:                                          mm
```

```
 7   R: is there was there a particular snippet there that you . . . can
 8      remember in that respect?
 9  LJ: um (2.0) I think . . . the emphysema one I think really went home
10      (.) that one um (1.0) and oh the very lonely people (.) I think
11      there were a couple of those who were very very lonely (1.0)
12      I felt sorry for those because you then think of people who are
13      in tha situation um and there must be thousands of people like
14      that all over (.) the world
```

Invoking the social group ('thousands of people like that all over the world', lines 13–14) seems to mitigate any experience of problems in relation to PSD in particular and of course, in relation to the particular instances of PSD in the stimulus material. In the group discussions, recognizing problematical elderly life circumstances regularly works to *deny* problems of listening to PSD (the issue the researcher was trying to explore quite systematically in the evaluative study). This process of contextualization is apparent in extract 7.9.

EXTRACT 7.9 (from DG6)

```
 1   R: was it just the . . . bereavement that you found might have been
 2      difficult to respond to or was there anything else?
 3  PE: well no just the general situation of old age . . . I mean it just
 4      seems to me that old age is very often a sad situation and I
 5      don't think there is an awful lot can be done about it
                                                 [
 6 MS:                                             I didn't find
 7      it difficult
          [
 8 ML:   no
 9  PE: I mean I didn't find it difficult either but I think that's the
10      situation it's it's you just accept that I mean when you're
11      talking to old people
          [
12 MS: they like to talk about their husband who passed away seven
13      years ago
          [
14  PE: yes I agree
          [
15 ML: yes
16 MS: they like to have a chat about it
```

17 ML: yes it's lovely it's yes yes and if you listen
                                        [   ]
18 MS: yes
19 ML: I mean you don't have to say anything
                                [   ]
20 MS: no
21 ML: just let them unburden

In answer to R's question, PE observes that 'old age is often a fairly sad situation' (line 4) and that little can be done about it. MS interjects to deny she finds PSD 'difficult' (lines 6–7) and PE seems to feel the need to match MS's denial and redress her earlier statement to some extent. ML even maintains that it is lovely (line 17) to listen to old people talking about lost loved ones, which appears to transform the suggestion of problematical recipiency into satisfaction at some sort of altruistic, perhaps therapeutic, involvement. So the discussion at this point works in various ways to deny what we have seen as the essence of PSD talk. It is now glossed as the elderly having 'a chat about it', and 'liking' to engage in such talk (line 16): an image of talk that is both enjoyable and superficial is constructed in the discussion discourse. Problematicality is subverted to the extent that ML claims 'I mean you don't have to say anything' (line 19): recipients are implied to be free from any significant involvement.

For some discussants, the very generality of what they perceive to be undesirable elderly behaviours in talk is used to downgrade the degree of problematicality they cause. For EB and RW, in extract 7.10, it is the fact of 'those' modes of talk being 'routine' (lines 7–8) that leads to their view that PSD in not problematic for them as listeners. This is a perplexing claim, until it is made clear by both RW and MC that they accept that elderly PSD is routinely unfounded. Their ageist suggestion is that 'you have to take it with . . . a pinch of salt' (lines 19–20), and that some elderly people 'play for sympathy' (line 23). MC finally invokes the classic inverted-U stereotype of the old as children (cf. chapter 1).

EXTRACT 7.10 (from DG5)

1   R: is there anyone here who feels that (.) um me asking the
2   question what was problematic doesn't doesn't really resonate
3   with how they felt does anyone feel (.) that they didn't find
4   (.) the ext responding to the snippets snippets of conversation

```
5        problematic? (1.5)
6  EB:  on the whole no=
7  RW:  =on the whole no because one's come across those before
                            [         ]        [      ]
8  EB:                       routine
9  NL:                                                    yes
                                                          [
10 EB:                                                    one's come
11       across those before . . .
            . . .
12 RW:  well I've got a granny of eighty-five who's continually saying
13       she's lonely she's not lonely at all because there's a visitor
                         [    ]
14  R:                   yes
15 RW:  just about every hour of the day into the house
                                             [
16  R:                                       mhm
17 RW:  but she says she's lonely and nobody comes to visit her
                                                   [
18  R:                                             mhm
19 RW:  and in some respects you have to take it with a little bit of a
20       pinch of salt=
21  R:  =mhm
22 RW:  um (.) what people say
23 MC:  yes they play for sympathy they're very much like some some
24       elderly people are very much like young children they want
25       to be the centre of attention for as long as possible
```

A discourse of elderly stereotyping[3] is, in fact, structurally integrated into other patterns of argumentation in the group discussions. Stereotyping operates here at different levels of inclusiveness, with both categorical and less inclusive characterizations (cf. Henwood, 1987) of the elderly. We find labels such as 'cantankerous' (GD in DG3), 'depressing' and 'moaning' (HP in DG3), 'boring' (ML in DG3), 'selfish' (KM in DG10), and 'rambling' or 'rattling on' in conversation (EK in DG5; KM in DG10). But this sort of stereotypical ascription is often counterbalanced by less pejorative themes, such as the discourse of sadness and sympathy for old people we referred to above. In the group discussions people will often focus on exceptions to the stereotyped norm, thereby apparently legitimizing their negative ascriptions to the out-group. In GD 4 NL says 'it can be a b rather boring to be with an old person for any length of time and a bit frustrating and you feel a bit resentful of the time you have to spend . . . it's the sort of duty thing'. She then immediately restricts the currency of her observations with 'it's an exceptional person that makes you feel like that', and the more positive global view is bolstered by another participant's (HP's) contribution that 'some of the conversations [in the stimulus material] were quite buoyant . . . it was an elated sort of conversation'. Pejoration seems to be in turn enabled by this upswing; HP adds 'but some were very downcasting very sort of moaning type conversations'.

The ebb and flow of stereotyping and counter-stereotyping in the discussion data seems to reflect a normative constraint: that in a liberal democracy naked categorical assertions about social groups are undesirable. Once 'isms' gain some currency in public discourse (and awareness of ageism (see chapter 1) has certainly lagged behind racism, sexism and classism in the UK and, to an extent, in the US consciousness (see Nairn and McCreanor, in press; van Dijk, 1987)) they tend to proscribe openly pejorative statements in public settings. But we are prepared to construe a good deal of the more positive ascriptions within the stereotyping talk as a *veneer* of tolerance and liberal sentiment over some generally endorsed beliefs about the elderly as undesirable interactional partners and problematical conversationalists. Of course, as we noted earlier, people's actual beliefs are not open to analysis. What seems most significant in the group-discussion data is the readiness with which young discussants appeal to group formulations – positive, negative or both – in the context of questioning about particular sequences of PSD. The pervasive denial of specific problems associated with PSD recipiency is achieved *only* through adopting the broader perspective. Such problems, as we construed them, are either dissolved into highly general, recognized inadequacies of intergenerational talk or are reduced to an irrelevance by comparison with considerations of the elderly's 'problematical' lives. Either way, the availability of group-salient, stereotypical formulations of old people intervenes crucially in what we originally conceived as an exercise of evaluation and response.

Overview

Reviewing the intergenerational PSD sequences in the light of the evaluative study findings, it still appears entirely reasonable to see them as an interactional mode that is substantially enabled and supported by disclosers and recipients alike. PSD reflects complementary instrumental goals for cross-generation talk, realized by complementary sociolinguistic behaviours. But the group-discussion data suggest we need to see goals operating at different levels and in multiple dimensions (see Tracy, 1991; Tracy and Coupland, 1990). The interlocking goals that people of different ages appear to bring with them to accomplish intergenerational talk can be traced to the sorts of prior assumptions about the 'treatment' of the elderly as a social group that surfaced in the discussions. These 'deeper' identity and relational goals sustain and promote conflict at an intergroup level, through endorsing and revitalizing social stereotypes.

The PSD sequence can appropriately be considered a conversational *routine*, in Coulmas's (1981) sense of a sociolinguistically regulated pattern of interchange, but also in the sense of being self-regulating. We are not dealing with a simple formula in talk (as most of the instances in the Coulmas collection are), but an integrated social, cognitive and linguistic design for intergroup attitudes, social relations and face-to-face talk. The consonance of goals for procedural aspects of talk appears to derive from stereotype-consistent beliefs young people hold about elderly identity and the possibilities and priorities for talk with the old. But the complementary discourse roles not only stem from, but may also confirm, dissonant generational goals and beliefs, which come, or continue, to be seen as 'the way things predictably are'.

Future research could very valuably explore the ways in which elderly groups, too, rationalize cross-generation encounters, and draw out the stereotypes that, no doubt, *they* subscribe to. We are aware that there is a risk of an unbalanced perspective that takes elderly people's, but not younger people's, discourse strategies at face value. Study of both sexes is another obvious need, to supplement the female bias in this study and this book as a whole. Still, we feel the chapter has shown how the role of young people as recipients of PSD is ultimately highly ambiguous. Recipients do a substantial amount of work to bring about accommodative interactional patterns that may still *distance* them from their interlocutors. Goal consonance is reflected in patterns of elderly self-disclosure and young elicitation, mutual tolerance of counter-normative and face-threatening intimacy, and the young's repertoire of sustaining and supporting moves. But all of this may be possible only because young people often construct such negative identities for the old, as depressed and depressing, and as dull, grouchy and unreliable conversationalists. Good procedural fit belies complex group-evaluative processes that are a barrier to cross-generation relations. Perceived 'problems' in talk, that would appear to be an inevitable consequence of intimate self-disclosing to strangers, are contextualized and even denied through there being low expectations of interaction with elderly people. Talking to the old is perceived as a time-consuming duty and a necessary therapy rather than as relational development and broadening.

In the real-time of the group discussions we have seen intergenerational orientations and goals being not only expressed but perhaps also consolidated. These sequences may be representative of commonplace ingroup discourses (in the home or at work) through which experiences of interaction with elderly people are judged and goals for future contact are established. Through this process of transformation, we see problems in one sense denied, but in another sense perpetuated and consolidated. The ground is laid for new initiatives that guarantee that intergroup non-alignment and ideological conflict will continue. Young people come to evaluate elderly PSD positively only through, and at the cost of, perceiving the elderly as a disenfranchised out-group needing special consideration. Responding to elderly PSD is to be regarded positively only to the extent that intergenerational conversation is pseudo-consultation. In our data the young seem to accept, often enthusiastically, their opportunity to make a therapeutic intervention in the lives of the elderly. However appropriate this might be in particular cases, it inevitably constrains the roles older and younger adults can fulfil in intergenerational talk. The more general consequence is that a rigidly intergroup frame is imposed on talk between younger and older adults, and this must perpetuate the social alienation elderly people so often consider their greatest handicap.

The accommodation model we introduced in chapter 2 captures the complexity of these processes quite well. Referring back to figure 2.1, let us assume that 'sociolinguistic encoding' represents elderly

PSD and young people's supportive responses to PSD. Younger speakers may, then, perceive their own and interlocutors' behaviours as (respectively) overaccommodative and underaccommodative. The elderly are seen as underaccommodating in that they make insufficient allowance for the burden (affective and interactional) that PSD imposes upon recipients. The young see themselves as overaccommodating: having to transcend what they perceive to be the normal bounds of the recipiency role. In the past we have tended to assume that these evaluative labels signal some sort of miscommunication and probable interactional dissatisfaction with problems in interaction. However, the discussion data in this chapter show young people, in their talk, attributing elderly PSD largely to 'situation' (an option specified in the model), in terms of elderly life circumstances, beliefs about talk and needs for talk, plus their own responsibilities *vis-à-vis* 'therapeutic' intervention.

In the process of making these attributions young people's potentially negative evaluations of elderly PSD (again specified in the model) are often recast as, or transformed into, more positive evaluations through mediating considerations of elderly stereotypes. Subsequently (again in the model's terms), these evaluations enter the 'context' component as a form of learned or reproduced 'knowledge' about the old and about intergenerational talk, which again predisposes recipients (as 'Individuals B' in the model) to adopt presumably quite convergent psychological orientations to the elderly in future encounters. If so, the classic 'positive attuning' interactional goals of promoting social approval (maintaining and responding supportively to PSD) and communication efficiency (selecting discourse strategies, such as elicitation and expressing sympathy) are adopted and talk will go ahead according to a conventional intergenerational schema.

Ultimately, we have a cyclical process explaining the transmission of intergroup attitudes, including predispositions for modes of talk, through experiences of talk. If the accommodation model has captured some of the complexities of multiparty PSD management, it may prove to have some more general use in understanding intergroup communication – perhaps in gender, occupational, ethnic or religious contexts, and certainly in other aspects of intergenerational communication than we have considered here. In the final chapter we assess what pragmatic potential our approaches to accommodation and self-disclosure may have in those medical and caring contexts involving older people.

8

Sociolinguistics and Gerontology: Applied Concerns

There is no shortage of applied settings where an integrated sociolinguistic account of ageing could bear fruit. Much published work has been devoted to developing the communication skills of professionals and carers routinely involved with the elderly (cf. Dreher, 1987; Gravell, 1988; Portnoy, 1985; Wooliscroft, Calhoun, Maxim and Wolf, 1984). Social skills training with the elderly is an established practice (for example, Lopez, 1980) that has tried to remedy some of the reported difficulty that withdrawn elderly residents have with interpersonal relationships (Kuypers and Bengston, 1973). Future interchange between these practical, interventionist efforts and sociolinguistic work should advance not only our understanding of language-related processes but also our social practices in the gerontological sphere.

This is not to underestimate the disjunction between descriptive *post hoc* analyses of talk and prescriptions for talk. In fact, the priorities we have stressed throughout this book, the need to appreciate strategy, sequence and context in accounts of sociolinguistic phenomena, are themselves an argument *against* formulating simple principles to guide practice and training. This is why attempts to specify 'how to interact with your elderly patient' are overoptimistic if not counter-productive. At the same time, a sociolinguistics that does not *aspire* to application misses its potential, and perhaps its vocation. And on theoretical grounds it follows from the social constructivist tradition we have been endorsing in this book that we do have the resources for intervention. If, as we have been arguing, talk is the relational key to age identities and to significant dimensions of ageing itself, then it is through talk that change may conceivably come about. The constructivist paradigm at least offers the prospect of morally acceptable and relationally satisfying cross-generation encounters being within the grasp of interactants who are sensitive to the active potential of talk.

As yet there are no extensive analyses of cross-generation talk *in situ*. A major aim of this book has been to show what might be feasible in this direction and to stimulate activity in this new research area. On the other hand, we are able to show how the fundamental ideas we have developed can and do cross-refer to interactional concerns in health and in caring settings. First, we show how existing interventionist attempts to develop communication skills for practitioners working with the elderly are already concerned with several of the discursive issues we have been discussing. A case-study of prescriptions for talk to elderly people, outlined in course materials for trainee domiciliary workers, shows how ambivalent specific initiatives can be. We suggest that these attempts to guide practitioners' behaviours need to be refined by more detailed discourse analyses. Then, as the principal and final section of the chapter, we review recent studies that have explored age-identity management processes and, in particular, the discourse of troubles-telling, in two contexts of care for the elderly, the domiciliary, or home-help, service and long-stay residential hospitals.

Communicating with Older People: The 'Skills' Approach

Awareness of the trend to an older Western society is being followed, though slowly, by an awareness of the need to provide a more adequate and comprehensive system of caring for the elderly. With the growing recognition that 'health' needs to be defined very broadly and positively, as 'a state of complete physical, mental and social well-being and not merely the absence of disease or infirmity' (World Health Organisation, 1968, p. 453), communication processes are increasingly acknowledged to provide access to a dimension of health (see Giles, Coupland and Wiemann, 1990; Williams, Giles, Coupland, Dalby and Manasse, 1990). Findings that stereotypical inferences intervene in talk to the elderly and that communicative styles attribute social roles, positions and identities are therefore central considerations in health care for the elderly.

In this section we review two recent interventionist treatments of 'communication and the elderly', Dreher (1987) and Gravell (1988). The starting point for each of these books is wholistic care for the elderly, care that concerns itself with the opportunities for, and quality of, inter- and intragenerational communication. Dreher and Gravell both aim to teach practitioners who are concerned with specific elderly speech and hearing disorders and often with the institutionalized elderly, but their experience of the communication environment of the elderly is also related explicitly to the world of 'normal ageing'.

Dreher's broadly based book is aimed at 'employees in the health and helping professions' and she intends to offer 'practical techniques as well as new methods for enhancing communication with aged clients' (p. xii) based on firsthand experience. But the question relevant to our present concerns is whether the specification of 'techniques' (practical exercises are suggested at the end of each chapter) is adequately detailed in characterizing the communicative means and methods with which to provide wholistic care. Dreher offers case-studies to illustrate elderly personality types she terms 'extrovert' and 'introvert'. But there is, in fact, little detailed description of how these different supposed types communicate. Dreher comments on simultaneous monologuing as a feature of the conversational style of elderly 'extroverts' (p. 11ff.), but it is difficult to appreciate the significance of a stylistic feature this abstractly defined. Is simultaneous monologuing associated, for example, with Gold et al.'s notion of elderly 'off-target verbosity' (see chapter 1), or with some *non*-age-specific orientation to talk ('extrovert')?

Both the structure and the function of this speech style are underanalysed in Dreher's account. In an investigation (related to the 'beliefs about talk' paradigm – see chapter 1) of group discussions among elderly day centre members Giles, Coupland and Wiemann (1990) also commented on simultaneous monologuing, though this is ultimately an inappropriate label for the complexities of topic interrelation between participants' discourses that we commented on there. Giles et al. argue there is a social (as opposed to a thematic) cumulativity realized through such a discourse as a whole, but that this finds its force through highly supportive individual contributions that *are* topically attuned despite speech often being simultaneous.

Both Dreher and Gravell consider the implications of there being restricted interaction opportunities for many older people. Dreher addresses problems engendered by a youth-oriented Western culture, where even the physical appearance of elderly people may impede intergenerational communication. Young–old interaction is explored (p. 40ff.) in terms of 'levels of disclosure'. Low-level disclosure is said to comprise 'ritualized greetings, simple inquiries, comments about the weather and surroundings' and is said to be 'the way most interactions begin' (p. 40); it would more commonly be identified, then, as phatic talk (cf. chapter 2). Dreher advises strategies for promoting 'middle-level disclosure' . . . events, hobbies, sports, travel, holidays and such', so that 'old persons can get beyond their current physical selves and talk about past experience and accomplishments' (p. 41). However, in chapter 2 of this book we highlighted these precise topic areas as an arena for potential intergenerational *non*-alignment, where a younger interactant may, for example, feel herself to be emphasizing disengagement in an elderly person who lacks a current social calendar.

As high-level (intimate) disclosure, Dreher describes 'trusting' disclosure by the elderly, which deals with 'personal problems, successes and failures'. The successes are easy to respond to, but how should carers respond to the problems and failures? Dreher prescribes a policy of low intervention: 'perhaps the best responses are reflective – a simple reiteration or rephrasing of the speaker's current emotions, perceptions and plans' (p. 44). In our investigations of PSD management (chapters 4 and 5) we have found that the neutral ground that Dreher recommends shows up *rarely* in situated talk, and that it is even more rarely adequate. The threats to positive and negative face inherent in responding to PSD often force a younger listener to choose from a range of dispreferred alternatives.

So the prescriptive literature has again raised issues of central importance to intergenerational communication, but, arguably, without the sustained analysis on which to base well-founded practical advice. Despite this, it is crucially important that grass-roots experience of caring for older people arrives at the *general* constructivist position that, on theoretical grounds, the discourse perspective has adopted. In common with Gravell, who stresses the importance of the 'cognitive representation of objective reality' (p. 10), Dreher says that morale among older people is more closely linked to perception of self than to objectively measured circumstances. This is the core of the wholistic ideology of care; to illustrate it, Dreher quotes Goethe: 'Treat people as if they were what they ought to be and you help them to become what they are capable of being' (p.129). Only if the caring institutions acknowledge older people's needs for talk and provide them with conducive opportunities for intergenerational and intra-generational talk will positive age- and health-identities be able to ensue.

Gravell's important goal is to outline a broader, communicative approach than the traditional specialized treatment of elderly speech disorders, one that fosters a 'high-quality' interactional environment. Gravell's review of the effects of ageing on communication does not link ageing *per se* with encroaching deficit as readily as many of the studies it cites (cf. our own review in chapter 1). Her conclusion is that, owing to changes in the central nervous system or the anatomical structures necessary for speech 'ageing . . . results not in a defective ability to communicate, but in a different system' (p. 15). It is this notion of difference as opposed to decrement that her book is at pains to illustrate and accommodate. In her discussion of counselling, for example, Gravell comments on elderly people's need to talk about the many and perhaps painful changes in life circumstances they may have been subject to: 'Old age leads to a number of enforced changes . . . reduced strength, poor health, lack of employment, the loss of family and friends, relocation into a sheltered environment or institution, and . . . loss of independence . . . anyone working with elderly people needs to be aware of their need to express grief at such events' (p. 48). Her emphasis is on the importance of listening as an active rather than a passive process, whereby the problems of accepting age, and death and dying, need to be discussed without embarrassment. There is certainly still work to be done on how Gravell's prescribed active listening may be actualized in specific interactional strategies, though our own analyses of response options (particularly in chapter 7) may provide a basis.

Particularly revealing is Gravell's view that the institutional environment is commonly 'communication-impaired' (p. 110), with limited reasons for talk, carers offering little support for elderly talk, residents' physical and emotional withdrawal, and so on (see also J. Coupland, Nussbaum and Coupland, 1991). Gravell discusses the interactional and personal damage that can be caused by the generalized use of 'baby-talk', which may have a nurturing effect if used with patients of lower functional ability but is more likely to create self-fulfilling prophesies by promoting learned dependency if used more consistently to all patients or residents. Again it seems important to present care-givers with a more discriminating analysis of baby-talk (perhaps in terms of our substrategies of overaccommodation in chapter 2) and of the contextual factors that are relevant to its production and evaluation.

Applied treatments like those of Gravell and Dreher go some considerable way to highlighting ignorance, ageist attitudes and practices in communicating care, set against the special communicative problems and needs of elderly care-receivers. We can learn how these problems arise and how in general they might be ameliorated. But as Gravell herself comments, 'education on ageing bodes well for the quality of life of elderly people only if the new philosophy is translated into practical methods of care' (p. 158). And it is unfair both on those who work with the elderly and their clients that carers are 'expected to pick up the relevant knowledge and skills as they go' (p. 99). The next stage is to provide detailed training experiences and materials for such carers built on a stronger empirical research base than is now available. Discourse analysis can usefully characterize the routine procedures that constitute experiences of care and institutional life. In fact, for some theorists, talk may be taken to constitute those institutions themselves (Fisher and Todd, 1986; Kress, 1985). Within medical and caring contexts, the interplay between individual or group identities and institutional assumptions and prescriptions are likely to surface in these interactional routines. Talk and its absence are more than the outcome or product of beliefs and policies about elderly care and more than an accompaniment to health-care provision. Rather, talk *embodies* critical aspects of caring itself and plays a part in the construction of caring norms and ideologies. However, as data reported in the following section show, the implementation of training initiatives and the working-through of ideologies of 'good care' are complex processes in themselves.

Ideologies of Accommodation in Training for Domiciliary Care

The UK home-help service was introduced in 1918 as a supplement to domiciliary maternity services, but it is now a primary agency involved in provision for older people living at home. Traditionally, the service has been seen as a domestic cleaning service, though current trends are to develop 'a personal caring service with less and less emphasis on domestic tasks' (Clarke, 1984, p. 60). The home-help service is therefore one context where relational and communicative dimensions of 'care' are currently being renegotiated, and where ideologies of care and communication are available for inspection. In particular, K. Atkinson and Coupland (1988) examined how over-accommodation (in the sense defined in chapter 2) features, overtly and covertly, in current training initiatives for home helps in the UK.[1]

The starting assumption is that strategies of talk can embody the relational, moral and political considerations that define much of the ideological essence of caring institutions for the elderly. In this study, then, the focus is less on overaccommodation as a cluster of observable strategies of intergenerational talk and more on over-accommodation, and its avoidance, as a disembodied, reified 'problem issue' that surfaces in *evaluations of* talk and in discussions of 'good care' and 'professional conduct'. In line with general discussions of ideological formations (Kress and Hodge, 1979; Potter and Wetherell, 1987), Atkinson and Coupland expected overaccommodation in this sense to play some active role in the reproduction of home-help and other institutional networks, to embody inconsistent and contradictory elements, and to make positive use of such inconsistency for their own ends.

For example, it is predictably the case that 'baby-talking the elderly' (which can be specified as different forms of overaccom-modation) is an established component of recognized bad practice and a risk identified as a particular characteristic of community services (H. Levin and Lin, 1988). It is correspondingly to be expected that 'overaccommodation avoidance' will feature as an endorsed liberal principle that informs the ideology of 'good care'. In fact, the home-help service is at pains to show itself aware of overaccommodation avoidance as good care, though there is also the paradox that caring can itself *presuppose* dependency. To the extent that the service needs to show itself as 'caring', it simultaneously has a vested interest in portraying its primary clientele – older people – stereotypically as dependent in some sense, and perhaps also as 'difficult to care for'. Atkinson and Coupland's analyses therefore focus on the tensions in home-help training materials between prescriptions of overaccommodation avoidance on the one hand and displayed tolerance of, and even prescriptions of, overaccommodation on the other hand. Text analyses showed how simple prescriptions for 'talk to the elderly' are, in fact, embedded in highly complex moral and political considerations.

To take just a few instances from K. Atkinson and Coupland's data (1988, p. 323, ff.), overaccommodation avoidance is commonly prescribed in the form of overt policy statements in training materials for home helps. It is advocated that home helps should counteract elderly stereotypes and dependency, and that older people should be thought of as individuals with autonomous rights. The Local Government Training Board Manual (1981) advises that it is 'important to encourage clients to do as much as possible for themselves to help them maintain independence and to keep their minds and limbs active'; 'taking over' is said to be 'counter-productive in many ways' (p. 45). In an extended series of simulated interactions between a prototypical home help and diverse clients (a tape–slide package known to be employed by most regional UK authorities), the model home help endorses these views in comments she makes to the trainee audience and through particular illustrated strategies of talk to elderly clients portrayed in the film.

Extracts 8.1 and 8.2 are from the tape–slide package. In extract 8.1 the prototypical home help (Betty) is being advised by the more senior home help organizer (HHO) on how to handle a 'difficult' client (Mrs Hogarth). In the second extract, Betty is making an aside to the audience when visiting Mrs Hogarth's home:

EXTRACT 8.1

```
1 HHO:  [to Betty] Mrs Hogarth's (.) a bit of an eccentric
2        not too keen on keeping the house clean (.) it's a
3        bit run down to say the least
4 Betty: needs a complete overhaul you mean?
5 HHO:  well no it's more a question of accepting that Mrs
6        Hogarth is leading her life her way (.) and will go
7        on doing so (.) and other things are more important
8        to her than a clean cooker
```

EXTRACT 8.2

```
1 Betty: [to audience] aha (.) I see what Mrs Davies
2        [HHO] means this is how she lives (.) and who wants
3        to change it if she's happy (1.5) I'm not the one
4        to change her little ways . . . better just get to know
```

5   each other a bit (.) you know hear a few stories (.)
6   a few moans [*laughs*] and learn a lot too (1.0) I'd no
7   idea how to grow gentians or (.) use garlic to cure
8   a cough

The overt theme of both fragments is the need to accommodate individual rights to make autonomous decisions. Respecting these rights is clearly intended as an instantiation of good care through the expressed views of the experienced HHO, endorsed by her junior. But the principle of overaccommodation avoidance is subverted in the same extracts by an equally clear tolerance of (and in context therefore a *prescription* of) overaccommodation, feeding off the elderly client being cast in a stereotypical mould. Client Hogarth's individuality is glossed as 'eccentric' behaviour; her rights are patronizingly glossed as 'little ways'. Such positive qualities as client Hogarth is credited with are in the stereotyped domains of home-cures and gardening. In the supposed consideration of an individual and individualism itself, invoking elderly stereotypes transforms the perspective from interpersonal to intergroup (cf. chapter 7). Covertly, this shift, and the overaccommodation implicit in it, are legitimized through portraying the client as herself *under*accommodative: Betty anticipates hearing 'a few stories (.) a few moans'. Ultimately, the advice about returning power and choice to the elderly person is ambiguous in these messages, though arguably an accurate reflection of the broader ideological tensions to which the developing home-help institution is subject.

Troubles-talk and Identity in Caring Contexts

Although there is an extensive literature on interaction and medical encounters generally (for example, see reviews by Street, 1991; West and Frankel, 1991), researchers have not systematically begun the task of analysing the discourses of the health and caring institutions as they involve *ageing* populations. Against this background, some recent exploratory studies have examined the identity consequences of talk to the elderly in domiciliary care and in long-stay hospitals for elderly people (Grainger, Atkinson and Coupland, 1990; see also N. Coupland, Grainger and Coupland, 1988). While these two settings and talk within them contrast along very many dimensions, they show some similarities in the ways in which *troubles-talk* by elderly care-receivers is managed and, in particular, *deflected* by care-givers. The data again raise questions to do with age- and health-identity for older people and the qualitative experience of care. In this section we review the Grainger et al. analysis of care-givers' deflection strategies as an important extension of the intergenerational PSD data reported in earlier chapters in everyday caring contexts.[2]

The sources for this study were 60 audio recordings of home help and client interactions (taking place in clients' own homes), and 30 audio recordings of nurse and patient interactions in three long-stay geriatric hospital wards. In both settings data were obtained through home helps or nurses carrying microrecorders over predetermined periods of time while performing their routine occupational tasks. Recordings were made with the informed consent of all participants and with the ethical approval of appropriate hospital and administrative authorities.

In medical and explicitly caring contexts, how elderly troubles-talk is managed takes on additional layers of social and political significance. Elderly people's telling of troubles to carers is open to multiple attributions and interpretations, for example, as the expression of more or less immediate medical or other caring needs or, at the other extreme, as fulfilling a stereotypically 'elderly' mode of talk. Responses to troubles-talk can achieve very diverse social processes: the provision of specific sorts of health care, the building of personal and professional relationships, the construction of personal, group and institutional identities.

In caring settings, where 'troubles' can span very local or enduring medical complaints as well as affective states, we clearly need to refine the gross notion of 'a trouble'. Grainger et al. assumed that response patterns would reflect the nature of the trouble so that it was important to isolate particular dimensions along which troubles could be located. For example, the *affective load* of a trouble is an estimate of how emotionally distressing the trouble is for an elderly person, either intrinsically or in the act of recounting it. Troubles may or may not relate to *physical or physiological* symptoms. Another dimension is the inferable *responsibility* for troubles remediation, because some troubles fall naturally within the spheres of professional competence of the people to whom they are addressed and others do not. For example, according to official, institutional criteria, auxiliary nurses and home helps (at least traditionally, see the previous section) are primarily responsible for non-medical dimensions of care, routine tasks such as preparing food, shopping, dressing and bathing. Still, their duties may be taken to include some responsibility for social welfare. Trained nursing staff are offically responsible for the more medical troubles.

A trouble's *temporal relevance* (is the trouble the source of a current discomfort or not?) may influence carers' perceptions of their obligation to provide any solution or mitigation. Grainger et al. also consider the *duration* of a trouble (is it a temporary or lasting illness, pain, etc.?), its *range* (is it restricted to the teller or to a wider class of subjects?) and the extent to which it is perceived as amenable to any solution, its *resolvability*. The general argument here is that care-givers' response strategies will reflect at least these perceptual dimensions of the troubles being told.

The term *deflection* is intended in a figurative sense of its dictionary definition: the action of turning, or state of being turned from, a straight line or regular course. That is, Grainger et al.'s analyses chart the various ways in which carers avoid fully and directly accepting the impact of their elderly charges' troubles-talk or its implications for future action. Instances of deflection, which are common in the two sets of conversational data, and the forms and contexts in which they occur give us some insight into the specific roles that interaction creates for carers and care recipients in these settings.

Predictably, local and medical troubles that have readily identifiable solutions can involve little or no deflection. So apparently treatable medical problems that are causing distress at the time of telling are often responded to supportively, with sympathy, understanding and the offer of a plausible solution. In the nursing context such concerns fall within the nurse's expertise and responsibilities (see extract 8.3).[3]

EXTRACT 8.3

```
1   P:  ... [crying] oh I didn't know I ((had it in me I'm in pain))
2  TN: I'll get you something for it now (1.5) shall I take give
3       you a tablet now? (.) would you like something now? a a
4       tablet for the pain? (.) all right I'll get it for you
5   P: I'll take anything as long as ((it doesn't hurt))
                                      [
6  TN:                               all right love
7       (.) all right
```

8   P: [*crying*] it's burning
          (2.0)
9 TN: is it your bottom?
10   P: it's driving me crazy
11 TN: mm (.) all right (.) I know what I can do for that (.) I've
12   got something for that . . .

Sequences like the one in extract 8.3 give us several verbal clues to a nurse's generally sympathetic orientation to the trouble, involving acknowledgements, requests for more information, invitations to express discomfort, attributions of a probable cause of the trouble, offers of plausible partial solutions, etc. But there are some instances of troubles-telling, still local and medical, where symptoms are probably amenable to treatment, where deflection does occur.

EXTRACT 8.4

1   P: I got a rotten cold
2 AN: I've got a cold as well Joe I think (.) caught it off
                                              [   ]
3   P: I think it's
4   ((all these)) draughts in this place
                                  [
5 AN: ((all of you)) (2.0)
6   [*sniffs*] no there's quite a few and I think once one
7   of you gets a cold (.) it's like=
              [   ]
8   P: yes
9 AN: =wildfire round the place (.) everybody gets a cold

In extract 8.4, AN's deflecting strategy is to try to reduce the load inherent in P's trouble by claiming that many other people, including AN herself, have also got a cold. Grainger et al. interpret this as an expanding of the 'range' of the trouble; as part of this process the complaint is depersonalized (notice the phrases 'all of you', 'there's quite a few' and 'one of you', emphasizing P's group membership in the institution). In this way, AN has *renegotiated* the trouble to a less serious level and as a result is perhaps under less pressure to respond with sympathy or to orient to a solution. AN here is not a trained nurse and may not have access to drugs, though she could hand on the complaint. Clearly, time and effort are at premium in this context and Grainger et al. assume AN may believe the complaint need not be given priority over the task of the moment (bathing P). It is interesting that P and AN *jointly* renegotiate the loading of the trouble when P agrees with AN's generalized framing of the complaint.

In the home-help context, predictably, solutions tend not to be offered to specifically health-focused troubles by carers who have no acknowledged medical expertise. In fact, the data reveal that responses here either make reference to a third party who might offer a solution (a doctor or a nurse) or provide a rationale for the trouble, accompanied by simple expressions of sympathy or empathy (see extract 8.5).

EXTRACT 8.5

```
 1 HH: are you any better this morning do you feel any better
                                                        [
 2 CL:                                               no (.) I
 3       do I do I don't feel a bit better (.) better
 4 HH: no (3.0) well anyroad the nurse is supposed to be c giving
 5       you a ring before she comes today
                                     [
 6 CL:                            yeah   (2.5) mm
 7 HH: she perhaps see she perhaps have seen the doctor for you
 8       you know
 9 CL: yeah (5.0) well it's that incontinent thing and then (.)
10       when I get on the toilet you know its (1.0) it's terrible
11       (.) black you know=
12 HH: =yeah well that's the iron you see you know I mean y you
13       get er (1.0) with iron
14 CL: everything's er
                     [
15 HH:             I had same myself when I was on iron you know
```

The handing on strategy is in its own way deflective, though entirely legitimate given the way the institution apportions its professional roles. The rationalization for the trouble in extract 8.5 ('yeah well that's the iron you see') also has a deflective function in that it removes some of the affective load from the trouble and reduces its seriousness. But in this case the effect is arguably soothing and reassuring. Other cases in the home-help data, however, show carers deflecting in diverse further ways, and again redefining troubles that are not obviously amenable to solution.

EXTRACT 8.6

```
1 CL: . . . I feel weak though you know I I (1.0) if I'd done
2        a hard day's I couldn't be ((more)) ((1 syllable))
3        . . . no different I don't seem to have any energy
4 HH: I think it does though doesn't it you know if you
5        keep getting a cold after cold it saps you
```

In extract 8.6 the open-ended trouble expressed by CL is trivialized when HH suggests there is a normal agency involved (getting a cold). This confines the trouble in both duration (implicitly, it will pass) and load (implicitly, it is a routine problem). There are many instances where minimizing a trouble is an explicitly negotiative effort. In extract 8.7 (from the hospital data) the two auxiliary nurses are about to put the elderly patient in the bath.

EXTRACT 8.7

```
 1 AN1: ((come on then)) let's get you in
 2 P: no no don't ((let me in))
 3 AN1: ((all right come on))
              [
 4 AN2:       that's a lovely bath (.) come on (.) two
 5            minutes and it'll be all over
 6 P: [moaning] oh
 7 AN2: there isn't that nice?
 8 P: no
 9 AN2: that's beautiful (.) come on you can go into bed then
10         (.) after you've had your bath
                      [        ]
11 P:                 [groans]
                      [
12 AN1:               down you go
13 P: [groaning] oh no
      [
14 AN2: there (.) there (.) it's lovely
             [    ]
15 P:        oh (.) mm oh no no
                    [
16 AN2:             there isn't that nice?
17 P: [quieter] no no
18 AN1: look at the bubbles
19 P: n n oh (.) oh
20 AN2: shut your eyes now Liz I'm going to wash your hair . . .
```

AN2 challenges P's perception of the bathing routine: it is 'a lovely bath', 'beautiful', 'lovely' and later 'nice', which will, furthermore, be only a brief penance (or a treat, depending upon the negotiative stance). Several of the strategies we identified (see figure 4.4) as moves towards closing PSD sequences – inversion, contextualization, face compensation and minimisation – surface again here. Notably, AN2 repeatedly seeks to invert the basis of the elderly resident's complaint, attempting to formulate a 'bright side' interpretation of events (cf. Jefferson, 1984b). Home helps similarly project bright responses to troubles told, routinely trying to relocate talk within a cheery key, as in the following two fragments.

EXTRACT 8.8

1 CL: oh dear I'm fed up (2.5)
2 HH ah you'll be all right (2.0) get them legs moving
3   (4.0) you'll be able to go out I'll be able t take
4   you town yourself

EXTRACT 8.9

1 CL: it's awful (.) terrible living on ((your own)) isn't it
2 HH: well Mrs Brent is home now so she'll probably pop in
3   to see you won't she?

Because there is a common assumption that elderly people must keep cheerful, home helps can claim there is some responsibility upon troubles tellers themselves not to break this code. In fact, reflexively, outlining the face-threatening nature of some troubles for recipients can come to function as a more elaborate deflecting strategy, as in the following instance.

EXTRACT 8.10

1 CL: ((1 syllable)) said if we hadn't agreed going on
2   ((our holidays)) ((2 syllables)) they ((can)) bury
3   me one day this week (7.5) she said what do you mean?
4   (.) I said because ((1 syllable)) I intend doing it
5   I'm intend doing it Kate I'll bloody do it=
6 HH: =oh go on now don't be starting that don't be saying
7   that to me when I'm here you'll have me all worried
8   to death

Some renegotiation of troubles can involve out-and-out contradiction, as in extract 8.11, where the nurses do not acknowledge that there can be different sensations of how cold or hot it is in the ward and therefore refuse to validate P's perception of his surroundings.

EXTRACT 8.11 [*P is being dried and dressed after a bath.*]

```
1    P:  I'm cold
2   AN:  you're cold? (.) it's like a sauna in here
3    P:  [coughs] (3.5) I'm cold nurse
4   AN:  well we'll have your jacket on now hang on a minute
5    P:  I'm cold nurse
6   TN:  shouldn't be
7   AN:  it's warm up here Albert
8    P:  ((it's cold though nurse))
9   AN:  ((it's not)) it's warm
10   P:  I'm cold anyway
              [        ]
11  AN:        are you?
12  TN:  soon have you in bed OK?
```

In contradicting the patient's perceptions, the nurses (strategically or not) relieve themselves of the need to address P's complaint, even though AN's offers (lines 4 and 12) of a resolution of the trouble in the near future ('we'll have your jacket on now' and 'soon have you in bed') tacitly recognize its validity.

In some cases contradiction can, of course, be a form of reassurance, and in more general terms Grainger et al. do *not* argue that deflection is always unwarranted or avoidable (and cf. Williams, Giles, Coupland, Dalby and Manasse's (1990) argument that low attuning by care-givers may in some circumstances *promote* positive health outcomes). All of the examples from the hospital context show troubles-talk being deflected by carers who are directly involved in the management of routine tasks – bathing, dressing, cleaning, etc. Deflection may be thought appropriate or necessary because getting on with the routine takes precedence over engaging with patients' troubles. We might therefore see deflection as a means of protecting the integrity and efficiency of the caring process itself. Often, the troubles being deflected arise out of the routines themselves, and if nurses did attend in more detail to the troubles expressed, established practices of 'good care' might suffer under pressures of time. It is perhaps not surprising, then, that troubles, and the speaking turns in which they occur, are sometimes ignored wholesale. In fact, getting on with the routine can be offered as an implicit account for not addressing the trouble in response, as in extract 8.12.

EXTRACT 8.12
[*P is in the bath being washed by Ns.*]

```
1   P: hurts my foot
2  TN: she's hurting your foot is she? (1.0) [laughs]
3  AN: cleaning your toes (2.5) cleaning in between your toes
```

The 'weightiest' troubles-telling sequences involve reports of acute depression, bitter expressions of global unhappiness and worries about death. In these instances carers cannot, certainly not without specific training, be expected to draw on unlimited resources for supportive responding. The possibilities of engaging with troubles telling here can be limited by carers' life experiences, maturity, emotional resolve or role-taking abilities. Response strategies may amount to a choice *among deflective* alternatives. Profound discontent-ment must be particularly threatening to nurses because they may carry inferences of blame: perhaps unwittingly, talk in this category raises an agenda of carers' responsibility for troubles that are almost certainly unresolvable. The nurse in the final extract we shall draw from Grainger et al.'s data (extract 8.13) confronts the paradox of needing to try to relieve P's distress and, therefore, having to try to modify P's perceptions of an enduring and global trouble; there is little option but to try to deflect a trouble that is not realistically amenable to deflection. N seems obliged to avoid telling P that she cannot go home and that she will probably die in hospital. She attempts to convey that the institution is P's home and that there are compensations to living there.

EXTRACT 8.13

```
1   P: oh I want to go home (1.0) [crying] ((where's my home
2      please?)) ((3-4 syllables))
3  TN: [quietly] I know (.) I know
4   P: ((where is it?))
5  TN: well this is your home now love
6   P: it isn't not forever (1.0) I don't want to stay here
7      (4.0) oh come on I'm cold
```

```
 8    P:   ((how long have I got to be here?))
 9   TN:   I don't know love (2.0) ((let's have this)) (3.0)
10    P:   ((not)) a long time is it? (3.0)
11   TN:   you've been with us now (.) what is it? eighteen
12         months? (.) about eighteen months
                    [
13    P:                  I (.) I haven't been here as long as that
14   TN:   haven't you?
15    P:   I hope I haven't [starts to cry] ((maybe I have though))
16   TN:   well Phillip [her son] comes to see you
17    P:   pardon?
18   TN:   Phillip comes to see you (.) and his wife
19    P:   [quietly] I know
20   TN:   so they know where you are don't they?
```

Outside of desperate cases like these where deflection seems to be a damage-limiting strategy, a major concern is that deflection may become a response-set (levity, minimization, generalization, denial, etc.) for 'dealing with' elderly talk about discomfort and other personal troubles in institutional settings. In the majority of instances that Grainger et al. consider, deflection seems to be highly censurable in interpersonal terms. To the extent that institutional pressures impinge on professional carers' communicative opportunities and practices, troubles deflecting may be to some extent inevitable. In evaluating nurse–patient talk, for example, we need to recognize how institutional frameworks constrain opportunities for talk and dictate modes of talk (cf. N. Coupland, Grainger and Coupland, 1988). The fact that nurses' involvement with elderly patients in long-stay hospitals consists almost exclusively of daily rounds of getting patients out of bed, dressing, bathing, administering drugs and providing meals inevitably reduces scope for focused interpersonal talk. At the same time, hospital routines themselves generate discomfort for patients and give rise to the telling of local troubles.

From the professionals' viewpoint, deflection might be seen as the most 'efficient' response strategies available to nurses if they are to keep within their role of caring professionals. The pervasively cheery manner that is considered to be a stereotypical feature of nurses' interactional style (Clark, 1981; Lanceley, 1985) may manage to signal positive affect without the nurse straying too far from the routine imposed on nurse and patient alike. Troubles-talk can certainly constitute a threat for nurses' role identity, arising out of a conflict of interests inherent in the job of a nurse in a long-stay geriatric ward – as both professional carer and capable and efficient worker or manager. The threat is not nearly so immediate for home helps, whose caring role is, in any case, institutionally less well consolidated, and whose work is intrinsically less intrusive and less regimented.

But if institutional considerations help us contextualize troubles deflecting, they do not mitigate the considerable impairment (as we interpret it) of the *quality* of elderly patients' experiences of interaction and of care. It is worth repeating the simple quantitive observation that for the institutionalized elderly, and often even for the elderly living in their own homes in the community, contact with professional carers can constitute the majority of available interactional experiences (cf. Nussbaum, Thompson and Robinson, 1989); for some long-stay hospital residents, they may, in fact, comprise the totality of these. In these circumstances we cannot ignore the multiply *alienating* function of routine deflection. In deflecting, carers regularly suggest and even insist on reformulations of elderly people's projections of their own experiences, states and sensations. Responding to troubles regularly asserts conflicting accounts of the elderly's already narrow environments. A bath that feels hot is 'in fact' cold; depression is 'the result of a cold'; weariness is a generic experience, and so on. There is a painful irony in documenting the conversational disorientating of populations for whom 'reality orientation' regimens, as a form of therapy, are commonplace. Relationally, deflection drives a wedge between care-recipients and care-givers, denying *each* group the potential fulfilment and health- and identity-bolstering of supportive discourse. In deflection we surely see one reason to believe that communication can be a factor in the 'survivability' of the nursing home environment (Nussbaum, 1990).

Because of the limited data-contexts that have as yet been studied, and in view of the contextual factors to be considered, we are not justified in making any generalized statements about the 'illegitimacy' of carers' deflecting responses to elderly troubles talk. On the other hand, and particularly if the data were to be replicated in other settings, we should be concerned that deflection strategies can epitomise some of the most disturbing interactional practices of care, potentially alienating elderly people, trivializing their worries and complaints, and subverting what would be construed as routinely accommodative discourse (cf. chapter 2) in other settings. Carers could profitably be made aware of these practices and their implications in their training. Therefore, we have another case of the need for relationships, language and interaction to be given explicit attention, ultimately as health concerns, in the gerontological context.

Epilogue

We are aware that in the course of this book we have probably stretched the conventional definition of sociolinguistics, to the extent there is one today. We have quite consciously attempted to maintain an interdisciplinary perspective, from the conviction that the (over)-descriptive tradition in sociolinguistics and the (over)theoretical bias of social psychology are, in their own ways, inadequate to understand the dynamics of intergenerational relations. We find it interesting that today, these paradigms are, in any case, equally under pressure to respect the realignment towards discourse and interaction that social studies generally have experienced in the 1980s.

But we do not want to end by voicing an appeal for more boundary hopping in the linguistic social sciences. This sort of appeal has too often been made, and ignored. Rather, we want to return to an extremely simple observation we made in the early pages of the book: that older people are underrepresented in *every* social area of language research. We hope therefore that this book will have helped to establish a research agenda for sociolinguistics in the broadest possible interpretation of that term. The social roles we require elderly people to play are rapidly changing, in the English-speaking world and far beyond; more and more older people are questioning the legitimacy and stability of these roles. Mapping the linguistic and discursive processes that will mirror and truly constitute the redefinitions of social ageing must be a sociolinguistic priority. In an academic climate where sociolinguistics is acknowledged to have made diverse but crucial contributions to the social scientific study of class, gender, ethnic and child studies, researchers of whatever subdiscipline urgently need to reconsider their neglect of our old folk and of their ageing selves.

Appendix

The issues we address in chapter 4 overlap with a line of conversation analysis research into troubles-talk: Jefferson, 1980, 1984a, 1984b, 1985; Lee and Jefferson, 1980. For purposes of comparison – to assess, on the one hand, the robustness, on the other hand, the context-specificity, of our own taxonomy – it will be valuable to summarize the basic schematization of troubles-talk (from Lee and Jefferson, 1980, pp. 10–11). We present these authors' structural summary (their 'candidate sequence') under their own category labels, adding some interpretive notes of our own, plus observations on overlaps and apparent inconsistencies with our own work. At the end of the appendix, we briefly discuss what appear to us to be the significant differences in focus between the two approaches as possible explanations for variation.

The candidate troubles-telling sequence

A Approach

1 Initiation
   (a) *Inquiry; for example, 'how are you today?'* Though the category overlaps with our 'direct elicitation', Lee and Jefferson's (L&J) data talk is between friends; hence, inquirers tend to know about ongoing troubles; if so, the issue of phaticity does not arise.
   (b) *Noticing; for example, 'do you have a sore throat?'* The noticing of possible trouble from paralinguistic features (hoarseness of

voice; coughing). Our schema would recognize this origin of talk on ill-health under the general category of textual determination. But between strangers (our data), there is, presumably, uncertainty about vocal characteristics being attributable to ill health or to setting (as permanent features of voice).

2   Trouble-premonitor
(a)   *Downgraded conventional response to inquiry; for example, 'oh, not so bad'; 'surviving I guess'* The speaker is orienting his or her co-participant to the presence or continuation of a trouble. This is a useful refinement of the structural account of disclosure initiations, which might be added to our taxonomy of pre-contexts to disclosure. L&J's category shows a subtle means by which disclosers-to-be may 'determine', in our sense, the disclosive outcome. However, familiars will be more predictably able or prepared to pick up on such subtle cueing, and we worry about the reliability of non-participants' (analysts') perceptions of these speech functions in context.
(b)   *Improvement marker*; for example, *'better'; 'much better'*. Again, not relevant to participants without a relational history. This category, as L&J's data show, will sometimes preface troubles talk, though we doubt it predicts it. Throughout, our own analysis tries to stress possible causal associations between pre-contexts and disclosive 'outcomes'; L&J's seems to favour structural observation.
(c)   *Lead-up*; for example, *'he went for his X-rays on Friday'; 'the next time you see me I'm gonna be looking like hell, you know why'*. This is said to be used in response to inquiry, but especially where talk about a trouble is being initiated by the teller. It indicates the presence of something 'untoward' and/or begins to tell the nature of the trouble. The category, like (a) above, can refine our analysis of the onset of disclosure, though it would fall within our phase 2 account of disclosures (themselves, not their pre-contexts).

3   Premonitor response
For example, *'mm', 'yeah', 'yes'* – a 'continuer' produced by recipients in order to show they are ready and expect to receive further talk. Just as our own analysis has not identified 'premonitors', so we have not distinguished a 'premonitor response' category. In our account these utterances are considered minimal back-channel moves by recipients during disclosures.

B Arrival

1 Announcement
For example, *'we got burgled yesterday'; 'her mother is terminal'; 'I had to have my toe-nail taken off'*. The equivalent of our core disclosure. It is interesting that L&J take announcements of troubles *not* to be integral elements of their delivery (the next major category). This suggests that, among familiars, to report painful experiences in summary form may be taken to be structurally incomplete; hence, another precursor to fuller telling. Such expectations are not clearly apparent in our own data-context, where 'announcements' may be the whole painful report, particularly in non-foregrounded disclosures; hence we see them as core elements, not in any sense precursory. This, importantly, suggests that functional categories and category systems are (and ought to be) altogether context-dependent.

2 Announcement response
For example, *'oh, really'; 'you did?'* – which elicits further talk on the trouble but does not necessarily 'align' the recipient with the teller; and, for example, *'nah, no'; 'oh shit!'* which 'commits' the recipient to the troubles-telling. Since for us these are responses to disclosures, they would feature as either neutral, sympathetic or empathetic minimal next-moves, the precise categorization depending heavily on prosodic enactment; cf. our stylistic encoding dimension (which L&J do not report, except in marking emphasis in the transcribed examples).

C Delivery

1 Exposition
Includes descriptions of 'symptoms', 'events', etc. This broad category is differentiated in our account under the various dimensions of elaboration: single versus chained; core versus core plus; minimal versus maximal detail.

2 Affiliation
For example, *'jesus!'; 'he's crazy!'; 'oh baby!'* Context again explains the non-occurrence of such emotional responses in our data. We suggest this general category of recipient utterances is

distributed across back-channelling and focused evaluative ('full') responses, depending on precise timing and details of encoding.

3   Affiliation response
For example, *'it just hurt so bad, Helen, I was crying'*. Emotionally heightened talk from the troubles-teller, giving descriptions of events, ailments, affective reaction to troubles. L&J note that C2 followed by C3 is not found in British data; even where C2 is found, C3 does not follow. C3 does not feature in our data either; necessarily, because we don't get emotional C2s.

D   Work-up
Consists of a range of activities including diagnoses, prognoses, reports of relevant other experiences, remedies, etc. The work-up positions the trouble by reference to more general circumstances so that talk starts out focused on the trouble but does not end up that way. Closure is becoming relevant, but not imminent. The work-up is achieved by teller *and/or* recipient, with no acknowledgement that quite different interactional motives, forces and consequences may be involved across these two conditions. To the extent that the unifying property of the work-up (to us, an otherwise amorphous category) is 'invoking the relevance of a move towards closure' (Lee and Jefferson 1980, p. 35), it seems difficult to differentiate the category, at least in functional terms, from E below. We suggest that a structurally based analysis like that of L&J may require the identification of multiple categories, while our more functional approach is happier to assign sequenced utterances to the same category when they are perceived to carry the same interactional force, albeit at different textual points.

E   Close implicature
1   Optimistic projection
For example, *'it'll iron itself out'*; *'I'm gonna be all right; the doctor says I'm doing fine.'* Examples (in the L&J discussion) in this category are all in the speech of tellers; to that extent, our nearest category is minimization as a discloser's move towards closing. Elderly disclosers in our data are probably less likely to be in a position to project optimistically, of course, in cases of severe health problems, sensory decrement, etc. However, recipients do, as we say, fabricate improbable solutions to (elderly) disclosers'

problems; cf., too, Jefferson 1984b, p. 363. The infelicitously labelled further possibility of 'substitute optimistic projection' (for example, *'whatever's to be's to be, that's all'*) is what we call resignation (by disclosers).

2 Invocation of the *status quo*
For example, *'oh God, we had the police round all night; it was hectic so I hardly got any work done.'* This re-engages the trouble with ordinary everyday activities, as shared by the two participants. In our data-context, of course, there is no such sharing, and *status quo* for them can be defined only as 'non-painful' talk. Once again, L&J's account does not distinguish participants' roles in achieving this. Hence, in our taxonomy, we identify a variety of perspective-changing and topic-shifting strategies variously used by disclosers and recipients.

3 Making light of the trouble
For example, *'well, you probably got at least a week . . . a week before you die.'* Again, either participant is said to make light of troubles, and generally involving laughter. Laughter does not occur in our data in connection with disclosure, though we do note instances where disclosers use a 'light' key in the course of disclosing. Certainly recipients in our data do not make light of troubles, beyond their attempts to invert and contextualize painful disclosures.

F Exit

1 Boundarying off
(a) *Conversation closure* – in the context of telephone calls, hanging up. Troubles-telling frequently occurs as topic of last exchanges of conversations in L&J's data. Quoted instances show confusing overlap with later subcategories; hanging up does not appear to be structurally prior to, or an alternative to, say, 'reference to getting together' (cf. below).
(b) *Conversation restart* A switch of topic (our subcategory) is brought about (clearly within the same conversation, in the more usual sense, though embarking on a quite new transactional field) by either participant.
(c) *Introduction of pending biographicals* A topic switch to an especially warranted new topic of prior concern to both. In relation to what we term both switches and shifts, it is important to

note the quite different underlying assumptions operative in the two data-contexts. Participants in L&J's data have a shared background of interpersonal knowledge, which can render what for our participants would be major switches in topics more like shifts – to different but already consolidated areas of common experience. The solitary effect of the topic changes L&J identify in this category cannot, therefore, be achieved in our data, where participants can manipulate interpersonal distance only symbolically, through degrees of discoursal accommodation.

(d)   *Reference to getting together;* for example, *'can you come out for a drink tonight?'; 'maybe next weekend if you and Freddy want to come up'* This established conversation closing strategy has a particular appositeness in the context of post-troubles-telling, showing affiliation. Since it is true (cf. above) that troubles-telling tends to be conversation-closing, it seems difficult to identify reference to getting together as part of the management of troubles-sequence-closing, rather than conversation closing as a whole.

2   Step-wise transition into other topics (cf. Jefferson, 1984a)
This detailed schematization is a particularly valuable elaboration of what our taxonomy simply labels as topic shifts and assigns to either participant. The model of progressive, interactive achieve-ment of topic transition is certainly likely to be a better reflection of the textual subtleties of moving out of painful self-disclosure, though we would still want to interpret the significance of each participant's efforts towards achieving closure.

Overall, then, several of the categories in Lee and Jefferson's and our own framework are motivated in direct response to the different interactional settings of talk – public versus private; involving strangers versus familiars. The relational histories of L&J's co-participants are a background against which new troubles (or new aspects of old troubles) are intrinsically salient and a highly predictable topic for talk. The structural development of troubles-telling can directly reflect this, as when 'noticed' paralinguistic cues can trigger elicitations of painful reports, or when troubles are 'announced' prior to being detailed. Our own starting point has been the assumption that, in our context, *any* recounting of, or even reference to, own painful experiences is interactionally 'charged' and salient – it is disclosive, a term not obviously appropriate to L&J's troubles-telling. The troubles-telling phone calls are more updates than self-disclosures, and less presentationally focused, hardly relevant to the projection and perception of social categories.

Beyond this, L&J's analytic focus is principally the structural mechanics of talk, as the shared construction of social events. Troubles-talk is discussed in terms of 'a progression through a template ordering' which 'constitutes an elegant and effective machinery by which the polar and competing relevancies of attention to business as usual and attention to the troubles can be managed' (Lee and Jefferson, 1980, p. 71). On the other hand, we have developed our taxonomy as a preliminary effort toward understanding interpersonal and intergroup processes, which requires us, *above all*, to attend to precisely *what* contributions to ordering are made *when*, *by whom*, even *why*, and *with what consequences*.

From the outset, we have conceptualized the disclosure of painful experiences as a locus for problematical interchange, within and across the generations. This focus is almost altogether lacking from L&J's discussion, not least because of the established relationships in which troubles-telling is exemplified. The troubles themselves are occasionally severe, including reports of terminal illness and hospital operations, as they are in our own data. But recipients in our context are exposed, unwittingly, to self-disclosures, and however resourceful they may be interactionally, they do not have the resource of relational back-up. Again, however, there is a difference of intention, even beyond the contextual disparities. When L&J do recognize interactional 'problems' occurring, it is interpreted in relation to sequence, not to participants. For example, extracts that show a recipient being 'troubles-resistive' (seeking to avoid being told a trouble) are discussed in terms of the interactants' being 'improperly aligned', which will result in the segment being 'topically and sequentially deranged' (p. 75). Disruption of the candidate sequence is a major consideration in the 1980 report, but its relation to *experienced* disruption (does the candidate sequence have any psychological validity as participants' preferred model of how troubles-telling will, or even should, best proceed?) is not at all clear. Lee and Jefferson, in fact, acknowledge that their ordering is 'not an index of problems in the running off of the sequence'. They do say it represents 'how the sequence ought to run' (p. 71), but is this as a descriptive generalization or a felt preference, whereby actors 'suffer' if the sequence is not fulfilled?

It is not that our taxonomy achieves this, but that we hope it may have some limited advantages over Lee and Jefferson's sequence in modelling interactional alternatives that can, as we intend, be taken into more explicitly evaluative empirical studies of responses to, and effects of, the disclosure of painful experiences.

Notes

Chapter 2   *Discourse, Accommodation and Intergenerational relations*

1 Sequences of talk in this and later chapters have been transcribed according to the following conventions:

● Conventional orthography is used wherever possible, though without capital letters (except in proper names and 'I') and generally without punctuation. However, questions marks and exclamation marks are retained as a rough indication of the illocutionary force of utterances.
● Identifying names and other information is replaced with fictional initials and/or an explanatory gloss.
● Syllables in italics receive heavy stress.
● Overlapping speech is marked by vertical alignment of text linked by square brackets.
● Brief (unmeasurable) pauses are shown as (.). Longer, measured pauses are timed in seconds, for example (2.0).
● Adjacent utterances that are 'latched' (end-to-end without an intervening pause) are linked with =.
● Inaudible sequences are marked as ((   )); where the number of syllables is identifiable, or where possible but uncertain interpretations are made, these are indicated within the double brackets; for example, ((2 syllables)).
● Commentaries on non-verbal, prosodic or paralinguistic features are given in italics within square brackets.

2 One of us is currently investigating the issues of vitality and institutional support of the elderly, and how these factors vary across cultures, in research with Susan Fox.

Chapter 3   *Formulating Age: Discursive Dimensions of Age Identity*

1 The following section derives from an extensive review of exisiting social psychological treatments of age identity written by Karen Henwood. We

gratefully acknowledge this source, though responsibility for the consequences of abstracting from it is entirely our own.

2   In the extracts and data fragments, numbers prefaced by I identify particular interactions; numbers prefaced by E and Y identify 'elderly' and 'young' participating individuals, respectively. Personal names and identifying place-names in extracts throughout the book are fictionalized.

3   There are at least two considerations in the interpretation of this particular instance: first, it is interesting that the 'old' self-categorization is invoked to a young interlocutor, whereas the out-group use of 'old' is to an elderly peer; second, it seems that projecting self as 'old' in this instance might well be a strategic self-presentation, perhaps inviting denial (as we suggest below).

4   This comment seems to make implicit reference to the medical profession's category label for childbearing women over the age of 27 (in our own cultural context, at least); the label is: 'geriatric mothers'.

Chapter 4   *'My Life in Your Hands': Processes of Intergenerational Self-disclosure*

1   At various points in this chapter (and in chapters 5 and 8), we cross- reference between our own analyses of painful self-disclosure (PSD) and Jefferson and colleagues' conversation analytic approach to 'troubles-telling'. Although Jefferson et al.'s research is a very rich source and valuably extends our own work, the two approaches have been developed independently and differ somewhat in their underlying goals and assumptions. The Appendix reviews the troubles-talk literature and highlights the points at which our own work on PSD differs from it.

2   Matters of coding reliability are not usually addressed in interpretive analysis of this sort, though we realize disciplines differ in the standards of self-justification researchers are required to meet. We certainly recognize that analysts, but also participants in interaction, may sometimes be unable to assign utterances uniquely to categories; this is a limitation of the taxonomic approach we adopt here.

3   Jefferson (1984b, p. 363) also notes the propensity of recipients in her data to propound extravagantly optimistic reassurances.

4   Miller, Berg and Archer (1986) have introduced the notion of conversational 'openers' to identify people who are particularly skilled in enabling self-disclosure, inducing others to 'open up'.

Chapter 5   *Troubles-telling, Facework and Age Identity*

1   Individual sequences were timed to 0.001 minutes and include all talk on the particular PSD topic with whatever filled and unfilled pauses (of up to 0.02 minute) occurred within that span. Raw scores for each cell (two-minute period) of tables 5.1 to 5.3 are, of course, recoverable by doubling the pecentage shown and reading as × 0.01 minute.

2   Statistical checks (ANOVAs on amount of time devoted to PSD) on these observations were made wherever possible. We are grateful to Karen Henwood,

whose quantitative analyses are briefly summarized in this note. A 2×5 ANOVA (first factor 'age' (between subjects); second factor 'time period' (within subjects)) was performed on the intergenerational data (see table 5.1) and another 2×5 ANOVA (same variables) on the peer-generational data (tables 5.2 and 5.3). Checks were not made, however, to compare the amount of PSD by each age group separately in intergenerational versus peer contexts. This was considered inappropriate given the disparity in number of observations between the two contexts: twice as many intergenerationally as in the peer contexts. Observations 4 and 5 therefore are not statistically corroborated. Not surprisingly, a highly significant main effect for age was found ($F = 21.64$; df $= 1, 38$; p $= 0.00$) for the intergenerational data. Hence, observation 3 is strongly supported. In the peer-generational context the main effect for age is only marginally significant ($F = 3.91$; df $= 1, 18$; p $= 0.06$). This may be partly attributable to the lower number of observations in the peer context. With respect to observation 6, no significant differences were found for effect of time period, nor were any significant interactions found between age and period. The relevant numerical values here are, for the intergenerational context main effect of period, $F = 0.23$; df $= 4, 152$; p $= 0.92$; for the intergenerational context age $\times$ period interaction, $F = 0.22$; df $= 4, 152$; p $= 0.93$; for the peer generational context main effect of period, $F = 0.42$, df $= 4, 72$; p $= 0.79$; and for the peer generational age $\times$ period interaction, $F = 0.23$; df $= 4, 72$; p $= 0.92$. Again, then, the observation is upheld.

3 In table 5.8 all PSDs within a chain, including the first, are counted as chained; in table 5.6, only the second and subsequent PSDs in a chain are shown as having 'own previous PSD' as a pre-context. Hence the score differences.

4 An interesting further qualification is that where elderly PSDs are structurally elaborated, they are nevertheless longer and more complex than those of the young.

5 It is therefore surprising, given Brown and Levinson's generally comprehensive documentation of instances, that their discussion makes no direct reference to self-disclosure in (i), (ii), (iii) on pp. 70–1 of the 1978 edition, though it perhaps does enter the category of Speaker threatening Hearer's positive face in 'expressions of violent emotions' (p. 71, ii, (a); or p. 72 (b); note also 'self-humiliation' on p. 73 (d); and the reference to 'pain' on p. 83).

Chapter 6 Telling Age in Later Life: A Strategic Analysis

1 Some current examples of the genre carry messages such as: 'Twenty-nine again??'; 'Forty isn't old . . . if you're a tree'; 'Still sporty at forty'; 'Still nifty at fifty'; 'Still sexy at sixty'; and 'Happy birthday to a unique person . . . most people your age are dead'.

2 Interviewers were, in fact, trained, for purposes beyond our immediate interests here, to question interviewees in accordance with very precise encoding guidelines, with prosodic uniformity as well as identical forms of words in scripted initial exchanges.

3 To claim that the young woman's assumptions are 'ageist' at this point is not to

accept that the elderly themselves do not possibly conspire in sustaining ageism (as, for example, in the accounting pattern discussed above in relation to E2 in extract 6.1).

Chapter 7   Intergenerational Talk: Consonance or Conflict

1   The evaluative study data were gathered, transcribed and analysed by Karen Henwood. We gratefully acknowledge this in reproducing some of the data and analyses developed in conjunction with her in this context.
2   Participants in the group discussions are referenced by pairs of, again, fictitious, initials. R designates the researcher leading the discussion groups. Individual group discussions are identified with the prefix GD.
3   Stereotypes of old age have been widely researched, cf. Braithwaite, 1986; Branco and Williamson, 1982; Brubaker and Powers, 1976; McTavish, 1971; Rosencrantz and McNevin, 1969; Sigall and Page, 1971. The discourse analytic perspective we are adopting here does not mesh well with these predominantly experimental and questionnaire-based studies. They have, for example, tended to use a restricted set of descriptive labels that do not relate easily to ascriptions of the elderly made by particular groups in contexts. See chapter 1 for a discussion of the language attitudes tradition of stereotype research.
4   See Tracy (1991) and Tracy and Coupland (1990) for a discussion of the complex relationship between goals and discourse generally.

Chapter 8   Sociolinguistics and Gerontology: Applied Concerns

1   The following analysis of ideological representations of accommodation processes in the home-help context was developed with Karen Atkinson, based on her own observational and interview data.
2   This section of the chapter draws extensively on data gathered by, and analyses developed with, Karen Grainger and Karen Atkinson in their doctoral research. We gratefully acknowledge their major contributions, therefore, to this discussion, and to this chapter generally.
3   Participants in the long-stay hospital data are identified by the abbreviations TN (trained nurse), AN (auxiliary nurse), N (nurse) and P (patient). Home-help encounters are shown using the abbreviations HH and CL (clients). Numerals after one of these abbreviations (TN1, TN2, etc.) identify nurses as different participants in particular extracts, not as uniquely labelled individuals.

References

Adams, C., Labouvie-Vief, G., Hobart, C. J. and Dorosz, M. (1990) Adult age group differences in story recall style. *Journal of Gerontology* 45, 1, 17–27.

Adelman, R., Greene, M. G. and Charon, R. (in press) Issues in elderly patient–physician interaction. *Ageing and Society*.

Ainley, S. C. and Redfoot, D. L. (1982) Ageing and identity-in-the-world: A phenomenological analysis. *International Journal of Ageing and Human Development*, 15, 1–15.

Arkin, R. M. and Baumgardner, A. H. (1985) Self-handicapping. In J. H. Harvey and G. Weary (eds), *Attribution: Basic Issues and Applications*, Orlando, Fla: Academic, 169–202.

Ashburn, G. and Gordon, A. (1981) Features of a simplified register in speech to elderly conversationalists. *International Journal of Psycholinguistics*, 8, 7–31.

Atkinson, J.M. and Heritage, J. (eds), (1984) *Structures of Social Action: Studies in Conversation Analysis*. Cambridge: CUP.

Atkinson, K. and Coupland, N. (1988) Accommodation as ideology. *Language and Communication*, 8, 3/4 321–8.

Barbato, C. A. and Feezel, J. D. (1987) The language of aging in different age-groups. *The Gerontological Society of America*, 27, 4, 527–31.

Bayles, K. A. and Kaszniak, A. W. (1987) *Communication and Cognition in Normal Aging and Dementia*. London: Taylor and Francis.

Baxter, L. A. and Wilmot, W. W. (1984) 'Secret texts': Social strategies for acquiring information about the state of the relationship. *Human Communication Research*, 11, 171–202.

Beasley, D. S. and Davis, G. A. (eds), (1981) *Aging: Communication Processes and Disorders*. New York: Grune and Stratton.

Bengston, V. L. (1973) *The Social Psychology of Aging*. New York: Bobbs-Merrill.

Bengston, V. L., Kasschau, P. L. and Ragan, P. K. (1977) The impact of social structure on aging individuals. In J. E. Birren and K. W. Schaie (eds), *Handbook of the Psychology of Aging*. New York: Van Nostrand Reinhold.

Bengston, V. L. and Kuypers, J. (1971) Generational differences and the developmental stake. *Aging and Human Development*, 2, 246–60.

Bengston, V. L., Reedy, M. N. and Gordon, C. (1985) Aging and self-conceptions, personality processes and social contexts. In J. E. Birren and K. Warner Schaie (eds), *Handbook of Psychology and Aging*. New York: Van Nostrand Reinhold, 544–93.

Berger, C. R. (1979) Beyond initial interaction: Uncertainty, understanding, and the development of interpersonal relationships. In H. Giles and R. N. St. Clair (eds), *Language and Social Psychology*. Oxford: Basil Blackwell, 122–44.

Berger, C. R. and Bradac, J. S. (1983) *Language and Social Knowledge: Uncertainty in Interpersonal Relationships*. London: Edward Arnold.

Berger, P. and Luckmann, T. (1967) *The Social Construction of Reality*. Harmondsworth: Penguin.

Berman, L. and Sobkowska-Ashcroft, I. (1986) The old in language and literature. *Language and Communication*, 6, 1/2, 139–45.

Blau, Z. S. (1956) Changes in status and age identification. *American Sociological Review*, 21, 198–203.

Boden, D. and Bielby, D. (1983) The past as resource: A conversational analysis of elderly talk. *Human Development*, 26, 308–19.

Boden, D. and Bielby, D. (1986) The way it was: Topical organisation in elderly conversation. *Language and Communication*, 6, 73–89.

Boone, D. R., Bayles, K. A. and Koopmann, C. F. Jr (1982) Communicative aspects of aging. *Otolaryngologic Clinics of North America*, 15, 2, 313–27.

Borgatta, E. F. and Montgomery, R. J. V. (1987) Aging policy and societal values. In E. F. Borgatta and R. J. V. Montgomery (eds.) *Critical Issues in Aging Policy: Linking Research and Values*. Newbury Park, Calif: Sage, 7–27.

Bradac, J. J. (1982) A rose by any other name: Attitudinal consequences of lexical variation. In E. B. Ryan and H. Giles (eds), *Attitudes Towards Language Variation: Social and Applied Contexts*. London: Edward Arnold, 99–115.

Braithwaite, V. A. (1986) Old age stereotypes: Reconciling contradictions. *Journal of Gerontology*, 41, 3, 353–60.

Branco, K. J. and Williamson, J. B. (1982) The stereotyping process and the life-cycle: Views of aging and the aged. In A. G. Miller (ed), *In The Eye of the Beholder: Contemporary Issues in Stereotyping*, New York: Praeger.

Brewer, M. B., Dull, V. and Lui, L. (1981) Perceptions of the elderly: Stereotypes as prototypes. *Journal of Personality and Social Psychology* 41, 656–70.

Brown, J. and Rogers, L. E. (1991) Openness, uncertainty and intimacy: An epistemological reformulation. In N. Coupland, H. Giles and J. Wiemann (eds), *"Miscommunication" and Problematic Talk*, Newbury Park, Calif: Sage, 146–65.

Brown, P. and Levinson, S. (1978) Universals in language usage: Politeness phenomena. In E. N. Goody (ed.), *Questions and Politeness*, Cambridge: CUP, 56–289.

Brown, P. and Levinson, S. (1987) *Politeness: Some Universals in Language Usage*. Cambridge: CUP.

Brown, P. and Yule, G. (1983) *Discourse Analysis*. Cambridge: CUP.

Brown, R. (1977) Introduction. In C. E. Snow and C. A. Ferguson (eds), *Talking to Children: Language Input and Acquisition*, Cambridge: CUP, 1–12.

Brubaker, T. H. and Powers, E. A. (1976) The stereotype of 'old': A review and alternative approach. *Journal of Gerontology*, 31, 4, 441–7.

Bultena, G. L. and Powers, E. A. (1978) Denial of ageing: Age identification and reference group orientation. *Journal of Gerontology*, 33, 748–54.

Bunzel, J. H. (1972) Note on the history of a concept: Gerontophobia. *Gerontologist*, 12, 116–203.

Butler, R. N. (1969) Age-ism: another form of bigotry. *Gerontologist*, 9, 243–6.

Caporael, L. (1981) The paralanguage of caregiving: baby talk to the institutionalized aged. *Journal of Personality and Social Psychology*, 40, 5, 876–84.

Caporael, L., Lucaszewski, M. P. and Culbertson, G. H. (1983) Secondary baby talk: Judgements by institutionalized elderly and their caregivers. *Journal of Personality and Social Psychology*, 44, 4, 746–54.

Caporael, L. and Culbertson, G. H. (1986) Verbal response modes of baby talk and other speech at institutions for the aged. *Language and Communication*, 6, 1/2, 99–112.

Carver, C. S. and de la Garza, N. H. (1984) Schema-guided information search in stereotyping of the elderly. *Journal of Applied Social Psychology*, 14, 69–81.

Chappell, N. L. and Orbach, H. L. (1986) Socialisation in old age: A Meadian perspective. In V. W. Marshall (ed.), *Later Life: The Social Psychology of Ageing*, London: Sage.

Cicourel, A. (1973) *Cognitive Sociology*. Harmondsworth: Penguin.

Clark, J. (1981) Communication in nursing. *Nursing Times*, 77, 12–18.

Clarke, L. (1984) *Domiciliary Services for the Elderly*. London: Croom Helm.

Cline, R. (1986) The effects of biological sex and psychological gender on reported behavioural intimacy and control of self-disclosure. *Communication Quarterly*, 34, 41–54.

Clyne, M. (1977) Bilingualism of the elderly. *Talanya*, 4, 45–65.

Coates, J. (1986) *Women, Men and Language*. London: Longman.

Cody, M. J. and McLaughlin, M. L. (1990) Interpersonal accounting. In H. Giles and W. P. Robinson (eds), *Handbook of Language and Social Psychology*. Chichester: Wiley, 227–56.

Cohen, G. and Faulkner, D, (1986) Does 'elderspeak' work? The effect of intonation and stress on comprehension and recall of spoken discourse in old age. *Language and Communication*, 6, 1/2, 91–8.

Cohen, S., Sherrod, D. R. and Clark, M. S. (1986) Social skills and the stress-protective role of social support. *Journal of Personality and Social Psychology*, 50, 963–73.

Cole, T. R. and Gadow, S. A. (eds), (1986) *What does it mean to grow old?: Reflections from the Humanities*. Durham, NC: Duke University Press.

Coleman, P. G. (1989) *Ageing and Reminiscence Processes: Social and Clinical Implications*. Chichester: Wiley.

Cooper, P. V. (1990) Discourse production and normal aging: Performance on oral picture description tasks. *Journal of Gerontology (Psychological Sciences)*, 45, 5, 210–14.

Coulmas, F. (1981) *Conversational Routine: Explorations in Standardized Communication Situations and Prepatterned Speech*. Amsterdam: Mouton.

Coulthard, M. and Montgomery, M. (eds), (1982) *Studies in Discourse Analysis*. London: Routledge and Kegan Paul.

Coupland, J. (1989) Review of B. B. Dreher *Communication Skills for Working with Elders*, New York: Springer, 1987; and R. Gravell *Communication Problems in Elderly People: Practical Approaches to Management*, London: Croom Helm, 1988. *Journal of Language and Social Psychology*, 8, 2, 155–60.

Coupland, J., Coupland, N., Giles, H. and Henwood, K. (in press) Formulating age: The management of age identity in intergenerational talk. *Discourse Processes*.

Coupland, J., Coupland, N., Giles, H. and Wiemann, J. (1988) My life in your hands: Processes of self-disclosure in intergenerational talk. In N. Coupland (ed.), *Styles of Discourse*, London: Croom Helm, 201–53.

Coupland, J., Coupland, N. and Grainger, K. (in press) Intergenerational discourse: Contextual 'versions' of ageing and elderliness. *Ageing and Society*.

Coupland, J., Nussbaum, J. and Coupland, N. (1991) Miscommunication and older adults. In N. Coupland, H. Giles and J. Wiemann (1991) *'Miscommunication' and Problematic Talk*. Newbury Park, Calif.: Sage, pp. 85–102.

Coupland, N. (1983) Patterns of encounter management: Further arguments for discourse variables. *Language in Society* 12, 459–76.

Coupland, N. (ed.) (1988) *Styles of Discourse*. London: Croom Helm.

Coupland, N. and Coupland, J. (1989) Age identity and elderly disclosure of chronological age. *York Papers in Linguistics*, 13, 77–88.

Coupland, N. and Coupland, J. (1990) Language and later life: The diachrony and decrement predicament. In H. Giles and W. P. Robinson (eds), *Handbook of Language and Social Psychology*, Chichester: Wiley, 451–68.

Coupland, N., Coupland, J. and Giles, H. (1989) Telling age in later life: Identity and face implications. *Text*, 9, 2, 129–51.

Coupland, N., Coupland, J. and Giles, H. (eds), (in press) *Sociolinguistic Issues in Ageing*. 1991 issue of *Ageing and Society*.

Coupland, N., Coupland, J., Giles, H. and Henwood, K. (1988) Accommodating the elderly: Invoking and extending a theory. *Language in Society*, 17, 1 1–42.

Coupland, N., Coupland, J., Giles, H. and Henwood, K. (1991) Intergenerational talk: Goal consonance and intergroup dissonance. In K. Tracy (ed.), *Understanding Face-to-face Interaction: Issues Linking Goals and Discourse*, Hillsdale, NJ: Lawrence Erlbaum.

Coupland, N., Coupland, J., Giles, H., Henwood, K. and Wiemann, J. (1988) Elderly self-disclosure: Interactional and intergroup issues. *Language and Communication*, 8, 2, 109–33.

Coupland, N. and Giles, H. (eds), (1988) *Communication Accommodation Theory: Recent Developments*. Special issue of *Language and Communication*, 8, 3/4.

Coupland, N., Giles, H. and Benn, W. (1986) Language, communication and the blind: Research agenda. *Journal of Language and Social Psychology*, 5, 52–63.

Coupland, N., Giles, H. and Wiemann, J. (1991) *"Miscommunication": Problem Talk in Context*. Newbury Park, Calif.: Sage.

Coupland, N., Grainger, K. and Coupland, J. (1988) (Review article) Politeness in context: Intergenerational issues. Review of P. Brown and S. C. Levinson (1987) *Politeness: Some Universals in Language Usage* Cambridge: CUP. *Language in Society*, 17, 2, 253–62.

Coupland, N., Henwood, K., Coupland, J. and Giles, H. (1990) Accommodating troubles-talk: The young's management of elderly self-disclosure. In G. McGregor and R. White (eds), *Reception and Response: Hearer Creativity and the Analysis of Spoken and Written Texts*. London: Croom Helm, 112–44.

Coupland, N. and Nussbaum, J. (eds), (in preparation) *Discourse and Lifespan Development*.

Covey, H. C. (1988) Historical terminology used to represent older people. *The Gerontologist* 28, 291–7.

Cozby, P. C. (1973) Self-disclosure: A literature review. *Psychological Bulletin*, 79, 73–91.

Crockett, W. H., Press A. N. and Osterkamp, M. (1979) The effects of deviations from stereotyped expectations upon attitudes·toward older persons. *Journal of Gerontology*, 34, 368–74.

Culbertson, G. H. and Caporael, L. (1983) Baby talk speech to the elderly: Complexity and content of messages. *Personality and Social Psychology Bulletin*, 9, 305–12.

Cumming, E. and Henry, W. E. (1961) *Growing Old: The Process of Disengagement*. New York: Basic Books.

Cummings, J. L., Benson, D. F., Hill, M. and Read, S. (1985) Aphasia in dementia of the Alzheimer type. *Neurology*, 34, 394–7.

De Paulo, B. M. and Coleman, L. M. (1986) Talking to children, foreigners and retarded adults. *Journal of Personality and Social Psychology*, 51, 945–59.

Doise, W. (1978) *Groups and Individuals: Explorations in Social Psychology*. Cambridge: CUP.

Dreher, B. B. (1987) *Communication Skills For Working With Elders*. New York: Springer.

Duck, S. (1982) A topography of relationship disengagement and dissolution. In S. Duck (ed.), *Personal Relationships 4: Dissolving Personal Relationships*. London: Academic Press, 141–62.

Dunkel-Shetter, C. and Wortman, C. B. (1982) The interpersonal dynamics of cancer: Problems in social relationships and their impact on the patient. In H. S. Friedman and M. R. DiMatteo (eds), *Interpersonal Issues in Health-Care*, New York: Academic, 60–100.

Emery, O. (1986) Linguistic decrement in normal ageing. *Language and Communication*, 6, 1/2, 47–64.

Emery, O. and Emery, P. (1983) Language in senile dementia of the Alzheimer type. *Psychiatric Journal of University of Ottawa*, 8, 169–78.

Feier, C. and Gerstman, L. (1980) Sentence comprehension abilities throughout the adult life span. *Journal of Gerontology*, 35, 722–8.

Ferguson, C. A. (1977) Baby talk as a simplified register. In C. E. Snow and C. A. Ferguson (eds), (1977) *Talking to Children: Language Input and Acquisition*, Cambridge: CUP, 219–36.

Ferguson, C. A. (1981) 'Foreigner Talk' as the name of a simplified register. *International Journal of the Sociology of Language*, 28, 9–18.

Festinger, L. (1954) A theory of social comparison processes. *Human Relations*, 7, 117–40.

Fisher, S. and Todd, A. (ed.) (1986) *Discourse and Institutional Authority: Medicine, Education and Law*. Norwood, NJ: Ablex.

Franklyn-Stokes, A., Harriman, J., Giles, H. and Coupland, N. (1988) Information seeking across the life span. *Journal of Social Psychology*, 128, 3, 419–21.

Gergen, K. J. (1985) The social constructionist movement in modern psychology. *American Psychologist*, 40, 3, 266–75.

Gergen, K. J. and Davis, K. E. (1985) *The Social Construction of the Person*. New York: Springer Verlag.

Giles, H. (1973) Accent mobility: A model and some data. *Anthropological Linguistics*, 15, 87–105.

Giles, H. (1979) Ethnicity markers in speech. In K. R. Scherer and H. Giles (eds), *Social Markers in Speech*. Cambridge: CUP. 251–90.

Giles, H. (ed.) (1984) *The Dynamics of Speech Accommodation*. (*International Journal of the Sociology of Language*, 46) Amsterdam: Mouton.

Giles, H. and Coupland, N. (1991a) *Language: Contexts and Consequences*. Milton Keynes: Open University Press.

Giles, H. and Coupland, N. (1991b) Language attitudes: Discursive, contextual and gerontological considerations. In A. G. Reynolds (ed.), *McGill Conference on Bilingualism, Multiculturalism and Second Language Learning: A Tribute to Wallace E. Lambert*, Hillsdale, NJ: Lawrence Erlbaum, 21–42.

Giles, H., Coupland, N. and Coupland, J. (eds), (1991) *Contexts of Accommodation: Developments in Applied Sociolinguistics*. Cambridge: CUP.

Giles, H., Coupland, N. and Wiemann, J. (eds), (1990) *Communication, Health and the Elderly. (Proceedings of Fulbright Colloquium 1988)*. Manchester: Manchester University Press.

Giles, H., Henwood, K., Coupland, N., Harriman, J. and Coupland, J. (submitted) Language Attitudes and Cognitive Mediation. *Human Communication Research*.

Giles, H. and Hewstone, M. (1982) Cognitive structures, speech and social situations: Two integrative models. *Language Sciences*, 4, 187–219.

Giles, H., Mulac, A., Bradac, J. and Johnston, P. (1987) Speech accommodation theory: The first decade and beyond. In M. L. McLaughlin (ed.), *Communication Yearbook 10*. Beverly Hills, Calif.: Sage, 13–48.

Giles, H. and Powesland, P.F. (1975) *Speech Style and Social Evaluation*. London: Academic Press.

Giles, H. and Ryan, E.B. (eds), (1986) *Language, Communication and the Elderly*. Special double issue of *Language and Communication*, 6, 1/2, Oxford: Pergamon Press.

Goethals, G. R. (1986) Social comparison theory: Psychology from the lost and found. *Personality and Social Psychology Bulletin*, 12, 261–78.

Goffman, E. (1955) On facework: An analysis of ritual elements in social interaction. *Psychiatry*, 18, 213–31.

Goffman, E. (1959) *The Presentation of Self in Everyday Life*. New York: Garden City.

Gold, D., Andres, D., Arbuckle, T. and Schwartzman, A. (1988) Measurements and correlates of verbosity in elderly people. *Journal of Gerontology: Psychological Sciences*, 43, 2, 27–33.

Goodglass, H. and Kaplan, E. (1972) *The Assessment of Aphasia and Related Disorders*. Philadelphia: Lea and Febiger.

Gordon, C. and Gergen, K. J. (1968) *The Self in Social Interaction*. New York: Wiley.

Gordon, S. K. and Clark, W. C. (1974) Application of signal detection theory to prose recall and recognition in elderly and young adults. *Journal of Gerontology*, 29, 64–72.

Grainger, K., Atkinson, K. and Coupland, N. (1990) Responding to the elderly: Troubles talk in the caring context. In H. Giles. N. Coupland and J. Wiemann (eds), *Communication, Health and Ageing (Proceedings of Fulbright International Colloquium 1988)*, Manchester: Manchester University Press, 192–212.

Gravell, R. (1988) *Communication Problems in Elderly People: Practical Approaches to Management*. London: Croom Helm.

Greene, M. G., Adelman, R., Charon, R. and Hoffman, S. (1986) Ageism in the medical encounter: An exploratory study of the doctor–elderly patient relationship. *Language and Communication*, 6, 1/2, 113–124.

Gregory, M. and Carroll, S. (1978) *Language and Situation: Language Varieties and their Social Contexts*. London: Routledge and Kegan Paul.

Grimshaw, A. D. (1980) Mishearings, misunderstandings, and other nonsuccesses in talk. *Sociological Inquiry*, 40, 3/4, 31–74.

Guggenbuhl-Craig, A. (1980) *Eros on Crutches: On the Nature of the Psychopath*. Dallas, Texas: Spring.

Guptill, C. S. (1969) A measure of age identification. *Gerontologist*, 9, 96–102.

Hagestad, G. O. (1985) Continuity and connectedness. In V. L. Bengston and J. F. Robertson (eds), *Grandparenthood*, Beverly Hills, Calif.: Sage, 31–48.

Halliday, M. A. K. (1978) *Language as Social Semiotic*. London: Edward Arnold.

Helfrich, H. (1979) Age markers in speech. In K. R. Scherer and H. Giles (eds), *Social Markers in Speech*. Cambridge: CUP, 63–108.

Henwood, K. L. (1987) The Social Psychology of Stereotypes: A Critical Assessment. Unpublished PhD Thesis, Bristol.

Henwood, K. and Giles, H. (1985) An investigation of the relationship between stereotypes of the elderly and interpersonal communication between young and old. Final Report to the Nuffield Foundation, London.

Hewitt, J. P. and Stokes, R. (1975) Disclaimers. *American Sociological Review*, 40, 1–11.

Hewstone, M. (1989) *Causal Attribution*. Oxford: Basil Blackwell.

Hewstone, M. and Brown, R. P. (eds), (1986) *Intergroup Contact*. Oxford: Basil Blackwell.

Hewstone, M. and Giles, H. (1986) Social groups and social stereotypes in intergroup communication: A review and model of intergroup communication breakdown. In W. B. Gudykunst (ed.) *Intergroup Communication*, London: Edward Arnold, 10–26.

Hollien, H. and Shipp, T. (1972) Speaking fundamental frequency and chronologic age in males. *Journal of Speech and Hearing Research*, 15, 155–9.

Holmes, J. (1984) Hedging your bets and sitting on the fence: Some evidence for hedges as support structures. *Te Reo*, 27, 47–62.

Holtgraves, T. (1990) The language of self-disclosure. In H. Giles and P. Robinson (eds), *Handbook of Language and Social Psychology*, Chichester: Wiley, 191–207.

Hopper, R. and Drummond, K. (1990) Goals and their emergence in a relationship turning point: The case of "Gordon and Denise". In K. Tracy and N. Coupland (eds), *Multiple Goals in Discourse*. Clevedon, Avon: Multilingual Matters, 39–66.

Hummert, M. L. (1990) Multiple stereotypes of elderly and young adults: A comparison of structure and evaluations. *Psychology and Aging*, 5, 182–93.

Husband, C. (1982) Introduction: Race, the continuity of a concept. In C. Husband (ed.) *'Race' in Britain: Continuity and Change*, London: Hutchinson.

Hymes, D. (1977) *Foundations in Sociolinguistics: An Ethnographic Approach*. London: Tavistock.

Hymes, D. (1972) Models of the interaction of language and social life. In J. J. Gumperz and D. Hymes (eds), *Directions in Sociolinguistics*, New York: Holt, Rhinehart and Winston, 35–71.

Jefferson, G. (1980) On 'trouble-premonitory' response to inquiry. *Sociological Inquiry*, 50, 153–5.

Jefferson, G. (1984a) On 'stepwise transition' from talk about a 'trouble' to inappropriately next-positioned matters. In J. Atkinson and J. Heritage (eds), *Structures of Social Action*, Cambridge: CUP, 191–222.

Jefferson, G. (1984b) On the organisation of laughter in talk about troubles. In J. Atkinson and J. Heritage (eds), *Structures of Social Action*, Cambridge: CUP, 346–69.

Jefferson, G. (1985) On the interactional unpackaging of a gloss. *Language in Society*, 14, 435–66.

Jourard, S. M. (1964) *The Transparent Self*. New York: Van Nostrand.

Kaplan, G., Barell, V. and Lusky, A. (1988) Subjective state of health and survival in elderly adults. *Journal of Gerontology*, 43, 114–120.

Kelly, H. H. (1967) Attribution theory in social psychology. In D. Levine (ed.) *Nebraska Symposium on Motivation*. Lincoln, Neb.: University of Nebraska Press.

Kemper, S. (1986) Imitation of complex syntactic constructions by elderly adults. *Applied Psycholinguistics*, 7, 277–88.

Kessler, S. J. and McKenna, W. (1978) *Gender: An Ethnomethodological Approach*. New York: Wiley.

Kite, M. E. and Johnson, B. T. (1988) Attitudes to older and younger adults: A meta-analysis. *Psychology and Ageing*, 3, 233–44.

Kogan, N. (1979) Beliefs, attitudes, and stereotypes about old people. *Research on Aging*, 1, 11–36.

Krause, N. (1986) Social support, stress and wellbeing among older adults. *Journal of Gerontology*, 41, 512–19.

Kreps, G. L. (1986) Health communication and the elderly. *World Communication*, 15, 1, 55–70.

Kress, G. (1985) Ideological structures in discourse. In T. van Dijk (ed.) (1986) *Handbook of Discourse Analysis* (vol. 4), London: Academic Press, 27–42.

Kress, G. and Hodge, R. (1979) *Language as Ideology*. London: Routledge and Kegan Paul.

Kubey, R.W. (1980) Television and aging: Past, preent and future. *The Gerontologist*, 20, 16–35.

Kutner, B. (1962) The social nature of ageing. *The Gerontologist*, 2, 5–8.

Kuypers, J. A. and Bengston, V. L. (1973) Social breakdown and competence: A model of normal ageing. *Human Development*, 16, 181–201.

Kynette, D. and Kemper, S. (1986) Aging and the loss of grammatical forms: A cross-sectional study of language performance. *Language and Communication*, 6, 1/2, 65–72.

Labov, W. (1966) *The Social Stratification of English in New York City*. Washington, DC: Center for Applied Linguistics.

Labov, W. (1972) *Sociolinguistic Patterns*. Philadelphia: Pennsylvania University Press.

Laver, J. (1974) Communicative functions of phatic communion. *Work in Progress*, 7. Department of Linguistics, University of Edinburgh. 1–18.

Lanceley, A. (1985) Use of controlling language in the rehabilitation of the elderly. *Journal of Advanced Nursing*, 10, 125–135.

Lee, J. R. and Jefferson, G. (1980) On the Sequential Organisation of Troubles-

Talk in Ordinary Conversation. (Unpublished report to the Economic and Social Research Council)

LePage, R. B. and Tabouret-Keller, A. (1985) *Acts of Identity: Creole-based Approaches to Language and Ethnicity*. Cambridge: CUP.

Lesser, R. (1978) *Linguistic Investigations of Aphasia*. London: Edward Arnold.

Levin, H. and Lin, T. (1988) An accommodating witness. *Language and Communication*, 8, 3/4, 195–8.

Levin, J. and Levin, W. C. (1980) *Ageism: Prejudice and Discrimination Against the Elderly*. Belmont, Calif.: Wadsworth.

Levinson, S. C. (1983) *Pragmatics*. Cambridge: CUP.

Liss, J.M., Weismer, G. and Rosenbek, J.C. (1990) Selected acoustic characteristics of speech production in very old males. *Journal of Gerontology (Psychological Sciences)*, 45, 2, 35–45.

Local Government Training Board (1981) *Training Material for Home Helps*. Ref. No. SS0002.

Local Government Training Board (n.d.) 'Pink spots on her teapot'. Tape–slide training package. Ref. No. SS0005.

Lopez, M. A. (1980) Social skills training with institutionalized elderly: Effects of precounseling structuring and overlearning on skill acquisition and transfer. *Journal of Counseling Psychology*, 27, 3, 293–6.

Ludwig, D., Franco, J. N. and Malloy, J. E. (1986) Effects of reciprocity and self-monitoring on self-disclosure with a new acquaintance. *Journal of Personality and Social Psychology*, 50, 6, 1077–82.

Lutsky, N. S. (1980) Attitudes toward old age and elderly persons. *Annual Review of Gerontology and Geriatrics*, 1, 287–336.

McCready, W. C. (1985) Styles of grandparenting among white ethnics. In V. L. Bengston and J. F. Robertson (eds), *Grandparenthood*. Beverly Hills, Calif.: Sage, 349–60

McTavish, D. G. (1971) Perceptions of old people: A review of research methodologies and findings. *The Gerontologist*, 11, 90–101.

Markides, K. S. and Mindel, C. H. (1987) *Aging and Ethnicity*. Newbury Park, Calif.: Sage.

Martel, M. U. (1968) Age-sex roles in magazine fiction. In B. L. Neugarten (ed.), *Middle Age and Aging*, Chicago: University of Chicago Press.

Maxim, J. and Thompson, I. (1990) *Language and the Elderly: A Clinical Perspective*. London: Edward Arnold.

Maynard, D. (1988) Language, interaction and social problems. *Social Problems*, 35, 4, 311–34.

Miller, L. (1987) The professional construction of aging. *Journal of Gerontological Social Work*, 10, 3/4, 141–153.

Miller, L. C., Berg, J. H. and Archer, R. L. (1986) Openers: Individuals who elicit intimate self-disclosure. *Journal of Personality and Social Psychology*, 44, 1234–44.

Montgomery, M. (1988) D-J talk. In N. Coupland (ed.), *Styles of Discourse*, London: Croom Helm, 85–104.

Montpare, J. M. and Lachman, M. E. (1989) 'You're only as old as you feel': Self perceptions of age, fears of aging and life satisfaction from adolescence to old age. *Psychology and Aging*, 4, 73–8.

Morrell, R. W., Park, D. C. and Poon, L. W. (1990) Effects of labeling techniques on memory and comprehension of prescription information in young and old adults. *Journal of Gerontology (Psychological Sciences)*, 45,4, 166–72.

Mutran, E. and Burke, P. J. (1979) Personalism as a component of old age identity. *Research on Ageing*, 1, 37–63.

Mutran, E. and Reitzes, D. C. (1981) Retirement, identity and wellbeing: Realignment of role-relationships. *Journal of Gerontology*, 36,6, 733–40.

Mysak, E. D. (1959) Pitch and duration characteristics of older males. *Journal of Speech and Hearing Research*, 2, 1, 46–54

Nairn, R. G. and McCreanor, T. N. (in press) Insensitivity and hypersensitivity: An imbalance in Pakeha accounts of racial conflict. *Journal of Language and Social Psychology*.

Nebes, R. D. and Andrews-Kulis, M. S. (1976) The effect of age on the speed of sentence formation and incidental learning. *Experimental Aging Research*, 2, 315–31.

Neugarten, B. L., Crotty, W. J. and Tobin, S. (1964) Personality types in an aged population. In B. L. Neugarten (ed.) *Personality in Middle and Later Life*, New York: Van Nostrand Reinhold.

Norman, A. (1987) *Aspects of ageism: A discussion paper*. London: Centre for Policy on Ageing.

Notarius, C. I. and Herrick, L. R. (1988) Listener response strategies to a distressed other. *Journal of Social and Personal Relationships*, 5, 97–108.

Nuessel, F. (1982) The language of ageism. *The Gerontologist*, 22, 273–6.

Nuessel, F. (1984) Ageist language. *Maledicta*, 8, 17–28.

Nussbaum, J. (ed.) (1989) *Life-span Communication: Normative Processes*. Hillsdale, NJ.: Lawrence Erlbaum.

Nussbaum, J. (1990) Communication and the nursing home environment: Survivability as a function of resident-nursing staff affinity. In H. Giles, N. Coupland and J. Wiemann (eds), *Communication, Health and the Elderly (Proceedings of Fulbright International Colloquium 1988)*, Manchester: Manchester University Press, 155–71.

Nussbaum, J., Thompson, T. and Robinson, J.D. (1989) *Communication and Aging*. New York: Harper and Row.

Obler, L. K. (1980) Narrative discourse style in the elderly. In L. K. Obler and M. L. Albert (eds), *Language and Communication in the Elderly*, Lexington, Mass. Lexington Books, 75–90.

Obler, L. K. and Albert, M. L. (1980) *Language and Communication in the Elderly: Clinical, Therapeutic and Experimental Issues*. Lexington, Mass.: Lexington Books.

Obler, L. K., Nicholas, M., Albert, M. L. and Woodward, S. (1985) On comprehension across the adult life span. *Cortex*, 21, p.273–80.

Oyer, H. J. and Oyer, E. (1976) *Aging and Communication*. Baltimore, Md: University Park Press.

Palmore, E. (1971) Attitudes toward aging as shown by humour. *The Gerontologist*, 11, 181–6.

Palmore, E. (1975) *The Honorable Elders*. Durham NC: Duke University Press.

Pearce, W. B. and Sharp, S. M. (1973) Self-disclosing communication. *Journal of Communication* 23, 409–25.

Penman, R. (1990) Facework and politeness: Multiple goals in courtroom discourse. In K. Tracy and N. Coupland (eds), *Multiple Goals in Discourse*, Clevedon, Avon: Multilingual Matters. 15–38.

Petros, T. V., Norgaard, L., Olson, K. and Tabor, L. (1989) Effects of text genre and verbal ability on adult age differences in sensitivity to text structure. *Psychology and Aging*, 4,2, 247–50.

Platt, J. and Weber, H. (1984) Speech convergence miscarried: An investigation into inappropriate accommodation strategies. *International Journal of the Sociology of Language*, 46, 131–46.

Portnoy, E. (1985) Enhancing communication with elderly patients. *American Pharmacy*, 25, 8, 50–5.

Potter, J. (1988) Cutting cakes: A study of psychologists' social categorisations. *Philosophical Psychology*, 1, 1, 17–33.

Potter, J. and Litton, I. (1985) Some problems underlying the theory of social representations. *British Journal of Social Psychology*, 24, 81–90.

Potter, J. and Wetherell, M. (1987) *Discourse and Social Psychology: Beyond Attitudes and Behaviour*. London: Sage.

Ptacek, P. H. and Sander, E. K. (1966) Age recognition from voice. *Journal of Speech and Hearing Research*, 9, 273–7.

Ramig, L. A. (1983) Effects of physiological aging on vowel spectral noise. *Journal of Gerontology*, 38, 2, 223–5.

Riley, M. W. and Foner, A. (1968) *Ageing and Society, Volume 1*. New York: Russell Sage Foundation.

Robinson, W. P. (1972) *Language and Social Behaviour*. Harmondsworth: Penguin.

Robinson, W. P. (1979) Speech markers and social class. In K. R. Scherer and H. Giles (eds), *Social Markers in Speech*. Cambridge: CUP, 211–50.

Rook, K. S. and Pietromonaco, P. (1987) Close relationships: Ties that heal or ties that bind? *Advances in Personal Relationships*, 1, 1–35.

Rosnow, I. (1973) The social context of the ageing self. *The Gerontologist*, 13, 82–7.

Rozencrantz, H. A. and McNevin, T. E. (1969) A factor analytic analysis of attitudes toward the aged. *The Gerontologist*, 9, 55–9.

Rubin, A. M. (1986) Television, aging and information seeking. *Language and Communication*, 6, 125–38.

Rubin, A. M. and Rubin, R. B. (1982) Contextual age and television use. *Human Communication Research*, 8, 228–44.

Rubin, A. M. and Rubin, R. B. (1986) Contextual age as a life-position index. *International Journal of Ageing and Human Development*, 23,1, 27–45.

Rubin, K. H. and Brown, J. (1975) A life-span look at person perception and its relationship to communicative interaction. *Journal of Gerontology*, 30, 461–8.

Ryan, E. B. and Cole, R. (1990) Perceptions of interpersonal communication with elders: Implications for health professionals. In H. Giles, N. Coupland and J. Wiemann (eds), *Communication, Health and the Elderly (Proceedings of Fulbright Colloquium 1988)*. Manchester: Manchester University Press, 172–91.

Ryan, E. B., Giles, H., Bartolucci, G. and Henwood, H. (1986) Psycholinguistic and social psychological components of communication by and with the elderly. *Language and Communication* 6, 1/2, 1–24.

Ryan, E. B. and Johnston, D. G. (1987) The influence of communication effectiveness on evaluations of younger and older adult speakers. *Journal of Gerontology*, 42, 2, 163–4.

Schegloff, E. G. and Sacks, H. (1973) Opening up closings. *Semiotica*, 8, 4, 289–327.

Searle, J. (1969) *Speech Acts*. Cambridge: CUP.

Searle, J. (1979) *Expression and Meaning*. Cambridge: CUP.

Shadden, B. B. (ed.) (1988) *Communication Behavior and Aging: A Sourcebook for Clinicians*. Baltimore, Md: Williams and Wilkins.

Shotter, J. and Gergen, K. (eds), (1989) *Texts of Identity*. London: Sage.

Sigall, H. and Page R. (1971) Current stereotypes: A little fading, a little faking. *Journal of Personality and Social Psychology*, 18, 2, 247–55.

Sinclair, J. McH. and Coulthard, M. (1975) *Towards an Analysis of Discourse*. Oxford: OUP.

Smith, M. J., Reinheimer, R. E. and Gabbard-Alley, A. (1981) Crowding, task performance, and communicative interaction in youth and old age. *Human Communication Research*, 7, 3, 259–72.

Smith, P. M. (1985) *Language, the Sexes and Society*. Oxford: Basil Blackwell.

Smith, P. M., Giles, H. and Hewstone, M. (1980) Sociolinguistics: A social psychological perspective. In R. N. St Clair and H. Giles (eds), *The Social and Psychological Contexts of Language*, Hillsdale, NJ: Lawrence Erlbaum, 283–98.

Snow, C. E. and Ferguson, C. A. (eds), (1977) *Talking to Children: Language Input and Acquisition*. Cambridge: CUP.

Solano, C. H., Batten, P. G. and Parrish, E. A. (1982) Loneliness and patterns of self-disclosure. *Journal of Personality and Social Psychology*, 43, 524–31.

Spence, D. L. (1986) Some contributions of symbolic interactionism to the study of growing old. In V. W. Marshall (ed.), *Later Life: The Social Psychology of Ageing*, London: Sage.

Stewart, M. A. and Ryan, E. B. (1982) Attitudes toward younger and older adult speakers: Effects of varying speech rates. *Journal of Language and Social Psychology*, 1, 91–109.

Street, R. L. (1991) Accommodation in medical consultations. In H. Giles, J. Coupland and N. Coupland (eds), *Contexts of Accommodation: Developments in Applied Sociolinguistics*. Cambridge: CUP.

Street, R. L. and Cappella, J. N. (1985) *Sequence and Pattern in Communicative Behaviour*. London: Edward Arnold.

Street, R. L. and Hopper, R. (1982) A model of speech style evaluation. In E. B. Ryan and H. Giles (eds), *Attitudes Towards Language Variation: Social and Applied Contexts*, London: Edward Arnold, 175–88.

Stubbs, M. (1982) *Discourse Analysis: The Sociolinguistic Analysis of Natural Language*. Oxford: Basil Blackwell.

Suls, J. M. and Miller, R. L. (1977) *Social Comparison Processes: Theoretical and Empirical Perspectives*. Washington, DC: Hemisphere.

Tajfel, H. (1974) Social identity and intergroup behaviour. *Social Science Information*, 13, 65–93.

Tajfel, H. (1978) *Differentiation between Social Groups*. London: Academic.

Tannen, D. and Saville-Troike, M. (eds), (1985) *Perspectives on Silence*. Norwood, NJ: Ablex.

Taylor, B. (1987) Elderly identity in conversation: Producing frailty. Paper presented at the Speech Communication Association, Boston, Mass.

Thakerar, J. N., Giles, H. and Cheshire, J. (1982) Psychological and linguistic parameters of speech accommodation theory. In C. Fraser and K. R. Scherer (eds), *Advances in the Social Psychology of Language*, Cambridge: CUP, 205–55.

Thorsheim, H. and Roberts, B. (1990) Empowerment through storysharing: Communication and reciprocal social support among older persons. In H. Giles,

N. Coupland and J. Wiemann (eds), *Communication, Health and the Elderly* (*Proceedings of Fulbright Colloquium 1988*), Manchester: Manchester University Press, 114–25.

Tinker, A. (1984) *The Elderly in Modern Society*. London: Longman.

Tracy, K. (ed.) (1991) *Understanding Face-to-face Interaction :Issues Linking Goals and Discourse*. Hillsdale, NJ.: Lawrence Erlbaum.

Tracy, K. and Coupland, N. (eds), (1990) *Multiple Goals in Discourse*. Clevedon, Avon: Multilingual Matters.

Trudgill, P. (1974) *The Social Differentiation of English in Norwich*. London: Edward Arnold.

Tuckman, J. and Lavell, M. (1957) Self-classification as old or not old. *Geriatrics*, 12, 666–71.

Tuckman, J. and Lorge, I. (1954) Classification of the self as young, middle aged or old. *Geriatrics*, 9, 534–6.

Tun, P. A. (1990) Age differences in processing expository and narrative text. *Journal of Gerontology (Psychological Sciences)*, 44,1, 9–15.

Turner, J. C. (1982) Towards a redefinition of the social group. In H. Tajfel (ed.), *Social Identity and Intergroup Relations*. Cambridge: CUP, 15–40.

Turner, J. C. (1986) *Rediscovering the Social Group: A Self-Categorization Theory*. Oxford: Basil Blackwell.

Tyler, W. (1986) Structural ageism as a phenomenon in British society. *Journal of Educational Gerontology*, 1, 2, 38–46.

Ulatowska, H. K., Cannito, M. P., Hayashi, M. M. and Fleming, S. G. (1985) Language abilities in the elderly. In H. K. Ulatowska (ed.), *The Aging Brain: Communication in the Elderly*, San Diego, Calif.: College-Hill Press, (125–39).

Ulatowska, H. K., Hayashi, M. M., Cannito, M. P. and Fleming, S. G. (1986) Disruption of reference. *Brain and Language*, 28, 24–41.

Valdman, A. (1981) Sociolinguistic aspects of foreigner talk. *International Journal of the Sociology of Language*, 28, 41–52.

van Dijk, T. A. (1986) *Handbook of Discourse Analysis* (4 vols.). London: Academic Press.

van Dijk, T. A. (1987) *Communicating Racism*. Newbury Park: Sage.

Ward, R. A. (1984) The marginality amd salience of being old: When is age relevant? *The Gerontologist*, 24, 227–37.

West, C. and Frankel, R. H. (1991) Miscommunication in medicine. In N. Coupland, H. Giles and J. Wiemann (eds), *"Miscommunication" and Problematic Talk*. Newbury Park, Calif.: Sage. 166–94.

West, C. and Zimmerman, D. (1985) Gender, language and discourse. In T. van Dijk (ed.) *Handbook of Discourse Analysis*, Vol.4. London: Academic Press, 103–24.

Wiemann, J., Gravell, R. and Wiemann, M. (1990) Communication with the elderly: Implications for health care and social support. In H. Giles. N. Coupland and J. Wiemann (eds), *Communication, Health and Ageing (Proceedings of Fulbright International Colloquium 1988)*, Manchester: Manchester University Press, 229–42.

Wilder, C. N. and Weinstein, B. E. (1984) *Aging and Communication: Problems in Management*. New York: Haworth.

Williams, A. and Giles, H. (in press) Sociopsychological perspectives on older people's language and communication. *Ageing and Society*.

Williams, A., Giles, H., Coupland, N., Dalby, M. and Manasse, H. (1990) The communicative contexts of elderly social support and health: A theoretical model. *Health Communication*, 2, 3, 123–44.

Won-Doornik, M. J. (1985) Self-disclosure and reciprocity in conversation: A cross-national study. *Social Psychology Quarterly*, 48, 2, 97–107.

Wood, L. and Ryan, E. B. (in press) Talk to elders: Social structure, attitudes and forms of address. *Ageing and Society*.

Woolliscroft, J. O., Calhoun, J. G., Maxim, B. R. and Wolf, F. M. (1984) Medical education in facilities for the elderly. *Journal of the American Medical Association*, 252, 3382–5.

World Health Organisation (1968) *The First Ten Years of the World Health Organisation*. Geneva.

Zola, I. K. (1962) Feelings about age among older people. *Journal of Gerontology*, 17, 65–8.

Index